BEING THERE
Titanic, Marlon Brando and the Luger Pistol

BEING THERE
Titanic, Marlon Brando and the Luger Pistol

PETER WILLIAMS
FOREWORD BY SIR JEREMY ISAACS AND SIR CLIVE JONES

ALSO BY PETER WILLIAMS:

In Black and White, the story of a coalfield, its life and death

Winner Stakes All, a profile of Lynn Davies, Olympic Gold Medallist

McIndoe's Army, the badly-burned airmen, reconstructed by
Sir Archibald McIndoe (with Ted Harrison)

Unit 731, the Japanese Army's biological warfare experiments on human beings
(with David Wallace)

Feature-length Documentary Films (a selection):

Test Tube Explosion

Ruth Ellis – The Last Woman to Hang

UNIT 731 – Did the Emperor Know?

D-Day – The Shortest Day

The Queen and Her Ceremonial Horses

Hilary Lister – A Race Against Time

The Challenge (for Salon Pictures)

A Canterbury Tale – The Battle for Hill 112

A Century of Coal, the unique story of the Kent coalfield

Titanic – A Question of Murder

The Night Football Changed For Ever, the formation of the Premier League

The Clone a Human Being

Hillary on Everest, Sir Edmund Hillary's conquest of Everest
(with Tom Scott Productions)

To my mother and father
Gladys Mary and William Edgar
and to my wife and best friend
Jo Taylor Williams

CONTENTS

INTRODUCTION

Circumstance during 70 years in journalism, both in newspapers and television, have led to privileged access to some of the world's milestone events, mostly planned but sometimes by accident. On these occasions, the access means that one finds oneself inside a situation or event, with the world's press outside, looking in. Most of the experiences involve a very personal element; my father, Edgar, for instance, was a victim of the Spanish flu pandemic of 1918 (see Chapter 15).

As time has passed, then, I may now be able to add a context to the record of what happened where and when and who did what to whom. It was that brave and doughty writer, Martha Gellhorn, who once told me as a young man, that the first duty of a journalist, the only thing that really mattered, was to "get it on the record". So, in this volume, that is what I have tried to do in suggesting why certain things happened and sometimes why they didn't.

If Gellhorn indicated the mission, it was my father, William Edgar Williams who, through his tenacity, set the example of how it could be done. By rights, he should have been disabled all his life. He lied about his age and volunteered for service in the Royal Navy in World War I. At the age of 17, he was a wireless operator on board a merchant vessel that was armed with concealed heavy artillery. They were called 'Q-ships' and were designed to surprise German U-boats which, to conserve their small arsenal of torpedoes, often surfaced to finish off their victims with gunfire. The Q-ships had a number of conspicuous successes and sank numerous German submarines. But Edgar Williams contracted Spanish flu and tuberculosis during his two years' service and lost a lung. I remember him as an invalid for most of his life, coming home and straight to bed at the end of his working day. He frequently coughed up blood. I remember, so often on my knees, praying, that God would allow him to stop that wracking cough. He too was a journalist, first on the *South Wales Echo* and then Editor of the *Great Yarmouth Independent* before moving in 1934 to edit the *Tamworth Herald* in Staffordshire. A year after I was born, he suffered a recurrence of his tuberculosis and thereafter was regularly confined in sanatoria, for months at a time. The family moved back to Cardiff. This coincided with World War II. We were blitzed in Cardiff and Edgar moved us all to Plymouth in order to avoid further Nazi bombs. This, on reflection, was a bad move, as the range of Germany's Heinkel and Dornier bombers soon embraced Plymouth. An incendiary bomb hit our home in Houndiscombe Road, Plymouth and failed to explode.* I was hurriedly evacuated with my mother, Gladys, to the Devonshire village of South Brent, spending four of the most influential years of my life in the countryside, while my father commuted to bomb-torn Plymouth every day to work for the *Western Morning News* and *Evening Herald*.

Ten years later, in Bristol, I informed my father that I wanted to become a journalist. There was a vacancy at the local paper for an office-boy. I was 15 years old and had just matriculated** from grammar school. He was less than pleased. He warned that it was a hard, exacting and unpredictable job. He was a living example of that, of course. A day later, he said: "Look, Peter, if you can stay out of journalism, stay out of it," by which I gathered that he felt I would be happy as a journalist, only if I believed it to be a duty. And if I wasn't willing to give that commitment, don't bother. For Edgar Williams, journalism in newspapers and television was an instrument for social change and betterment. It was a vocation. I've yet to hear a better definition of the art.

I was born in 1933. It was the year when Joseph Geobbels began destroying the written word in Nazi Germany, consigning books to a bonfire in order to destroy the record of anything with which he disagreed…

---

* I kept this bomb, which had landed on my bed while we were all taking refuge in a reinforced cupboard under the stairs. It was silver, about 2 feet long and, years later, I eventually handed it to the police who understandably chided me for my irresponsibility. But I'd become quite attached to it. I gather they took it to 'a safe place' where they exploded it.

** Matriculated: a standard that qualified a student for university entrance.

FOREWORD

Sir Clive Jones.
Source: Sightsavers.org

"The great virtue of *BEING THERE* – from the discovery of the sunken tomb that was the *Titanic* by Bob Ballard, through the ethical and scientific dilemmas to deliver the first test tube baby, the fatal errors that led the last woman in the UK to be hanged, plus decades of investigative journalism and countless current affairs scoops and, finally, to the wrongful fall from power of Greg Dyke as Director General of the BBC – is the fact that Peter really WAS there.

Across seven decades, from a local newspaper reporter to respected television correspondent, Peter has told truth to power, held our masters to account and celebrated extraordinary people. This is a remarkable book by a remarkable journalist."

Sir Clive Jones CBE

Sir Jeremy Issacs.
Source: Alamy

As a reporter, director and producer, Peter Williams made television programmes of high quality, neither tangling us with detailed complexity, nor over-simplifying for sensational effect.

He established the facts, checked that he'd got them right and presented them to us with clarity and zest. He was always worth reading. And, after 50 years, he still is.

To see for yourself, read on…

Sir Jeremy Isaacs

Chapter 1

TITANIC - *The Pride and the Fall*

Few events in a lifetime make the world pause. The assassination of John Fitzgerald Kennedy, the terrorist attack on the Twin Towers on 9/11, the shooting of Archduke Franz Ferdinand in 1914. The loss of the *Titanic* stands as one of those moments.

The sinking of the Titanic in 1912 stunned the world. Practically, it at last changed maritime law so that vessels were legally bound to carry enough lifeboats for every soul on board. But the impact of the disaster was greater than that. It made mankind examine itself and assess how far progress had altered life and attitudes. Every corner of the world shared the shock of bereavement – passengers from Europe, North and South America, Africa, Asia, Australia all died and on the ship that was 'unsinkable'. The arrogance of this assertion had certainly influenced the design of the great ship and the vessel's impregnability was a view widely held by those who sailed in *Titanic* on her short and tragic maiden voyage. This was technology at its finest. With these skills at his fingertips, mankind could – perhaps would – become invulnerable.

The loss of the *Titanic* was the greatest news story of modern times, to quote *Titanic* historian Walter Lord.[1] He summed up its worldwide influence thus: "In 1912, people

1. The Night Lives On, Walter Lord, p19

had confidence ... they were sure the world's wrongs could be righted. Now nobody is sure of anything and the more uncertain we become, the more we long for a happier era when we felt we knew the answers. The *Titanic* symbolises that era, and more poignantly, the end of it. The worse things get today, the more we think of her, and all who went down with her."

Her sinking was 'the end of a dream', the dramatic tragedy that shattered confidence in mechanical and technological mastery. It gave birth to the more healthy assertion today among planners and engineers that if anything can possibly go wrong, it will.

Given the part played by *Titanic* in this fundamental shift in attitude, we will consider her story in some detail.

* * *

The killing blow, when it came, was more of a caress. So soft that those who were about to die scarcely felt it, yet so final that the great ship had no chance of surviving. The *Titanic* took 2 hours 20 minutes in the dying; most of the 1,500 or so passengers and crew who died lasted a little longer.

Altogether, 2,223 passengers and 860 crew members were on board the night of April 14th–15th 1912. Most were in their cabins, asleep. Some were playing cards or talking in the staterooms of this most luxurious ocean liner. Others were ending the fourth day of the maiden voyage with just another nightcap. A few, in the galleys, on the bridge and in the engine rooms, were still hard at work. It was only here, in the heart of the ship, that the gravity of the blow was immediately apparent...

The iceberg struck like a dagger, piercing, tearing and distorting. The ship lunged on, like a grievously injured animal. The wound stretched and gaped until it was perhaps

100 metres long and, through it, poured the Atlantic Ocean. Some of the firemen working on *Titanic*'s 29 boilers were already dead; others would die in those first few minutes. But none of this was yet known to those who had paid up to £870 ($4,350) to sail on what was *Titanic*'s maiden voyage. They were a cross section of society – millionaires and their retinues, young men with their eyes set on opportunity and emigrants who had begun the journey from the Middle East to the New World five weeks earlier on the back of a camel. As the great liner freed itself from the cutting edge of the iceberg, it gradually slowed. Then, it stopped. The rhythm of the ship, constant through four days and nights, changed – and the passengers noticed. Some woke up.

Others asked a passing steward if the delay would be a long one and they were reassured.

Privately, among the crew, there was speculation that there was a mechanical failure; perhaps she had thrown a blade of a propeller and she would have to limp into harbour for repairs. There was no alarm because there was no need for alarm. *Titanic*, after all, was the ship that was unsinkable…

In only one cabin were preparations to cope with disaster already far advanced. Mrs Esther Hart was already fully dressed, snug in her warmest clothing that included layer after layer of underwear. She had sat thus throughout every night since the *Titanic* had left Southampton. She had known, from the start, that the ship would never reach New York; she had had a premonition about the journey, a feeling of unease that had grown into certainty when she discovered the name of the ship aboard which she, her husband and their seven-year-old daughter, Eva, were due to travel. Benjamin Hart's building business in Ilford had not been flourishing as he hoped so he had determined to try his luck in a fresh environment. They had intended to cross the Atlantic in a smaller vessel, the *Philadelphia*. But there had been a strike in Britain's coalfields and, because of the shortage of coal, numerous sailings had been cancelled. Even the *Titanic* had made its maiden voyage only through the courtesy of her sister ship, the *Olympic*, from which she borrowed hundreds of tons of coal. So the Hart family had themselves transferred to the *Titanic* – which pleased Benjamin Hart intensely. The world's biggest liner… a maiden voyage on the most opulent vessel afloat – he would arrive in style to see his brother in Canada.

But the change in plans did not please Mrs Hart. Her daughter, Eva,[2] remembered: "As soon as she knew it was the *Titanic*, she said, 'Ah, now I know why I'm frightened. It's because they've declared the ship is unsinkable – and that's flying in the face of God.'"

Mrs Hart tried to dissuade her husband by every possible means. She pleaded desperately. No ship was unsinkable: she was positive something dreadful would happen. Eva continued: "As we got to the gangplank to go on board, I remember she stopped, put her hand on his arm and said, 'I'll ask you once more. Will you please not go?' But he told her she was foolish – and aboard we went."

The Harts adopted a bizarre pattern of life on board ship. Mrs Hart was convinced that the disaster, when it came, would happen at night. So she slept during the day and, at night, sat up in a chair while the rest of the ship slumbered. She occupied herself with crochet, needlework and reading. She then took breakfast with her husband and child before repairing to her bunk, from which she emerged only for

---

2. Eva Hart was seven when the Titanic sank. She became a family friend in her later years, having pursued a distinguished career as a professional singer in Australia and a teacher of music when she returned to the UK. She spent Christmas with the Williams family when, in her nineties, she delivered the unforgettable line as I helped her from the sitting-room to the dining-room: "By the way, Jo (my wife) knows that I don't like turkey, doesn't she?" Author, 2021

dinner. They spent the hour after the meal together – mother, father and daughter. Mrs Hart then slipped out of her flowing, ankle-length dress to don her unorthodox but practical night attire, topped by the thickest of overcoats. Mr Hart judged this behaviour at the least, eccentric; he retired early and slept soundly, as did seven-year-old Eva, who remembers chiefly the joy of her father's undivided attention every day, plus her surprise at the depth of her mother's conviction: "She sat there all night – literally waiting for it to happen."

On the third night of the voyage, April 13th, there was a false alarm. *Titanic* was thrusting at speed through ice floes – Mrs Hart had awakened her husband and asked him to go on deck to find out if all was well. She feared the ice would damage the hull. He had grumbled and gone.

Now, on April 14th, at just before midnight, Mrs Hart felt what she was later to describe as 'a slight bump'. Because she was awake, she was immediately alert. She went again to her husband.

"Father was less inclined to get up for the second night running" said Eva. "But mother was convinced. She said she didn't know what 'it' was but she knew it was this terrible something that had been hanging over her for weeks. Precisely what it was she neither knew nor cared.

"It was 'it'."

Once he had been persuaded, Benjamin Hart had shrugged on a heavy overcoat and left to find out what was happening. When he returned to the second class cabin, he found his wife and daughter waiting expectantly. Eva Hart remembers:

"He came back, his face very white. He said nothing about the details of the crisis; very probably he didn't know. He simply said to my mother, 'You had better wear this thick coat of mine, you'll need it'. He put his coat on my mother, pulled out another coat for himself, wrapped me in a warm blanket and, in his arms, he carried me up to the deck."

The Hart family were among the first to take any action to save themselves that night…

* * *

In midsummer 1911, *The Shipbuilder* magazine, published four times a year, produced a 'Souvenir number' entitled '*The White Star's Triple Screw Atlantic Liners Olympic and Titanic*: 45,000 tonnes – the largest steamships in the world'. It was, they said, to mark the addition of 'yet another triumph of shipbuilding and engineering skill to the splendid list of vessels built for the Atlantic passenger service'. They added:

'In no other trade have such remarkable developments taken place in the size of ships and in the comfort and luxury provided for passengers. Competition between the great shipping companies engaged has been very keen, and efforts to secure pre-eminence have been quickly followed by the endeavours of rival lines to go one better.'

The major rivals for the rich pickings on the Atlantic run were Cunard, their British-owned fleet led by the *Lusitania* and the *Mauretania* and the White Star Line – or to be more precise, The Oceanic Steam Navigation Company, formed in 1896, sailing under the British Red Ensign but buttressed by American money. The editors of *The Shipbuilder* paid White Star a pretty compliment:

'…the building of the *Olympic* and *Titanic* makes it evident that the characteristic policy of enterprise and foresight is being worthily maintained…'

The builders, inevitably, were Messrs Harland & Wolff, of Belfast. Inevitably, because the two vessels were the 52nd and 53rd ships the White Star Line had ordered from the Northern Ireland shipyard. The relationship between the two companies was close, so close that the head of the shipbuilding company, Lord Pirrie, was also one of only three directors of the White Star Line. The size of the vessels focused attention from the moment they were conceived – more than 820 feet long, 92 feet in the beam and 64 feet deep. They were almost 100 feet longer than their Cunard rivals, the *Mauretania* and the *Lusitania*. As it turned out, the *Titanic* was 825 feet and 6 inches long when she was launched – factually the world's largest ship, 30 inches or so longer than her sister.

Special slipways had been built at Harland & Wolff's Queen's Island works to accommodate the new giants, before the *Olympic*'s keel was laid on December 16th 1908. They grew side by side; *Olympic* first and *Titanic* a few months behind her. They were to be powered by a combination of reciprocating engines with a low-pressure turbine; White Star had proved the effectiveness and economy of this type of harnessed power in an earlier vessel, the *Laurentic*, in 1909. There was a double bottom to each vessel, about 5 feet from the keel, so that if she ran aground, the integrity of the ship would be protected. And there were 15 separate, watertight compartments. *The Shipbuilder* declared:

'The watertight compartments of the *Olympic* and the *Titanic* is *(sic)* very complete and is *(sic)* so arranged that any two main compartments may be flooded without in any way involving the safety of the ship…

'The watertight doors giving communication between the various boiler rooms and engine rooms are arranged, as is usual in White Star vessels, on the drop system. They are of Messrs Harland & Wolff's special design of massive construction … (and) can be instantly released by means of a powerful electro-magnet, controlled from the captain's bridge, so that in the event of an accident or at any time when it may be considered advisable, the captain can, by simply moving an electric switch, instantly close the doors throughout and make the vessel practically unsinkable.'

That phrase was to hang like an albatross around the neck

of the *Titanic*. 'Practically unsinkable'. Whether or not it was believed by those who built her, or by those who bought her, the phrase infiltrated the public consciousness. This assertion was not a figment of popular imagination, an assumption by a lay, uncritical, ill-informed readership. The judgment was considered and authoritative. For *The Shipbuilder* was a highly respected, widely read trade magazine. It dealt in specification rather than sensationalism. The *Olympic* and *Titanic* were, in practical terms, unsinkable.

On her boatdeck, she carried 16 lifeboats, each 30 feet long and 9 feet wide, and four Englehardt collapsible liferafts. There was, therefore, room in the lifeboats for only one in three of the 3,457 passengers and crew who could sail in her. But, on an 'unsinkable' ship, lifeboats were something of an irrelevance, an extra encumbrance, a safeguard necessary only to comply with Board of Trade regulations…

* * *

The elevator to the boat deck was close to the second class cabin the Harts had occupied throughout the four-day voyage. Eva Hart remembers that it was "cold, so cold" as she was awakened from her deep sleep and carried out into the still, night air. There was confusion, she remembers, but no panic. After all, wasn't the *Titanic* unsinkable?

"Father went off to find (out) what was happening. He came back saying he didn't think the lifeboats were going to be lowered and he asked us to stay where we were, at the side of one of the boats.

"I often wonder whether, for all the efforts he made to pooh-pooh my mother's premonition, he hadn't realised that there were far too few lifeboats on board to take all the passengers and crew. He was a native of Hull and he'd been to sea a great deal. All the time he was running around the ship all through the day, amusing me, he must have noticed how few lifeboats there were. Anyway, he knew precisely and exactly where to go – and we'd had no lifeboat drill at any time. There were hundreds of people on that ship who didn't even know where the boats were…"

By now, past midnight, the decks were thronged with people.

"They were milling around. There was a sense of disaster, obvious even to one as young as me. I was frightened and crying and father came back again and again and said, 'Yes, they *are* going to launch the boats because we've hit an iceberg. But it's just a precaution and you'll probably be back by morning, in time for breakfast.'"

Which was the moment that Mrs Hart realised that her husband wouldn't be coming with her. It was to be women and children first…

Eva said: "He put me into the lifeboat and he said, 'Now, you take care of Mummy', and the boat was lowered over the side. He stood back with all the other men. It was a terribly long way down to the dark sea and I remember looking up and seeing him leaning over, saying again, 'Be good, look after Mummy'. And that was the last I saw of him.

"He made no attempt to get into a lifeboat, nor did most of the other men. As we swung from the davits we saw him help other women and children into the boats but he made no attempt to save himself. He was a very powerful swimmer but no-one was going to be able to live long in those icy waters. And though I was too young to reason out why, I had this dreadful feeling. I knew that I would never see him again."

Eva Hart and her mother were now in lifeboat No 14 on the port side of the ship. Fifth Officer Harold Lowe fired three shots from his revolver to warn off a crowd of passengers pressing up against the rails. As the boat was lowered, a young man climbed over the rails and tried to hide under the seats. Lowe ordered him to leave at gunpoint. Another male passenger, Daniel Buckley, did manage to get into Boat No 14 thanks to a female passenger who concealed him under her shawl.

As the lifeboat dropped to the calm sea, Eva lost sight of her father. Then, the passengers leaned into their oars and pulled away from the great ship, which was silhouetted against the clear night sky. Eva could see again the scurrying figures on deck – near enough to watch the frantic activity, but too far away to identify the precise fate of her father.

"All the lights on board were on. In other circumstances it would have been a beautiful sight. On our side of the ship, you could hear music, too. It wasn't the full ship's orchestra, just a small group. They were playing *Nearer, My God, to Thee*. And they went on playing.

"From the lifeboat, we watched her sinking. There was a tremendous amount of noise – the hissing of steam and crying and shouting. I couldn't do anything but stare. Most of the other children in the lifeboat were so cold and sleepy that they didn't watch it, but I certainly did.

"There was no real panic, I would say, until it was discovered that the lifeboats were full and there were still more than 1,500 people on board, left behind..."

But the lifeboats were <u>not</u> all full and that is another twist in the tragedy. For some passengers were not eager to step off the 'unsinkable' ship. They delayed – and the lifeboats kept leaving, places empty...

"After what seemed a long time people began screaming and running from side to side on the ship. Gradually, she went down by the nose and her stern reared up in the air. The people scrambled towards the stern. It was almost as if they still believed she wouldn't sink."

Eva Hart watched, transfixed. Some passengers were now leaping or falling from the deck of the *Titanic* into the sea.

Then Eva was whisked back into an awareness of her own predicament. "Our lifeboat was overfilled. We were packed like sardines. But there was room in some of the other boats, particularly the ones which had been got away early on. So, the officer in charge of our boat (Fifth Officer Lowe) called the boats together in order that some people could be transferred out of our boat and other boats could take their fair share. Four survivors into this boat, five into that one. He wanted to make room to go back and pick up some more people.

"Suddenly, I was picked up, separated from my mother. I was terrified; I thought I was being thrown over the side. It was all so very dark except for the lights from the ship. I started to yell very loudly – and someone sat down next to me and put an arm around me. And that frightened me very much as well. I thought I'd lost Mother too…"

Mrs Hart was just as terrified. She thought Eva had dropped into the sea. She tried to tell the other passengers. She must look for her little girl in the water between the lifeboats. But the lifeboats were moving again; there were other priorities to be considered. Mrs Hart screamed – and collapsed.

Eva continued to record what was going on around her.

"I never closed my eyes. It was like all those paintings you've ever seen. We saw her sinking with all her lights still alight. She started to go down, nose first, and then it seemed to me that her stern sort of turned sideways as she actually slid beneath the surface. I felt she broke in half…

"…And everyone who was left on board was suddenly in the water. And then we heard the people drowning. I can't tell you what that was like – it was the peak of all the horror. It frightened me more than anything. The screams."

Now that he had empty seats, Lowe took his boat back to the scene of the sinking ship to try to find survivors. Lifeboat 4 was the only other lifeboat to rescue people from the sea, which was littered with the bodies of hundreds of people who had already died of hypothermia. Four men were pulled from the water into Lowe's boat. One of them, William Hoyt, died in lifeboat No 14, but the other three survived.

Eva Hart, tiny and terrified, remembers: "Everything was silent, quite suddenly. After all the cries and the hissing of steam and the crashing and the panic, all the noise that went with the disaster – suddenly it was over. The people were dead and their screams had stopped. It was a dreadful silence. As if the world was standing still."

The world was only now learning a garbled version of the disaster. Ships were racing to *Titanic's* aid. 'All safe' was the first rumour that found its way into print in New York. The first to gain a clear picture of the enormity of the disaster were the captain and crew of the Cunard steamship, *Carpathia*. She had cast caution to the winds and had raced at full speed the 58 miles through the ice to *Titanic's* last reported position. She picked up some survivors – frozen, injured, some of them dying. It was six hours or so since Titanic had gone down; it had been to quote Eva Hart, "an intensely cold night." The survivors were given food, hot drinks, blankets, somewhere to sleep. They settled down, looked for their friends and loved ones; Eva was reunited with her mother. Then the count began. Early reports said that 712 people had been saved – 189 members of the crew, 129 male passengers and 394 women and children. One survivor died aboard *Carpathia* on the passage to New York. Of the *Titanic's* complement of passengers and crew, it was believed that at least 1,503 had died.

But the reckoning was only just beginning...[3]

* * *

---

3. The actual death toll has always been a subject of dispute. One estimate has put it as high as 1,523. The current 'official' figure is 1,496; source, David Scott-Beddard, British Titanic Society, 2021

Why, then, did 1,503 people die in the greatest loss of life in maritime history? At its most basic, they died because the world's largest ship had struck an iceberg and sunk before they could be rescued. In the abstract, there were those who argued that they had died because – to quote Mrs Hart – to describe a ship as unsinkable was "to fly in the face of God". Man was being taught a lesson, they insisted; pride came before a fall and, regrettable as it was, 1,503 deaths were a salutary reminder from the Almighty of the vulnerability of even the best laid plans.

Then there were those who insisted that it was all just bad luck, an accident that could never happen again – bad luck to hit the iceberg when many thousands of similar journeys by other vessels through the same waters had resulted in no such disaster; bad luck that the collision with the iceberg had been with the most vulnerable part of the hull of the vessel and bad luck that the distress radio signals were not heard and acted upon by vessels closer than the 58 miles that the *Carpathia* had to cover, to effect a rescue.

Walter Lord listed what he called the "if onlys": if only (*Titanic*) had paid more attention to the warnings she received … if only the last (radio) warning had reached the bridge … if only the wireless operator hadn't cut off one final attempt to reach her … if only she had sighted the iceberg a few seconds earlier … if only there had been enough lifeboats … if only the watertight bulkheads had gone one deck higher … if only that (unidentified) ship on the horizon had come … if only, if only.[4]

Survivor Eva Hart was quite clear where a major part of the blame lay. She accepted that, having struck an iceberg, there were bound to be casualties. But she criticised the

---

4. The Night Lives On, Walter Lord, p16

owners, the White Star Line, for failing to provide enough lifeboats for everyone on board the *Titanic*. She said: "If a ship is torpedoed, that's war. If she strikes a rock in a storm, that's a natural disaster. But for so many people to die because there weren't enough lifeboats, that's ridiculous."[5]

Personally, and unsurprisingly, the trauma of the *Titanic* sinking cast a shadow on her life. Her mother died in 1928 when Eva, then 23, confronted her fears of travelling by sea again by deciding to travel to Singapore in a passenger ship. It was 15 years since the *Titanic* had sunk. "The voyage brought back so many memories I had tried to bury. I couldn't leave my cabin for four days. Eventually, a friendly stewardess persuaded me to open the cabin door and go with her on deck. The sea still seemed so grey and vast and unforgiving..."[6]

* * *

In July 1985, a French group mounted an expedition to find, among other more military objectives, *Titanic*'s last resting place on the sea bed. In the final days of that expedition, they had established where the wreck was but they ran out of time to explore it more closely.

Robert Duane Ballard was part of this French-US exploration. He was a retired US Navy officer and a professor of oceanography at the University of Rhode Island. His speciality was underwater archaeology. Having sighted the wreck, he was determined to find it again and chronicle her secrets. *Titanic*, he said, was his "Mount Everest ... with the French we hadn't actually found anything, but the evidence suggested we were in the right area. There was a box of 100 square nautical miles where most of us believed the *Titanic*

---

5. Conversation with author, 1992
6. Ibid

had gone down. I was sure, if we went again, we had a good chance of finding her".[7]

On the southernmost tip of Cape Cod, Massachusetts, Woods Hole is the USA's leading oceanographic institution. It is dedicated to ocean research, exploration and education. It has an annual budget of more than $200 million and 500 scientists work there, among them Bob Ballard. Ballard is both able and ambitious. He was determined to 'discover' *Titanic* and to tell her story. Woods Hole supplied the muscle to match his determination. Ballard and the US mother ship, *Knorr*, left Woods Hole again in August 1985 to return to the site and, in the early morning of September 1st 1985, they followed a trail of debris across the ocean bed and identified a piece of wreckage as a boiler from the *Titanic*. Jubilant, they returned to Woods Hole. They now knew where *Titanic* had come to rest. But it would need more sophisticated equipment to record properly what remained of the great liner.

Nine months later, on July 12th 1986, Ballard set sail again, this time aboard *Atlantis II*, carrying a submersible named *Alvin* and a small, remotely operated vehicle called *Jason Junior* (or *JJ*) which carried a camera that would be able to fit through the small openings they anticipated finding among the wreckage. In this way they could view the interior of *Titanic*.[8]

How much was still recognisable? How much of the great vessel had been preserved? What had happened to her as she sank beneath the waters, 2½ miles down to the sea bed? The difficulties facing Ballard's team were immense. They were seeking top quality video and photographs of the wreck. But *Titanic* was lying 4,000 metres (12,400 feet) deep and it was dark down there. The temperature was freezing. The

---

7. Conversation with author, at Woods Hole, 1986
8. TVS, a British ITV company, for which I was then a Controller, negotiated to accompany Ballard on this voyage, see Appendix One

pressures were around 6,000 lbs per square inch. Almost straight away they found the debris trail again and followed it to the wreck itself. Ballard later wrote[9] that the shape of *Titanic* "came out of the dark like this huge shark. Terrifying. Absolutely terrifying. We started whoopin' and hollerin'. We were dancing around the ship. 'We've found it! We've found it!' Then somebody noticed that the time was 2 am and he said, 'She went down at 2.20 am. She sank in 20 minutes...' We were embarrassed. We felt we were dancing on dead bones.

"You could see these images on the screens. Pairs of shoes lying exactly where the people had died. Some people lying on their back. A man on his front. There was nothing left of the bodies – they'd either been eaten or dissolved – but the shoes were untouched, probably because of the tannic acid. At 2.20 am we stopped the ship and had a memorial service. We had found the lost souls."[10]

Ballard is a religious man. He describes the ocean as "Godlike. It's a force that's bigger than you and me". The Ballard team dived 12 times on the *Titanic* wreck, each dive taking 2½ hours down and 2½ hours back to the surface. Film director, Graham Hurley, was there throughout the voyage. His take on Ballard is interesting:

"There was always something slightly godlike about Ballard. He had the looks, the height, the charm and the knowledge. He could handle himself in pretty much any company. He is a clever man and he is physically brave as well, but he has a sense of presence that can, on too many occasions, be close to overwhelming.

"Watching him closely and later, when in 1989 he tried to find the wreck of the German battleship, *Bismarck*, and

9. The Sunday Times: Best of Times, Worst of Times, 1987
10. Ibid

failed, it struck me that he was starring in a movie of his own making. This was a clever trick to pull off. Very few people have the nerve and knowledge to carry them to the brink of global stardom but Ballard was there, on the very edge of doing something huge and, reading his own account of the voyages, I was struck by the roles he seemed to have assigned himself. On a good day, he was Chuck Yeager, the legendary test pilot immortalised by Tom Wolfe in *The Right Stuff*. On a bad day, he was General Patton."[11]

Not for nothing was US General Patton – flamboyant and ruthless – nicknamed 'Blood and Guts'.

Ballard's pursuit of success came at a significant time for the United States. Space travel, in which they now led the world, had become almost routine. Launches no longer dominated the front pages while a nation held its breath. But in January 1986, a tragedy had thrust space travel back into the public's consciousness; the Space Shuttle *Challenger* had blown up after take-off. The entire crew were killed. Investigations determined that NASA had forgotten the 'safety first' attitude which had characterised the most successful years of the USA's space programme. They had set ambitious, dangerous targets for the Space Shuttle *Challenger* – 24 flights a year, which resulted in unreal expectations and "created pressure throughout the Agency that directly contributed to unsafe launch operations".[12]

Evidence of hubris high and low now revealed in space as well as on the sea bed; over-confidence that can reap a bitter harvest of human lives. Ballard's success now reassured

---

11. Graham Hurley directed our film of the Titanic exploration, The Nightmare and The Dream. His summary of the experience is in Appendix One. He also accompanied Ballard to film his expedition to the wreck of the German battleship, Bismarck. After a distinguished career in television (ITV), Graham went on to become a successful novelist and thriller writer

12. US House of Representatives Report, Washington, 1986

a nation that technology could be harnessed safely to explore the world's frontiers. Yet, the arrogance of Man that had characterised the Space Shuttle *Challenger* disaster echoed that of the men who had confidently sent the unsinkable *Titanic* to sea, from the port of Southampton, 74 years before.

Chapter 2

TITANIC - *The Reckoning*

There were two official inquiries into the *Titanic* disaster in 1912 – one in the United States within a week of the *Titanic* going down, the other in Britain, in London, between the beginning of May and the end of July 1912. They probed the design of the vessel, the effectiveness of the watertight compartments, the motivation of various ships' captains involved and the conduct of passengers and company presidents.[13]

Yet, among the thousands of words, hours of claim and counter-claim, one incontrovertible truth emerges: many of the 1,500 people died because there were not sufficient lifeboats to carry them to safety.

It is also clear now that, two years before *Titanic* was launched, there *were* those who warned that she needed to be fitted with three, even four times as many lifeboats as were being planned for her. Enough to carry to safety every passenger and every member of the crew. Enough to save every soul. Just in case the unsinkable sank...

* * *

The building stands alone in the Northern Ireland village of

---

13. I quote heavily from the report of both inquiries, by the Board of Trade in London from May 2nd to July 3rd 1912 and by the US Senate Commerce Committee from April 19th to May 25th 1912

Comber; tall, austere, and unremarkable. It is a tribute to one of the heroes of the *Titanic* disaster. It is used as a school now and bears the legend, the Thomas Andrews Memorial Hall. Thomas Andrews Jr, after whom the hall is named, was one of the naval architects of the *Titanic* and her sister ship, the *Olympic*. He perished in the ship he had helped to build.

Young Thomas Andrews was 39 when *Titanic* sank. He died a hero because he had refused to take a place in a lifeboat – though J Bruce Ismay, the White Star Line's president, had done so. They said of him that "his last great monument lies a full two miles deep in blue water … He could have saved himself a dozen times over … (but he went) down for the sake of his chief concern in life – the passengers".[14]

The building of the *Titanic* was almost a family affair. Thomas Andrews was a managing director and in charge of the drafting department at Harland & Wolff, who built the vessel, working with his uncle, Lord Pirrie and Pirrie's brother-in-law, Alexander Carlisle, who had married Pirrie's sister, Margaret, in 1879.

Pirrie and Carlisle were Northern Ireland Privy Counsellors – advisors to the King. Both were powerful figures in Harland & Wolff, the Belfast yard where the new giant vessels were constructed. Pirrie's role was particularly influential, as he was a director of both the builders, Harland & Wolff, *and* the White Star Line, who were placing the order.

Alexander Carlisle was one of Harland & Wolff's most senior executives. Managing Directors were appointed to run each of the major sections of the great yard and, when important decisions were to be taken, they met in committee. Carlisle was chairman of that committee of managing directors – he was also general manager of the whole works.

The idea for *Olympic* and *Titanic* was born at a dinner

---

14. The Observer, April 27th 1912

party at the London home of J Bruce Ismay, president and chairman of the White Star Line. He discussed the idea with Pirrie and White Star and Harland & Wolff embarked on a series of secret meetings to thrash out the principles, costs and details to which they would work.

Harland & Wolff were represented by Lord Pirrie and Alexander Carlisle at all these meetings.

White Star Line's views were put forward by Ismay and Harold A Sanderson, another senior director.

It was a close-knit, cosy team.

We know that the four men met in October 1909 and in January 1910, as they discussed and modified their plans for the new liners. There is broad agreement between White Star and Harland & Wolff about the routine of the meetings. According to Mr Sanderson of White Star: "The plans are submitted to us and we discuss them ... We go over (the details) with them (Harland & Wolff) and we have the advantage of having Lord Pirrie himself (for further discussions) in London..."

According to Alexander Carlisle, for Harland & Wolff: "The details, the decorations, the equipment and general arrangements all came under me ... Mr Ismay, Mr Sanderson, Lord Pirrie and myself spent about four hours together ... on each occasion. We generally arranged that only two should talk so as not to lose time. Generally, if Lord Pirrie was present, he did the talking on one side and Mr Ismay on the other."

But on one crucial issue, there is profound disagreement. According to Carlisle, for the builders, plans were submitted that would have provided four times as many lifeboats for *Titanic* and *Olympic*. This was supported by Thomas Andrews, who oversaw the building of both *Titanic* and *Olympic* and who advised that the ship should have at least

46 lifeboats.[15] But, according to Ismay and Sanderson, the owners, no such plans were submitted. Carlisle insisted that at least 'five or ten minutes' had been spent at each of these meetings discussing the need to provide more boats for the passengers in the event of disaster. According to Ismay and Sanderson, no such discussions took place.

The British inquiry into the disaster was held by the Board of Trade in May 1912, at the London Scottish Hall, which used to be just around the corner from Buckingham Palace. It heard the evidence and supported White Star's version of events. Crucially, Pirrie did not give evidence; he was ill and there was a question of clash of interests in that he held senior positions in both companies. Carlisle, for the builders Harland & Wolff, gave evidence on June 10th 1912 and was vigorously cross-examined, rather in the manner of a hostile witness by the Board of Trade's Commissioner, Lord Mersey, as the following exchange indicates:

Q: "Who was the person at Harland & Wolff's responsible for saying: 'so far with lifeboats and no further...' Were you?"

Carlisle: "If I had been there, I very likely might–"

Q: "Were *you*?"

Carlisle:"Was I?"

Q: "Yes."

Carlisle: "No."

Q: "Well, that seems to me to be a very grudging 'no.'"

Carlisle: "Not in the very least."

Q: "Well, who was?"

---

15. Thomas Andrews – A Talented Designer, Titianicuniverse.com, September 2014. Titanic sailed carrying 20 lifeboats

Carlisle: "The owners in the first place, who would have to pay for them, would be consulted."

Q: "But we know perfectly well that the owners left it to Harland & Wolff. Now, who was responsible?"

Carlisle: "The White Star and other friends give us a great deal of liberty but at the same time we cannot build a ship any bigger than they order, or put anything in her more than they are prepared to pay for. We have a very free hand … and I do not think that we could possibly have supplied any more boats to the ship without getting the sanction and the order of the White Star Line."

Now, either the two sides discussed the need for more lifeboats, or they didn't. On so emotive a subject and after 1,500 people had died, there can be no valid argument for lapses of memory. In short, someone was lying. So let us weigh the evidence – some of it produced at the time, some of it accumulated during many months of investigation.

This is what happened, according to shipbuilder Alexander Carlisle. When working out the designs of *Titanic* and *Olympic*, he had decided that it was necessary to explore the practicality of increasing the number of lifeboats on board. Lifeboats are slung from small cranes, known as davits. They had always been slung singly, one to each davit. But Carlisle reasoned that if more than one lifeboat could be handled by each davit, this would be a novel way of solving the problem of additional boats without lining the flanks of the ships with a multitude of davits. He drew a sketch plan. Then, he contacted Axel Welin, a Swede whom he knew had already designed an adjustable davit for the Union-Castle Line, capable of carrying two lifeboats. Carlisle wanted *four* boats on each of his davits. Welin was interested in the challenge.

Carlisle told the inquiry that in 1909 he had put the sketch design "before Lord Pirrie and the directors of the White Star. Then, when I pointed out that I expected ... the Government would require much larger boat accommodation on these large ships, I was authorised to go ahead and get out full plans and designs so that if (the Government) did call upon us to fit anything more, we would have no extra trouble or extra expense".

Axel Welin, in his factory at Gothenburg, came back with a design for a revolutionary new davit. It would swing through a 180-degree arc and move lifeboats stacked on the deck beside them. It would be called the Welin Double-Acting Quadrant Davit. It would provide the facility to carry 64 lifeboats, without increasing the number of davits planned for *Titanic* and *Olympic*. The Welin davit was submitted to White Star. They accepted the design and as Carlisle insisted in his evidence to the British inquiry, the object of getting White Star's approval was not simply that they were paying the bills, but that they should "have an opportunity of deciding for themselves whether the plans suited them ... (that they should) have the opportunity of seeing whether they would have 20 boats or 64 boats which ... could be provided". Carlisle is quite clear about what happened next.

The plans were submitted to White Star and discussed "two or three times". Ismay and Sanderson were the White Star representatives. The revolutionary new davits, 16 pairs, were made and fitted on the *Titanic* and *Olympic*. Each ship could then take 64 lifeboats, four to each set of davits. Yet, the ships were eventually equipped with only 16. For the builders, Carlisle said: "Personally, I considered there were not enough lifeboats. I said so over and over again in the works ... I thought there ought to be three boats on each set of davits ... 48 boats in all. Whereas in point of fact there were only 16."

That, then, is Carlisle's version of what had happened.

The White Star version is much simpler. Neither Ismay nor Sanderson had "any recollection" of seeing any such plans.

Ismay said that he remembered seeing plans for the "fitting up" of lifeboats but, as for any suggestions that this should be as many as 40 lifeboats, he had "never seen any such design".

In fact, he did not think "any special attention was given" to the question of providing additional lifeboat accommodation for the extra thousands of passengers who would be carried.

Sanderson was even more adamant. "The managers of the White Star Line never saw (Welin's design) and never heard of it until *after* the *Titanic* accident."

Was there not correspondence, then, that indicated whether discussions *had* indeed taken place over the question of the lifeboats? "We should be very largely influenced by the builders on this matter."

Were there not documents to show (a) what the builders had put forward, (b) what White Star's marine adviser had suggested, or (c) what White Star had eventually decided upon? "I doubt it very much. Plans (for the whole ship) are submitted to us and we examine them around a table and talk over the different points and make little notes..."

The Commissioner, Lord Mersey, was moved mildly to remark, "I should have thought that there would have been correspondence on the subject (of lifeboats)." And Sanderson replied, "There may be, but I have no recollection of it ... I am pretty sure (there is nothing). I will have it traced if there is."

The rebuttal was total. The implication was clear. Carlisle was lying.

* * *

On June 30th 1910, eleven months before *Titanic* was launched and, according to Carlisle, six months after he had forcefully expressed his view on the matter of lifeboats, Alexander Carlisle retired from Harland & Wolff. In August he went to join Axel Welin, the designer of the new davits then being built for the *Titanic* and *Olympic*.

* * *

Horatio William Bottomley, who was born in 1860 and died in 1933, was a rogue. Of that, there can be little doubt, though it is fair to add that there were millions who, during the first 50 years of his life, would have found that assertion difficult to believe.

For Horatio Bottomley was also a spellbinder – a man of split personality who defrauded a public dazzled by the brilliance of his words out of hundreds of thousands of pounds through a series of questionable ventures. In a little more than ten years, he promoted nearly 50 companies with a total estimated capital of £20 million. As his business methods were called into question between 1901 and 1905, 67 bankruptcy petitions were filed against him.

Yet in 1906, he ran for Parliament in the London borough of South Hackney – and won. He stood as a Liberal; the political label scarcely mattered because it was as a populist that he was elected. Bottomley knew how to communicate. He did it from the platform, his stocky body radiating both energy and sincerity. Most importantly, he did it through his writing. For whatever his morals in the world of finance – and in March 1922 he was eventually to be found guilty at Bow Street Magistrates' Court on 23 out of 24 charges of fraudulent conversion – he was a vigorous, colourful, campaigning journalist. He had bought *The Sun* newspaper in 1898 and in 1906 he founded a new style of weekly magazine. He called it *John Bull* and, through it, he pursued his own political ambitions, berated his own Establishment enemies, paraded his own florid patriotism – and launched his own simply-stated campaigns. Often he was inaccurate and over-hasty. Frequently, he was cruel. Sometimes he was correct. Which is where the extraordinary life of Horatio Bottomley touches the story of the *Titanic*.

Whether or not Bottomley had himself seen the model of the ship, we shall never know. Perhaps it was noticed by one of the excellent journalists who were attracted to him and his publications and clung to his coat-tails through year after stormy year. Whichever way he came by the information, on November 22nd 1910, Bottomley asked, in the House of Commons:

"Has the President of the Board of Trade's attention been called to the fact that the new White Star Liner, the *Olympic*,[16] now being built – and a model of which is being exhibited in Piccadilly – is provided with only 14 lifeboats … and will he make representations to the owners on this matter…?"

The answer, from Mr Tennant for the Board of Trade, was this: "I understand the *Olympic* will be provided with 14 lifeboats and two ordinary boats, of an aggregate capacity of 9,752 cubic feet, which is in excess of the requirements of the statutory rules…"[17]

It was an answer that did not satisfy Horatio Bottomley. The model of the *Olympic*, virtually identical to the *Titanic*, was on show in Piccadilly, as part of a publicity campaign launched by the White Star Line to convince those wishing to travel across the Atlantic that they should do so by White Star Line vessels rather than by, say, Cunard. After *Olympic* would come *Titanic* and then *Gigantic*. The battle for the transatlantic market was becoming keener month by month. Apart from any legitimate concern he may have had about

---

16. Olympic, sister ship of Titanic, was being built beside her in Belfast
17. Hansard, November 22nd 1910

the lifeboat regulations, Bottomley sensed a good story.

He renewed his attack through the pages of *John Bull*, thus:

THE WHITE STAR'S *OLYMPIC*
A Serious Insufficiency of Lifeboats

Our attention has been directed to the model of the *Olympic*, the monster steamship of 45,000 tons now building for the White Star Line. This model may be seen under the Piccadilly Hotel. An examination will show that the new ship is to have only 16 boats. The *Mauretania* and *Lusitania*, very much smaller ships, have 40 boats and rafts. The *Europa*, which is about to be built for the Hamburg-American Line, and will be 5,000 tons larger than *Olympic*, will have no fewer than 80 boats. How, then, can 16 boats be sufficient for the *Olympic*? The explanation given by the Company is that the ship is practically unsinkable, and that for life-saving purposes boats will not be required. That is a most unsatisfactory explanation. No vessel can be considered unsinkable if it meets with certain concussions. And presumably the *Europa* will be as unsinkable as the *Olympic*, but the builders of the German vessel do not suggest that life-saving apparatus will be unnecessary. What does the Board of Trade say?

Encouraged by this, an anonymous naval architect wrote to *John Bull* in December 1910. He said:

"Towards the end of 1909, Mr A M Carlisle and myself ... worked out special davits for the *Titanic* and *Olympic* ... each capable of carrying three or even four lifeboats. These davits are actually being fitted and although I have personally no idea how many boats the builders or owners are likely to fit in these ships prior to their departure..."

Whether or not Bottomley knew it, the anonymous

naval architect was of course, Axel Welin, now working in partnership with Carlisle and owner of the company making the revolutionary davits.

On December 31st 1910, Bottomley fired his next shot – at the alleged 'unsinkability' of the *Olympic* and *Titanic*. He referred to the British liner *Pericles*, which had sunk on March 31st 1910. He quoted a survivor of the disaster thus:

"The statement of the 'unsinkability' of modern ships is all bunkum. Taking the case of *Pericles*, although she was equipped with a double bottom, airtight compartments, submarine signalling and all the 'other paraphernalia' supposed to render a ship unsinkable, she foundered, shortly after striking a reef off Cape Ludwig, the same as any ordinary vessel would have done."

Bottomley was also taking the opportunity of a sideswipe at a political opponent, a man who had been harrying him over financial dealings – Sydney Buxton, 1st Earl Buxton and President of the Board of Trade. He pointed out that the survivor had written to the Board of Trade, to its president (Buxton), enclosing his criticisms and the unfavourable comments of others. These included the serious charge against the shipping company that some of the lifeboat equipment was so corroded and so little used that they were impossible to lower. Bottomley continued:

"It might have been thought the President of the Board of Trade would have considered these grave allegations sufficiently important to warrant courteous acknowledgement as a matter of fact; although the letter was sent in April last, it remains unacknowledged."

In February 1911 – still more than a year before *Titanic* went down – Bottomley returned to the attack in the House of Commons. In a written question, he asked the President of the Board of Trade, now Winston Churchill, whether he would 'state the date of the last regulations made by the

Board in reference to the number of lifeboats necessary to be attached to passenger vessels; and whether having regard to the increased tonnage of modern ships, he will consider the desirableness of revising such regulations?' He had put his finger on a glaring weakness in British maritime law. From the Board of Trade he received the following written response:

'These regulations were last revised in 1894. The question of their further revision is engaging the serious attention of the Board of Trade and I have decided to refer the matter to the Mercantile Shipping Advisory Committee for consideration and advice...'

The British rules governing lifeboats, written in 1890 and slightly revised in 1894, were a peculiar affair. They were complex – and they were linked not to the number of passengers on board but to the gross tonnage of the vessels.

Any vessel of more than 10,000 tons, said the rules, had to carry lifeboats for about 1,000 people. More precisely, the maximum space any ship-owner would be expected to provide in lifeboats to save the lives of the passengers, was 9,625 cubic feet. Translate that space into people and it becomes 962 (if all are carried in lifeboats) or 1,133 (if some are assigned to lifeboats and others to collapsible dinghies). But since 1894 there had been an eruption in the size of the larger, passenger-carrying liners. RMS *Celtic*, launched at the turn of the century, was 21,000 tons. The *Lusitania*, launched in 1907, was 31,000 tons.

The ships grew but the rules did not change. *Titanic* and *Olympic*, each with a displacement of 45,000 tons and capable of carrying 3,547 passengers, had a legal requirement to carry lifeboats for only a third of that number of passengers – about 1,000. In retrospect, it was a scandalous situation. Nor were the authorities unaware of the need for change. Three days after Horatio Bottomley's question was parried in the

House of Commons, a circular letter was sent by the Board of Trade to the board's principal officers in the great ports of Liverpool, London and Glasgow. It asked each to draft their thoughts on how best the existing rules might be changed to meet the needs of those who would be – and were already – travelling on the breed of new giant liners.

From Glasgow, Principal Officer Harris replied within six days, on February 24th 1911. The principal officer in London, Mr Park, took three days longer and, in the following week, on March 3rd, Mr Young replied from Liverpool. All suggested a considerable increase in the number of lifeboats – and their promptness in reply indicated the priority they gave to the matter. The Board of Trade's principal ship surveyor, Mr William D Archer, produced a scale that would have provided 2,201 lifeboat places on *Titanic* – but he insisted that, because it would be "impossible" to provide a place for every member of passengers and crew, the ship-owners should be encouraged to "increase the floatability of the ships they built" and that "the way to encourage them was to *relax* the legal requirement as to (the number of) boats, as their plans advanced in that direction".[18]

The great object, said Mr Archer, was to build a ship which, in the event of a disaster, would be her own lifeboat. It was a thought and an aim that was to be adopted by the White Star Line. It was a sentence that would be repeated by them at the official British inquiry into the disaster.

These four reports from Young, Harris, Park and Archer were sent to the Board of Trade for consideration more than a year before *Titanic* set sail.

* * *

18. Lord Mersey, chair, in summary of British inquiry into Titanic disaster

Bottomley's question and his campaign in *John Bull*, had given a public voice to an anxiety that was being expressed throughout the world of shipping and shipbuilding. It had, to quote an internal Board of Trade memorandum (February 1911), raised 'very clearly the point whether the Board of Trade should consider the desirability of revising the Life-saving Apparatus rules...' Yet, however clearly the Board of Trade might now be considering the matter, the speed at which the British administrators reacted was anything but urgent. When *Titanic* struck her iceberg in April 1912, the rules were still precisely the same as they had been every year since 1894. Neither a word nor a comma had been altered for all the paperwork generated inside the Board of Trade. Lord Mersey was to say at the British inquiry:

"The omission during so many years, to revise the rules of 1894 ... was blameable... The gross tonnage of the vessel is not, in my opinion, a satisfactory basis on which to calculate the provision of boat accommodation ... There seems much more to be said in favour of making the number of lives carried the basis, and for providing boat or raft accommodation for all on board.

"The provision of (watertight) compartments is of supreme importance, but it is clear that it should not be sought at the expense of a decrease in boat accommodation. When naval architects have devised practical means for rendering ships unsinkable, the question of boat accommodation may have to be reconsidered, but until that time arrives, boat accommodation should, where practicable, be carried for *all* on board..."

Lord Mersey had the advantage of hindsight. But the Board of Trade had the opportunity at the very least, to see that other nations – Germany and the United States, for instance – had already taken action as they saw the size of the liners doubling and doubling again. The Americans had moved in 1907, extending their rules to cover vessels 'up to 20,000 tons gross' and containing a clause showing how 'the boat capacity is to be increased on vessels above that tonnage'. The Germans had changed their rules in 1909 specifying, 'the boats to be carried on vessels up to 17,500 tons gross' and indicating that 'for vessels of greater tonnage, the boats must be increased in number and capacity, in proportion'. Both these acknowledgements are quoted from an internal Board of Trade memorandum dated February 1911.

If *Titanic* had been German, she would have had to carry places in lifeboats or on rafts for more than 3,000 people. Had she been American, she would have needed 2,800 places in order to comply with the law. But she was registered in Britain – so she needed to carry lifeboat places to save only 962. It was not enough.

* * *

Early in 1911, a year before *Titanic* set sail, the British Government set up a committee especially to examine the question of safety at sea. The size of the passenger-carrying vessels was growing apace, outstripping the existing legislation. In May 1911, Alexander Carlisle was called to give evidence to their Merchant Shipping Advisory Committee. He had now been with Welin's company nine months, working on the new davits for *Titanic* and *Olympic*. He attended two meetings and took with him two plans; one, a modified scheme, based on the lifeboats originally mooted for *Titanic*, and the other on the new Welin davit, which was capable of carrying up to four lifeboats on each set. He said later: "The committee was practically at an end when I was asked to join it. I was only at the last two meetings and the majority of points had been well considered. They had (already) come to certain conclusions on certain points."

The committee, to quote its chairman, Sir Norman Hill, "were not satisfied" with Carlisle's schemes. They thought their scheme, which would have provided eight more lifeboats for *Titanic*, was "infinitely preferable to Mr Carlisle's plans (to have) open-decked lifeboats ... launched by rotation".

Carlisle later told the British Wreck Commissioner's inquiry into the sinking of the *Titanic* that he had continued to argue against the decisions of that committee. He did not consider their scheme to add just eight more lifeboats adequate and had told them so. But at least it was a step in the right direction and, because of that, he had agreed to sign the recommendations. He told the *Titanic* inquiry on June 10th 1912 that he was an unwilling partner. But a few more lifeboats were better than none.

Eight days later, Sir Norman Hill was called to the *Titanic* inquiry to give his version of what happened at that private meeting of the Merchant Shipping Advisory Committee. Sir Norman said that the account that Carlisle had given of what happened in the committee "was pure invention". Carlisle *had* put two plans before the committee but he had quite willingly gone along with the rejection of Welin's four-boats-to-a-davit scheme and he had agreed the modification of the second plan, which required only one boat under each set of davits. He had not opposed the committee's findings. "The greatest deference was paid to Mr Carlisle ... there was absolutely no pressure of any kind brought to bear on him."

When questioned, Sir Norman agreed that he had made the journey from Liverpool to the inquiry in London to correct the statement made by Mr Carlisle. In the Liverpool offices of Hill Dickinson & Co, 70 years later, I inspected a leather bound copy of the transcript of the evidence that had been given at the British inquiry. There, too, are Sir Norman's margin notes and scribbled comments on Carlisle's evidence.

Many of the points most contentious, most pertinent to

Carlisle's version of events, are heavily underscored. They are numbered and, as they accumulate, it is easy to imagine the mounting concern that Sir Norman must have felt in his office in Liverpool, that propelled him on his 300-mile journey to London. For Sir Norman Hill, the witness, was also a partner in the firm of solicitors instructing counsel for the ship-owners, the White Star Line. And White Star Line's version of events was being challenged.

His evidence was valuable support for White Star Line's version of events. Sir Norman was also secretary of the Liverpool Steamship Owners Association: it would not be surprising if he had the ship-owners' interests very much at heart...

* * *

"I am pretty sure there is nothing in writing ... but I will have it traced if there is ..." Thus, Mr Harold Sanderson, director of the White Star Line, in evidence to the British inquiry on June 5th 1912. So, was there any correspondence on the subject of lifeboats that might have helped the inquiry in its deliberations? Seventy years later, it was still possible to find in the Public Record Office, evidence of a brisk debate on the subject of the number of lifeboats to be carried by *Titanic* and *Olympic*.

On March 9th 1910, Axel Welin, davit builder, wrote to the Board of Trade. He enclosed a blueprint for the newly designed double acting davit. He stated: 'I confirm that the number of sets (of davits) is 32.' That's 16 davits for the *Titanic* and 16 for the *Olympic* – each vessel capable of carrying 64 lifeboats.

The Board of Trade replied a week later, on March 16th. They stated: 'The *Titanic* and *Olympic* are each to be fitted with 32 boats which are to be carried under 16 sets of double acting davits, eight on each side.'

Welin's layout positioned the extra lifeboats piled one on top of each other, beneath each davit (see plans, figures 1 and 5, page 223). Now, Carlisle firmly believed that both the *Olympic* and *Titanic* should be equipped, probably with 64 lifeboats or a minimum of 48 lifeboats. Yet, already, within seven days of the design being lodged with the Board of Trade, the 48 boats Carlisle had proposed as a minimum had become ... 32.

On March 23rd 1910, the Board of Trade declared: "The matter (of lifeboats) can be further gone into when the proposed new rule is settled..." The new rule, of course, was never settled – until *after* the *Titanic* had gone down, that is...

Carlisle left Harland & Wolff in 1910. And on July 1st that year, the Board of Trade heard from Harland & Wolff again: 'I beg to forward ... a print showing the number of the boats proposed to be carried...'

It showed: eight lifeboats each end: 16 lifeboats in all. The 48 lifeboats Carlisle had advised as a minimum had become 16 in four months.

In addition, six important files are missing from the Public Record Office – withdrawn and never returned. Among them, it transpires, was a report by the Emigration Officer of the Board of Trade on the day *Titanic* set sail, advising '50 per cent more lifeboats.'[19]

Is it conceivable, then, that this amount of documentation *could* have been chronicled without White Star being aware of a suggestion that *Titanic* needed to carry more lifeboats? For that was the stance that Ismay and Sanderson took in their scantily reported conflict with Alexander Carlisle. When *Titanic* sailed from Southampton on April 10th 1912, she was

19. See page 61

fitted with 16 sets of the revolutionary new davits designed by Axel Welin. The fact that only *one* lifeboat rested under each set was to be relevant only to those who were soon to die. Someone had paid for the development and installation of the new style of davits and that someone was the White Star Line. Is it likely that they paid out good money without finding out what they were buying? Regrettably, neither Ismay nor Sanderson was ever cross-examined about Carlisle's evidence; they were never asked the crucial questions:

Why did you buy Welin's new davits? What did you think the new davits were for? And, even if the law did not dictate, did you not think that in the interests of prudence a lifeboat place for every passenger would have been a sensible idea?

On March 29th 1912, only two weeks before *Titanic* sailed, Axel Welin was still trying to persuade the authorities of the folly of their decisions. He presented a paper on lifeboat installations to the Royal Institution of Naval Architects and wrote:

'On the boat deck of the White Star liner *Olympic*, and also of the *Titanic*, this double-acting type of davit has been fitted throughout in view of coming changes in official regulations. It was considered wise *by the owners*[20] that these changes should be thus anticipated, and so make it possible to double, or even treble, the number of boats without any structural alterations, should such increase ultimately prove to be necessary.'[21]

Even at this late stage, Welin hoped to influence the owners, White Star, to change their minds. In the record of that meeting, he revealed in discussion, his desperation:

MR AXEL WELIN (Associate): "Mr Chairman and Gentlemen, I am very grateful for the friendly criticism that

---

20. Author's italics
21. Precisely the evidence subsequently given by Alexander Carlisle to the Titanic inquiry

has been given in connection with this paper. Mr Robinson[22] suggested that owners might object to filling up the lower deck with lifeboats – well, they often object to boats wherever you place them. They dislike boats because they cannot earn money, and they fill up space..."[23]

* * *

The Merseyside Maritime Museum held a *Titanic* exhibition late in 1982. It was an imaginative, carefully-designed affair, the centrepiece of which was a huge model of *Titanic* that, for years, had rested at Blackpool Airport, assumed to be a replica of her sister ship, the *Olympic*.

But the museum had done its detective work. They had carefully taken the model apart as they renovated it – and they had found a number of fascinating contradictions in this 'model of *Olympic*'. First, each vessel in a shipyard carried a yard number. *Olympic*'s was 400. *Titanic*'s was 401. This model carried the number 401, which was *Titanic*'s identification number. Then the number of lifeboats had been altered, at least once – they could tell by the style of the craftsmanship.

She had once borne only 16 lifeboats but when she arrived at the museum, she carried 54. The museum's curiosity was aroused and, as Les Nelson Ewen drily put it, "Four years' work was complicated by the fact that we had to discard our original assumptions and change course in midstream..."

So, they went back to the beginning and examined the name on the bow. The lettering was crude. They cleaned part of it – and found scratched on the brass the letters 'Tit...' For more than 50 years, this model had hidden at Blackpool Airport, its identity quite deliberately changed and concealed.

22. Mr Robinson (a delegate)
23. The Arrangement of Boat Installations on Modern Ships, Axel Welin, to the Installation of Naval Architects, pp212 and 217

The museum's co-operation in our research was total. We were allowed to examine the model and have access to their documents. Many of the papers had belonged to Cunard, who had inherited them when they took over White Star in 1934. Cunard had passed them on to the museum in 1971. And among these documents, researcher, Kate Cross, and I, found a blueprint. It showed the suggested layout of the lifeboats aboard the *Titanic* and *Olympic*. It showed the new davits, and it showed something else – plans for an additional 16 lifeboats – capable of carrying another 800 people to safety. The document is an Axel Welin blueprint, drawn around 1910 (see photograph, page 221). It was found among the White Star Line's possessions.

The blueprint survives today through a series of pieces of good fortune. It had been stored, for years, in a sub-basement below Cunard House, at Liverpool's Pier Head. The sub-basement was regularly subject to flooding and many of the White Star documents that had been saved during the company merger had already been damaged beyond recall. Further, museum curator, Mike Stammers, admitted that "the whole job was done in a rush. Cunard were in a hurry to clear the space and we simply grabbed what we could – the rest they sent to the rubbish dump.

"We noticed there were some White Star documents – and anything from a defunct company like that is a bonus, so we took it."

On other blueprints rescued by the museum – deck plans, for instance – the word 'Titanic' has been erased. As with the 22 feet-long model, it was as if White Star wanted to excise *Titanic* from the company consciousness. But on the Welin document, the ship's name survives – overlooked in the aftermath of the disaster.

This blueprint, then, indicated that well before *Titanic* was launched, the shipping company *did* know of Carlisle's and

Welin's concerns that she would be carrying too few lifeboats. Further proof emerged in 2012, exactly 100 years after *Titanic* sank, in the salerooms of auctioneers Henry Aldridge & Son of Devizes in Wiltshire. Devizes is a country community of 30,000 souls, with a castle built in 1120 by Roger, Bishop of Salisbury, and the remains of a factory that, in the 18th century, produced an early version of cashmere, a cloth that found favour with the crowned heads of Europe and brought prosperity to this market town. On November 24th 2012, *Titanic* enthusiasts gathered in Henry Aldridge's auction rooms to bid for that rarity – a collection of original Board of Trade documents about *Titanic* bought by a solicitor more than 50 years before. It was probably the contents of one or more of the nine files missing from records of the British Inquiry in 1912.

The documents were bought by several anonymous bidders, for around £30,000. They revealed that, on the morning of her departure from Southampton, a Board of Trade employee, Maurice Clarke, boarded *Titanic* to check whether she could be granted a certificate to carry emigrant passengers. The notes Clarke made, for the record and for internal consumption, are damning to the White Star assertions at the inquiry. Clarke reported that it had not been possible to double the number of lifeboats because of 'cost and extra manning considerations'. But he recommended an increase of '50 per cent more' lifeboats to 30 in the event of a disaster that would 'allay a panic' and, tellingly, he acknowledged that if he had tried to insist on this increase 'I might be shifted (from my job), as is suggested to me by the owners if I enforced my views as to (this) efficiency'. Clarke's notes of the blueprint confirm that Ismay and Sanderson were lying as they professed ignorance of the conversations about the need for more lifeboats on the *Titanic*.

But when Mr Clarke was called to give evidence at the

British inquiry in London in July 1912, he backtracked and said he felt the *Titanic* was in "proper order" to go to sea. He did not mention his concern over the lifeboats. He toed the company line and kept his job. Maurice Clarke, employee of the Board of Trade, knew that, even in the sumptuous world of the *Titanic*, the profit motive was still an important consideration to the ship-owners.

For their part, White Star's counsel at the inquiry had clearly implied that it was Carlisle who had the financial motivation for not telling the truth. Had Carlisle not joined Welin's company, they asked? And was he not financially interested in the success of the new davits? But the suggestion does not bear examination. We shall never know why Carlisle voluntarily left Harland & Wolff in 1910. It could have been the disagreement with his co-director, Lord Pirrie, over the lifeboat issue. It is perhaps significant that in his 'anonymous' letter to *John Bull* in December 1910, Welin referred to both the White Star Line *and* Harland & Wolff when he said that he did not know how many boats would eventually go on board the giant ship when she sailed. He clearly felt there were two decision-makers.

Carlisle would hardly have left to join the Swedish firm to seek a commercial advancement, for Welin's was a small company struggling to launch a new idea. Harland & Wolff, at which Carlisle was a senior executive and a member of the 'family' that designed and built *Titanic*, was established as one of the world's richest and most prosperous shipbuilders.

The motivation for Ismay and Sanderson to lie is more obvious. Ismay was already shamed, rightly or wrongly, because he had taken a place in a *Titanic* lifeboat when others had stayed to die. The impact of this, added to the fact that the 'unsinkable' *Titanic had* sunk, was already having a serious effect on passengers' attitudes to White Star and her vessels. These were critical months for the company in

1912. How much more serious would it have been if it were admitted at the official inquiry that the company's chairman *had* considered providing seats in lifeboats for everyone on board – and then decided against it? That, as a surviving crew member was later to say,[24] would have been "almost like murder, wouldn't it..?"

Soon after the inquiry was over in 1913, chairman Bruce Ismay retired from the White Star Line and from public life. It was rumoured that he became a recluse, that he lived a solitary life on the West Coast of Ireland. In fact, he was embraced by a supportive family and died in October 1937. His body lies in Putney Vale Cemetery, London.

But what happened to the 'family' that had given birth to *Titanic*? Well, Thomas Andrews' reputation was secure. He died a hero with several witnesses saying that they had last seen him on board guiding passengers to the lifeboats. Steward, John Stewart, said that 15 minutes before *Titanic* sank, Andrews was standing in the first class smoking room, arms folded, his life jacket lying on a nearby table. Stewart asked him: "Aren't you going to have a try for it, Mr Andrews?" Andrews did not reply. "I think he was in a state of shock."[25] Several sources place Andrews on the bridge with Captain Smith, as the *Titanic* sank.

After *Titanic*, Lord Pirrie remained a dominant figure in Harland & Wolff. He was made a viscount in 1921 when King George V visited the Belfast yard. He died at sea in 1924 en route to South Africa.

After *Titanic*, Alexander Carlisle never again spoke publicly about the battle he had lost over the lifeboats. At the memorial service for the *Titanic's* dead in St Paul's Cathedral, he broke down in tears, a fact recorded in a headline in *The*

---

24. Survivor Frank Prentice, assistant purser, conversation with author, Southampton, 1993
25. The Sinking of the Titanic, Library of Ireland

Times newspaper. He died in 1926.

After *Titanic*, Axel Welin continued to develop, with Carlisle, his new style of davits and the Swedish business flourished, just as it does today, as Welin Lambie at Brierley Hill in the West Midlands. The company has since provided davits for the *QE2* and the Royal Yachts. Axel Welin died in July 1951.

The rules governing lifeboats were eventually changed, of course, and never again did a liner sail without sufficient lifeboats for everyone on board in the event of a disaster. In the wake of the sinking of the *Titanic* in 1912, business in life-saving equipment was never better...

Chapter 3

AND THEN WE WERE THREE...:
IVF – An Inside Story

The first words I ever spoke to Patrick Steptoe were: "What *exactly* are you doing, doctor?"

The question carried the traditional air of inquiry, seeking information. But beneath it was more than a hint of concern. It reflected the mood of the time, when in vitro fertilisation (IVF) was dismissed as a race to produce a 'test tube baby' through a scientific process that drew doubt or disapproval from pretty well every section of society, with the conspicuous exception of one.

The childless.

Infertility is defined by the World Health Organization (WHO) as a disease and a disability. To remedy it is, and never was, a self-indulgent exercise.

Now that perhaps nine million babies have been brought into the world through IVF, it is difficult to recall the invective aimed at those who wished to pursue this experimental work. It came from across the scientific, religious and political spectrum.

The first news of IVF broke in the *Sunday Times* in 1965 under a headline reflecting a science fiction attitude to this particular branch of medicine: 'Births by Proxy – experiments reminiscent of Huxley's Brave New World'. By 1970, IVF was in the eye of a media storm. The *News of the*

World led its front page with an inch-high headline: "'TEST TUBE BABY SENSATION... there's one on the way'.[26] Test tube babies were 'raising moral issues; they were a move to the threshold of genetic engineering'. *The Sun* shrieked 'Ban the Test Tube Baby'. In the USA, too, scientific journalists wrote of 'made to order human beings'.[27] The Vatican condemned IVF as 'immoral'. The Chief Rabbi of the United Hebrew Congregations of the Commonwealth, Dr Immanuel Jakobovits branded the work as 'indefensible'. It should be stopped immediately and the "stud farming methods" were "a debasement of human life". There was "no justification for the experiments already undertaken in this sacred sphere and a strict moratorium should be placed on further tests".[28] At the same time, Peregrine Worsthorne, a widely-read columnist and political commentator, wrote: 'The act of procreation, or rather human procreation, has always been regarded as rather a miraculous business, not so much a matter of sperm and ova, as of God moving in a mysterious way his wonders to perform.

'The process of conception, in short, is both mysterious and private, the one area of life, for most human beings, in which they withdraw from the web of social intercourse, from the ties of society in general, into an oasis sacred to themselves ... Prayer and death have always been social acts; but never the procreative act.

'Nothing would simplify the problem of social planning so much as to allow the State to determine the size and kind of its population. Nationalisation of the breeding process would put into the hands of the State incomparable new powers for good as well as evil.

'Yet even Hitler did no more than toy with such powers;

---

26. *News of the World*, November 1ˢᵗ 1970
27. Baby's life begins in test tube, Universal Science News, October 1970
28. *Sunday Express*, March 1st 1970

not even he dared fully to breach the taboos governing the procreative process. The question raised by the news last week of test-tube babies is surely whether scientific progress, put to human ends, is going to succeed in making this breach...

'Test-tube babies are State babies to an extent that has never been known before, and it is only a matter of time before they are treated as such.'[29]

Worsthorne was a popular, quirky communicator in print, on radio and on television. He wrote for *The Telegraph* group of newspapers. The group's circulation was nearly 600,000 a week. Worsthorne's views reflected a considerable body of opinion.

At the heart of this storm were two people – surgeon, Patrick Steptoe and scientist, Robert Edwards. There was a third member of the team, who remained very much in the background – but of her, more later. Edwards and Steptoe were a contrasting pair. Yorkshireman Edwards, a distinguished scientist, a socialist who was a Labour councillor in Cambridge, where he worked at the University; Steptoe, a patrician, fond of stylish cravats and never happier than when playing his grand piano. Edwards had set out on a career in agriculture at the University of Bangor in North Wales. A scholarship boy, second son in a working class family in Batley, Yorkshire, he had been commissioned during his National Service and the officers' mess had given him a glimpse of another world; one of "affluence and grace ... croquet on a green lawn".[30] As a schoolboy during World War II, he had been evacuated to the Yorkshire Dales away from the bombs and the batteries of anti-aircraft guns and had developed a love of the countryside. "I had watched with wonder the birth of calves, sheep, pigs and foals,

29. *The Sunday Telegraph*, March 1970
30. A Matter of Life by Robert Edwards and Patrick Steptoe, 1980, p15

as the warplanes droned ... overhead." At university, he now switched to the Department of Zoology and became fascinated by the early stages of animal life, embryology. He asked the question: *Why does only one spermatozoon enter a female's egg?* The question was the first step towards the birth in Oldham in 1978 of the world's first IVF baby, Louise Brown.

Patrick Steptoe was also a grammar schoolboy, from Witney in Oxfordshire. His father was Witney's Registrar. Patrick loved medicine and music and played piano in the local cinema as background to the silent films of Harold Lloyd and Rudolph Valentino. He was organist at the local church and director of the Christ Church Musical Society. He chose medicine rather than music as a career and later credited the "weight of the organ keys" for making his hands and fingers so strong in his career as a surgeon. His war service was in the Royal Navy, where he rose to the rank of lieutenant commander. He was torpedoed off Crete, was rescued by the Italian navy and spent the next three years as a prisoner of war, finding it an opportune time to fascinate his Italian captors with his knowledge of music and wine.

If one were choosing an Odd Couple in order to prove that, through partnership, nothing is impossible, Steptoe and Edwards would be high on the list. Two very different men sharing only a major drive for success.

Edwards would go on to be knighted and win the Nobel Prize in Physiology and Medicine in 2010 for his work on IVF. Steptoe was awarded the CBE in 1988, which, to quote his friend and partner Edwards "was regarded by many as an inadequate reward in view of the immense and revolutionary contribution he made to his country and his subject".

Their partnership survived daunting difficulties. In the early years, Edwards lived and worked in Cambridge; Steptoe 181 miles away in Oldham, Lancashire. They had met when

Edwards heard Steptoe speak at a conference on childlessness and the special surgical skills needed to harvest human eggs through laparoscopy.[31] Edwards was so impressed that he asked colleagues why a formidable a surgeon "with such a funny name"[32] was working in Oldham rather than in one of London's leading teaching hospitals. The two men talked, shared aims and the partnership began. Both men identified key milestones in that partnership.

In 1965, Edwards went to the USA to work with the husband-and-wife team of gynaecologists, Howard and Georgeanna Jones at Johns Hopkins University, Baltimore. In the laboratory at Cambridge, Edwards had been frustrated by a shortage of human tissue as he explored whether sperm and egg could be persuaded to join and fertilise *outside* the human body. In Baltimore, working with like-minded doctors, there was human tissue in plenty. Edwards would later describe those weeks in Baltimore as "decisive for me ... I felt confident that I would solve the problem". It was also the beginning of a relationship with the Joneses that would lead to the birth of the first IVF baby in the United States, 16 years later.[33]

In 1970, Edwards and Steptoe announced they would be ready "shortly" to carry out the world's first implant of an IVF embryo into the womb of a childless woman.[34] It provoked a storm in the world's press. Opposition was sustained and serious. The US journal *Medicine Today*, summed up the received wisdom on Steptoe and Edwards' work thus:

'SCIENCE TAKES OVER FROM WIFE: TEST-TUBE BABY HOPES GROW.' And it went on:

---

31. Laparoscopy: A surgical procedure by which a laparoscope is inserted into a woman's ovaries to extract an egg or eggs
32. Steptoe and Son was a top-rated comedy show on the BBC at this time
33. Elizabeth Jordan Carr, born December 28th 1981 at 7.46 am in Norfolk, Virginia
34. A Matter of Life, Edwards and Steptoe, 1980, p98

'Are these hopes for conception outside the womb well founded? What do these headlines mean for women who suffer from infertility and are willing to grasp at any chance to bear a child?

'Bold researchers talk enticingly of producing pregnancies in heretofore hopelessly infertile women, perhaps within a year. Their conservative colleagues, who are equally knowledgeable, say that such talk is deceitful; it raises hopes that cannot be fulfilled. Time will tell who is right.

'Conception normally occurs after a woman ovulates at mid-cycle. An egg passing down one of her two tubes – each about 4¼ inches long – is met and penetrated by an upward swimming sperm. A series of delicate arrangements of the two parent cells' genetic endowments follows, and the microscopic new being begins to grow by dividing and doubling its cells. Normally, it remains in the Fallopian tube for three to five days, then passes out into the uterus. It floats freely there a while, then attaches itself to the uterine wall, which has been prepared to receive it by the fertilized egg's very presence in the tube and womb.

'Fertilization thus is a critically-timed series of events that involves all of a woman's reproductive organs. These events may seem simple to duplicate outside a woman's body in a glass lab dish – 'in vitro' is the technical term. In fact, they are not at all simple.'

The article went on to summarise Edwards' and Steptoe's work, reporting the claim that they had 'developed a fluid that encourages human sperm to penetrate eggs with which they are placed'. They reported Edwards as saying: '"Suddenly, to our unbounded delight, the sperm started penetrating the eggs".'

Medicine Today quoted a number of US experts in the field, all doubting that the British team had achieved what they claimed. Dr Richard Blandau, a specialist in biologic structures at the University of Washington in Seattle, said:

"I don't believe they have achieved penetration ... Steptoe has gone overboard. To raise hopes in people with fertility problems that they can solve these problems in this decade is stretching things as thin as they can be stretched. I object to this violently. This is poor science. No-one knows what kind of baby they will get."

Medicine Today conjectured: 'Who will succeed in implanting the first test-tube baby – and when? The Steptoe-Edwards team generally is conceded to be in the lead. In mid-July, Dr (*sic*) Steptoe said no pregnancies had been achieved. "We're just about to publish a paper on how to do it – how to fertilize an egg and how to get it to grow. Then it won't be long before we do it." In the US, Dr Clyman[35] says: "Putting fertilized eggs back in the uterus at this moment is a little like science fiction.

"What, then, can a woman with blocked tubes do? No infertility counsellor today would tell her to abandon adoption attempts and wait for an in vitro fertilized baby. In all probability, the better part of the decade – at least – must pass before the procedure can be performed routinely."

In April 1971, Edward & Steptoe applied for a grant from the UK Medical Research Council (MRC) to continue their work on a programme of scientific and clinical 'studies on human reproduction'. The MRC rejected their application saying they had "serious doubts about ethical aspects of the proposed investigations". The MRC members assessed the IVF work as purely experimental, feared foetal abnormalities and wanted more experiments on primates to be carried out. They were also "antagonised by the applicants' high media profile". One of the scientific referees on the 1971 funding application began his report: "Dr Edwards feels the need

---

35. Dr Martin Clyman, Mount Sinai Hospital, New York City, who was also experimenting with IVF

to publicise his work on radio and television, and in the press, so that he can change public attitudes. I do not feel that an ill-informed general public is capable of evaluating the work… This publicity has antagonised a large number of Dr Edwards' scientific colleagues, of whom I am one." The other MRC referees agreed that Edwards' work was excellent but that, "on balance," the application did not merit support. The MRC's judgment said scientists who supported IVF, provided an 'insight into the then dominant attitudes of reproductive scientists and clinicians towards human conception research'.[36] They forget, some added, that the world was overpopulated already.

To Edwards and Steptoe, it was a profound blow. Edwards later confided: "I felt sick reading that letter. This opposition was wounding. I read it again and I felt angry. I lifted the phone to Patrick. 'I have some bad news, Patrick'. I don't recall exactly what he said."[37] The rejection set MRC policy and medicine's attitudes negatively for the next eight years.[38]

In October 1971, Robert Edwards was invited to attend a symposium on medical ethics by the Kennedy Foundation. It would be in Washington DC. At the dinner beforehand at the home of Sargent Shriver,[39] Edwards chatted to Dr James Watson, Nobel Prize winner in 1962, for his work with Francis Crick on the double helix structure of DNA. Edwards recalled later: "He was less than jocular." The next morning, Edwards spoke first in a session titled Fabricated Babies.

There were six other members on the panel and from two of them the attacks on his work were withering. Then James Watson spoke. He turned to Edwards and said:

---

36. Human Reproduction, Johnson MH, Franklin SB, Cottingham M and Hopwood N, September 2010
37. A Matter of Life, Edwards and Steptoe, 1980
38. Until, in fact, the successful birth of the first IVF baby, Louise Brown
39. Brother-in-law of President John F Kennedy

"*You can only go ahead if you accept the necessity of infanticide. There are going to be a lot of mistakes (in IVF). What are we going to do with these 'mistakes'? We must, we have to, think about things that we now refuse to think about.*"

The decision of the MRC *not* to fund IVF had been leaked to the press before the conference. Edwards commented later: "Though (we were) certain of the justice of our work, it would be wrong to pretend that all the hostility that Patrick and I were ... subjected to left us entirely unaffected."[40] To Edwards and Steptoe, the criticisms were "unrelenting..."

The criticism also affected personal and professional relationships. Scientists, as always, pursue different methods of achieving their objectives. Robert Winston[41] went to Hammersmith Hospital as a registrar and a Wellcome Research Fellow in 1970 and, five years later, was a scientific advisor to the World Health Organization on human reproduction. He concentrated on reducing human infertility through surgery on the female Fallopian tubes. This was his preferred way forward and he was allegedly critical of IVF. Andrew Steptoe, Patrick's son,[42] recalls: "At one of the most difficult times in the IVF programme, Robert Winston described IVF at a medical conference as being dangerous and not the right way to go. Tubal surgery offered more hope. Bob and my father were deeply upset. To criticise privately could have been helpful but to do so publicly was, they felt, unnecessarily hurtful."

Winston was a major figure in the field, with a big clinic at a major London hospital. What he was alleged to have said was obviously influential, criticising the work of a so-far unproven scientist in Cambridge and an unknown surgeon

40. A Matter of Life, Edwards and Steptoe, 1980, p111
41. Now Lord Winston
42. Andrew Steptoe, Head of Behavioural Sciences Health, University College, London

in Oldham. Andrew Steptoe said: "My father never held back if he felt something strongly. He dismissed the criticism from 'these bloody people'. But I know he felt that this intervention helped to set the IVF programme back some years."

Patrick Steptoe never forgave Winston. "Years later," says Andrew Steptoe, "Lord Winston offered an apology to my father for what he had said.

"My father refused to accept it."

In 1980, Robert Winston opened a reproductive clinic at Hammersmith Hospital and became Professor of Fertility Studies. The clinic offered IVF as a treatment and 'revolutionised in vitro fertilisation, leading to its place as one of the most successful units in the world'.[43]

* * *

This summary of the ten years leading up to July 25th 1978 is necessary in order to understand fully what happened that day at Dr Kershaw's Cottage Hospital (now Dr Kershaw's Hospice) in Oldham and in the months that followed the birth of Louise Joy Brown. Everything that had gone before every criticism, every disappointment had contributed to the growth of a siege mentality in the British team. Their work had been widely undermined; the MRC had doubted their governance and sense of responsibility and had even wanted them to move their laboratory work from Cambridge University so that they could give it closer inspection. Edwards and Steptoe felt battered and unloved. They trusted only their close friends and colleagues but the conviction remained that what they were doing was morally and ethically correct. They were determined to succeed, with or without the support of the medical Establishment; they were going to protect their

---

43. Robert Winston website, 2020

ability to make and implement their own decisions. They would continue as they were, with Edwards in Cambridge and Steptoe in Oldham, separated by 181 miles.

* * *

The public's eyes were fixed on Steptoe and Edwards. But there was a third person in this remarkable team – a nurse. Her name was Jean Marian Purdy. She was crucial to the success of IVF in two ways; for her skill in the laboratory and for her encouragement of the two men, particularly of Edwards, when the programme threatened to founder. She was perfectly equipped to complement and work with them. She loved music, which pleased Steptoe. She was hardworking and a brilliant technician, which established a huge respect in Edwards. Her fellow nurses in Oldham spoke of her unassuming willingness to help: "Nothing was too much trouble." She also had the priceless gift of putting at ease the patients she cared for; women who were, without exception, anxious as they entered a programme that was still experimental but which presented perhaps their only chance of having a child of their own. From 1968, Purdy, who trained at Addenbrooke's Hospital in Cambridge, worked for 17 years with Edwards as an embryologist on the oocytes[44] that Steptoe harvested. She kept the data and records for the team – much of it in her own hand, with amendments in red ink – including the laboratory results of the embryo transfers and even the meals and travel expenses. She systemised the data used for analysis and publication. She worked through the frantic years, which included carrying fertilised human eggs from Cambridge to Oldham inside the body of a live rabbit, to the endless, testing days in the 1970s when hopes

---

44. Oocyte – human egg

of a pregnancy were dashed again and again. It was always, she once said, "another day, another adjustment" in the technique. By 1974, Edwards was openly saying: "It was no longer just Patrick and me. We were a threesome."

In 1974, Edwards seriously considered giving up the IVF programme. He was flirting with a political career. As a Cambridge city councillor, he offered himself as the Labour candidate in the constituency's parliamentary seat. He was narrowly beaten by Jim Curran, who then lost the seat at the next General Election. This coincided with a period of relative inactivity in the IVF work. Purdy's mother died; she nursed her through her terminal cancer. Funds for IVF were short. Support was scarce. The press and peer group criticism was wounding. Discouraged by the lack of progress, Edwards considered switching his priorities to another project on which he was working, to revitalise the qualities of blood and to explore the future for stem cells. He asked for Purdy's opinion; would she like to join him on this new initiative? Purdy was adamant "in her restrained manner". A colleague remembers[45] that she was convinced of "the rightness of his vision of bringing IVF to the world". No personal or professional considerations should stand in the way of the IVF work. Jean "persisted alongside Bob despite the disappointments, setbacks and repetitive failures".[46] A committed Christian, Purdy firmly rejected the religious criticisms of their work.[47] During this period of self-doubt, she was "a major supporter of keeping things going and she worked – along with Patrick, who was a really tough, determined and optimistic man – to urge Bob to persist. She and Bob were … also good friends ... beyond a purely scientific association. The combination of professional and

---

45. Dr Joe Schulman, former clinical and laboratory research colleague on IVF
46. Ibid
47. Rosemary Carter, friend of Purdy

personal closeness was also true for Bob and Patrick".[48]

Without it, the IVF programme might not have survived.

* * *

Dr Kershaw's Cottage Hospital in Turf Lane, Royton, near Oldham was completed in 1929, at a total cost of £14,850. A charity was set up to be administered by a committee of nine, which "was not to include any clergyman or socialist".[49] It had opened in 1931, a hospital intended for medical and surgical patients only.[50] Preference would be given to Royton residents. Those who did not live in Royton would have to pay more for their treatment, though much later, this would not apply to IVF patients.[51] When the National Health Service (NHS) came into being in 1948, there were vigorous protests from Royton's residents opposing the takeover and transfer of the hospital to the NHS.[52] But the opposition barely delayed the move and the life of the hospital settled back into its traditional comforting presence in this Lancashire town. This was the hospital at which I first met Patrick Steptoe in the mid-1960s. This was his bailiwick. This was where he was, without exaggeration, adored. The contrast between Dr Kershaw's Cottage Hospital and the clinical vastness of a leading London teaching hospital could not have been greater.

The atmosphere at the hospital on the fifth day in the 39th week of Lesley Brown's pregnancy, July 25th 1978, was extraordinary. Bob Edwards was relaxing at his cottage in

---

48. The Oldham Notebooks, an analysis of IVF, 1969–78; the role of Jean Purdy reassessed, Johnson MH and Elder K
49. Which, of course, would have ruled out Robert Edwards
50. Infections, mental and chronic cases were not admitted
51. No IVF patient ever paid for treatment
52. Oldham Local Studies and Archives

Yorkshire. Jean Purdy was at the hospital checking the assays as they came through from the laboratories. Patrick Steptoe was in his office, waiting for test results on the progress of Lesley Brown's pregnancy, on which he would decide when her baby would be born. At 5 pm that day, the phone on Steptoe's desk rang with Lesley Brown's results, "and I knew", Steptoe would say later, "that I could deliver the baby and that its size and weight would be above the level usually described as premature". He felt very calm.

The atmosphere outside the hospital complex was anything but calm. Kershaw's, where Steptoe and Edwards had laid the scientific and medical foundations for this moment, is about a mile away from Oldham General Hospital (now Royal Oldham Hospital), where Lesley Brown was waiting to give birth; a natural birth, perhaps, or a Caesarean section in the operating theatre along the corridor. Security was tight. For those of us in the building, the pattern of what would now happen had been laid down for weeks. The medical team would embrace the moment with their normal efficiency as for any birth – except, of course, it was by no means a routine birth. Those wishing to record what should be the historic moment had been vying for the privilege. Shrewdly, the hospital had arranged for a film crew from the Central Office of Information (COI) to record the birth itself. There were, it seemed, hundreds of people, including the world's press, on the outside trying to be on the inside. One journalist had attempted to enter the building disguised as a hospital porter, but was unmasked. Steptoe faced the problem of how he could prepare Lesley Brown for the birth, without alerting those outside the inner circle that the first IVF birth was imminent. Lesley, for instance, must starve for eight hours before going to the theatre. He knew that any disturbance in her routine would be noticed. But Lesley must not eat her supper. Nil by mouth. As it happened, Sheena Steptoe, Patrick's wife, was visiting Lesley Brown that afternoon. Through her, a message was sent to Lesley: 'Don't eat anything'. When, as usual, Patrick Steptoe did his ward rounds in the late afternoon, the contents of the supper tray had been routinely delivered to Lesley Brown's bedside – and had been efficiently deposited into a polythene bag by Sheena Steptoe and, thence, into her shopping basket to be taken off site. Lesley's cup of tea now disappeared down the washbasin. Steptoe and his wife then went home. Media attention had reached "gigantic proportions".[53]

"There seemed literally hundreds of reporters everywhere, inside and outside the grounds of the hospital. As I drove home, I realised my patience was almost at an end," said Steptoe. "Medically, we were ready but the authorities had known about this impending birth for many weeks and, from a media point of view, had apparently given little thought to its importance till the last minute." [54]

Steptoe had a nagging headache. When he reached home, he relaxed at his piano for 10 minutes. He and Sheena had a meal together and returned to the hospital, entering by a side door. There, Steptoe met Edwards and Purdy and, together, the three of them made their way between rows of the Oldham police force to meet the rest of the clinical team. Lesley Brown remembers being prepared for the birth by torchlight. I now use Steptoe's own words:

"At 11.30 pm, Lesley Brown was wheeled into the anaesthetic room. Bob, Jean and I gathered in a little knot, wished each other luck and went our ways; they, into their masked positions in the theatre, and I to Lesley.

"We were alone for a few minutes. I took her hand and comforted her and she smiled. I think we both made our

---

53. A Matter of Life, Ibid, p168
54. Conversation with author, 1979

prayers in our own ways at that moment. I listened one last time to the foetal heart. Fifteen seconds noted on the clock, 38 beats counted loud and regular and 152 beats per minute.

"I checked that everyone was ready and proceeded to the scrub-up area. I turned on the taps and started to wash. We had done all we possibly could to bring off this event. Of that I was confident. All the tests for normality had been done; no step had been reckless or hurried in all those long struggles. The moment we had all awaited so long was at hand."[55]

At 11.47 pm on Tuesday July 25th 1978, was born to Lesley Brown, in Oldham General Hospital, Lancashire, a baby girl named Louise Joy Brown. She weighed 5 lb 12 oz.[56]

Her surgeon said of the event: "Glorious. She was chubby, full of muscular tone … She took a deep breath. Then she yelled and yelled and yelled … and how we all loved that wonderful sound."

Much later, Lesley Brown whispered to Patrick Steptoe: "Thank you for my baby. Thank you."

Patrick Steptoe said to himself: "I doubt I shall ever share such a moment as this in my life again."

* * *

Months earlier, Patrick Steptoe had declared, over a glass of claret, that the birth of the first IVF baby would be "as big a story as man landing on the moon". He was sitting in the drawing-room of his house in Blackfriars Street, Canterbury, in the shadow of Canterbury Cathedral and with the River Stour flowing along the bottom of his garden. His grand piano occupied a quarter of the room's floor space while his wife Sheena was in the small kitchen, supervising the preparation

---

55. Ibid
56. The birth by Caesarean section is detailed in A Matter of Life, Steptoe and Edwards, 1980

of something delicious. He had expanded on the theme: "I'm not sure the medical authorities realise this – probably because they don't think we will succeed." He said it without rancour but with a tired acceptance of the opposition they were now used to facing. This compact home was a well-kept secret, chosen by Sheena who was the daughter of a Kent general practitioner.[57] She had been a RADA-trained actress. She and Patrick came to Canterbury to avoid the storm of publicity that pursued them, year after year. It was here that they escaped again, in the days following the birth of Louise Brown.

First, it was to Sheena's family home in Mill Lane; later to Blackfriars Street where there was more room. The Steptoes were visited occasionally by their children, Andrew and Sally. "What they liked about Canterbury," says Andrew today, "is that no-one bothered them. My father's face was well-known but, though everyone was friendly, this life was the closest they could get to normality."

Canterbury, more like a village than a city, is like that. It is a city where the man sitting next you in the hairdresser's may be an archbishop.

Apart from the media demands from all over the world, there were important decisions to be made. IVF, and Louise Brown, became 'a property'. Keen-eyed lawyers met Steptoe, Edwards and Purdy around boardroom tables to discuss "the future" and "rights".[58] The brutal truth was that, as Edwards put it: "We had nowhere (suitable) to continue our studies. Facilities offered in Manchester were of no use to me since

---

57. Sheena Steptoe's father was the village doctor at Boughton under Blean between Faversham and Canterbury. There is a street named after him in the village, Arthur Kennedy Close

58. Thames Television negotiated the exclusive rights to the IVF story and I produced and reported 'To Mrs Brown, A Daughter' on September 7th 1978 and later, 'Test Tube Explosion', which was runner-up for the Prix Italia in 1980

the exhausting travel to and from Oldham had to end. Patrick had passed retirement age from the National Health Service and a large hospital was needed to cope with the hundreds of patients who were queuing up for IVF. This proved to be unobtainable in Cambridge."[59]

Then the Steptoes suffered a personal tragedy. They were taking a well-earned rest, a transatlantic cruise on the *QE2*, when Sheena suffered a serious cerebral haemorrhage. She would need constant medical support for the rest of her life. The IVF project needed a home. Conversations with the *Daily Mail*, a group that had supported IVF and obtained exclusive access to tell the Louise Brown story in print, led to more boardroom negotiations to find financial backers for a new medical centre. Edwards reflected that, if they had accepted the early media offers for exclusive access to the Louise Brown story – one was for more than a quarter of a million pounds – they would not be in this "odd situation". Patrick Steptoe's list of would-be patients was expanding by the day. It was Jean Purdy who found, and suggested, Bourn Hall in Bourn, Cambridgeshire, a huge Jacobean house in expansive grounds. She would become 'technical director' at the new Bourn Hall Clinic.[60] A company called Bouvier Investments decided to back the venture – and then withdrew when warned of the financial risk if a deformed baby were born through IVF. After further months of negotiation, ICFC (now 3i) stepped in and Bourn Hall opened in 1980, more than two years after Louise Brown's birth.

Edwards said: "It was vital that IVF became an acceptable and routine clinical procedure. This delay has been frustrating and potentially damaging."[61]

---

59. Conversation with author, 1979
60. Rosemary Carter, Ibid, quoted in The Oldham Notebooks, 1969–78, Johnson & Elder, see also Appendix 3
61. Conversation with author, 2009

Within a few months of Bourn Hall Clinic opening, 15 pregnancies were established.

* * *

In the USA, the first American IVF baby, Elizabeth Jordan Carr, was born to Roger and Judith Carr, on December 28th 1981. She weighed 5 lb 12 oz and, as the gynaecologists Howard and Georgeanna Jones[62] reported, she was "beautiful and perfectly normal". The birth took place at the Norfolk General Hospital, Virginia. For those of us inside the hospital,[63] the experience aroused memories of Oldham, three years before. The difference was that the Joneses, cannily, had managed to avoid much of the intense media interest that had attended the birth of Louise Brown. On the previous day, Howard had, just in case, prepared a press release to cover the possibility of Judy Carr's baby being born abnormal, adding that 'we have two more patients with ongoing pregnancies whom we hope will be normal in every way'. He said: "Georgeanna never shared these misgivings ... and she and I went home, stopping at a beauty parlour because (she said) her hair was a mess."[64]

Elizabeth Jordan Carr was born by Caesarean section at 7.43 am the next morning. The news was released to the media, almost immediately. A press conference would take place at 11 am. The Norfolk General Hospital was besieged by cameras, outside broadcast trucks, "and, it seemed, hundreds of reporters." Howard Jones was "flabbergasted, both by the huge interest and by the speed with which our news went

---

62. Edwards had spent crucial weeks working with the Jones team in the US in the 1960s
63. As a result of our coverage on the birth of Louise Brown, the Joneses invited us to document Elizabeth's birth
64. IVF Comes to America, Howard W Jones Jr, Jamestowne Bookworks, 2014

around the world".[65]

Elizabeth Jordan Carr's birth was another step towards IVF becoming accepted as "a routine clinical procedure", as Edwards put it. The local newspaper in Norfolk, *The Virginian-Pilot*, did not see it that way and produced a leading article, which maligned the US IVF team. The Joneses and the hospital authority sued the newspaper for $27,500,000. Soon after a date for the trial hearing was set, an off-the-record meeting was called. Georgeanna Jones met Frank Batten, owner of *The Virginian-Pilot*. A settlement was reached – and the settlement money was given to Norfolk Medical School.

Ironically, when she was in her teens, Elizabeth Jordan Carr spent six months as a newspaper intern – at *The Virginian-Pilot*.

* * *

For nearly eight years, Edwards and Steptoe ran the largest IVF clinic in the world at Bourn Hall. It had teams of clinicians, scientists, nurses, technicians and support staff, all working closely together. For three years, more than half the world's IVF babies were conceived there. Two smaller clinics were opened in London. Edwards, Steptoe, Purdy and the team were together treating up to 2,000 patients a year.

It is not possible to work so intimately with colleagues, day after day, in a continually stressful situation without becoming close. Robert Edwards and Patrick Steptoe knew each other well. Purdy, based in Cambridge, spent as much, if not more, time with Edwards, as she did with Steptoe. She adored Edwards and deeply respected Steptoe. In 1980, Edwards wrote to Oldham area's Health Authority, suggesting that plaques be displayed at the hospitals 'to do justice to the

---

65. Conversation with author, 2009

participants involved'. The wording on the plaques would honour all three – Purdy, Steptoe and Edwards. The reply from the Health Authority omitted Purdy's name. Sector administrator, David Killion, wrote[66] that the wording would be: 'Human In Vitro Fertilisation, followed by the world's first successful pregnancy, was performed in this hospital by Mr Patrick Steptoe, Dr Robert Edwards and their supporting staff in November 1977.' Killion added: 'I hope you will find it sufficiently acceptable … even if this does not describe it as fully or as clearly as you would wish.'

Edwards did *not* find it acceptable. "I feel strongly about the inclusion of (all) the names … I feel this especially about Jean Purdy, who travelled to Oldham with me for 10 years and contributed as much as I did to the project … I regard her as an equal contributor to Patrick Steptoe and myself."

The plaque went on display at Dr Kershaw's Cottage Hospital at Oldham in Lancashire. It did not have Jean Purdy's name on it.

Within three years, the British IVF team suffered two hammer blows. First, in 1985 Jean Purdy died from a melanoma. Then, in 1988, Patrick Steptoe died from a resurgence of his prostate cancer. Edwards wrote an obituary which contained these words:

'Patrick Steptoe never had any soft options offered him throughout his medical career yet he made things work. He was charming when he wished to be and brusque when he didn't! He was optimistic, good-natured, reliable, a deeply affectionate family man … staff and patients … admired him almost beyond belief.' Edwards would "never forget", he said, "his determination to continue when his mind was made up and his passionate loyalty to his patients and his friends".

Professor Sir Robert Edwards was knighted in 2011. His

---

66. Robert Edwards' private papers

deepest regret was that his friend Patrick Steptoe could not share the Nobel Prize for Medicine that he had been awarded a year earlier in 2010. Frail and housebound, Edwards was himself too ill to travel to Stockholm so his wife, Ruth, accepted it on his behalf. Bob Edwards died in 2013.

* * *

Some months after his death, 21 notebooks and 571 pages 'of loose sheets and scraps of paper', including revelatory letters between Edwards and his patients, were discovered at his home. The contents confirmed that the British team had been both solicitous in their care for their patients and single-minded in their pursuit of producing a healthy baby.[67] They revealed that Steptoe and Edwards were so worried about producing an abnormal baby that every patient, when accepted into the programme, signed an agreement to undergo amniocentesis, with its attendant risk to the foetus at around three to four months' gestation.

Edwards had been at pains to inform his female patients that they were taking part in an experimental programme. The IVF team felt that eventual success was achieved at Dr Kershaw's Cottage Hospital in Oldham "largely because of the unpaid, voluntary work of the nurses and laboratory staff, who worked long hours, day and night".

Steptoe revealed that, if an abnormality were identified, he would have advised a termination of the pregnancy.

Before Louise Brown's birth, Steptoe and Edwards insisted on X-raying the foetus (with the attendant risks) "to see if the foetus was in the right position" – but also to check the baby was perfect. They both recognised that, for the first

---

67. The Oldham Notebooks, 1969–78, The role of Jean Purdy reassessed, Martin H Johnson & Kay Elder

IVF baby to be born deformed "could have stopped the IVF programme in its tracks".

The cache of new papers, meticulously assembled and analysed by Martin H Johnson and Kay Elder, confirmed the concern that scientist Edwards and surgeon Steptoe felt for their patients. They indicated "a driving desire to be as 'transparent as possible'" and the figures of the number of patients, nuclear transfers and implantations assembled, mainly by Purdy, give a detailed context surrounding Louise Brown's birth.[68]

* * *

How important, then, is the discovery of in vitro fertilisation? To the childless, in their millions, it has been vital. To the world, IVF has moved from being an acronym for fear and suspicion, to one of acceptance, hope and joy, which was why 'Joy' was the chosen middle name for Louise Brown.

Robert Edwards always appreciated the sociological implications of success with IVF, as well as the medical and scientific challenges. He often talked about the social issues that would face society, in the fields of human cloning, same-sex parenthood and genetic modification. He pointed out that identical methods of engineering an embryo could both remove the possibility of a hereditary disease, or aim to produce, to order, a child of choice. Scientists today are pondering these options and many others and considering their attitudes to them. In this regard, IVF has changed the world. We have entered 'the age of biological control'.[69] IVF

---

68. The papers also indicate that the first two pregnancies, to which no publicity was given, were both abnormal on examination, after they had spontaneously aborted

69. Ian Wilmut, Keith Campbell, Colin Tudge, The Second Creation, 2000. Wilmut's team cloned Dolly the sheep in 1996

was introduced to give nature a helping hand. Today, it is clear that IVF offers much more than this, for it has enabled a whole new understanding of the biological events it was intended to replicate, in turn, allowing reproductive cells to be re-programmed and re-made in the context of stem cell science, cloning and regenerative medicine.[70] And, as Edwards once said to me: "There's no going back. Once we've done it, the only way is forward..."

* * *

The other principal players in this medical drama were the two families – Lesley and John Brown with baby Louise in Bristol, England, and Judy and Roger Carr with baby Elizabeth in Westminster, Massachusetts. Lesley and John went on four years later to have a second daughter through IVF, named Natalie and both Louise and Natalie had their own children. John Brown died in 2006 and Lesley Brown, six years later. In the USA, Roger Carr, an engineer, and Judy, a teacher, continued to pursue their careers and young Elizabeth became a journalist in Virginia and Maine and later with *The Boston Globe*. She then became editor of several content websites. Like Louise Brown before her, Elizabeth had a baby of her own in 2010, a son named Trevor James. She wrote of the birth: 'Little Trevor was conceived in the old-fashioned way.' Her view of IVF?: 'People who have fertility issues deserve to know they can now safely have a healthy, normal family.'

In 50 years, the sensational and the extraordinary has become, simply and joyfully, very ordinary.

* * *

---

70. Conception Through a Looking Glass, Sarah Franklin, 2013

On March 19ᵗʰ 2015, another plaque was unveiled at Dr Kershaw's Hospice in Oldham. It reads:

Patrick Steptoe 1913–1988
Sir Robert Edwards 1925–2103
Jean Purdy 1945–1985
developed IVF, leading to the world's first 'test tube' baby

And then there were three…

Chapter 4

Ruth Ellis and the Mystery Lover

On July 13th 1955, Ruth Ellis became the last woman to be hanged in Britain. The revulsion at her death, described by author Raymond Chandler[71] as evidence of the "medieval savagery of the law", hastened the abolition of the death penalty in Britain in 1965. Yet Ruth Ellis was undoubtedly guilty, as she herself insisted. Was she, however, solely responsible for the murder of her lover, David Blakely? I doubt that. Nor do I believe that she should have been hanged by the neck until she was dead, for the crime of murder.[72]

In 1977, 22 years after the event, I travelled to Australia to find a man who should have stood in the dock beside Ruth Ellis, to confront him with his alleged role in the murder. His name: Desmond Cussen. The journey had begun a year before with the appearance in the *This Week* office of a letter from the lawyer, John Bickford, who had represented Ruth Ellis in 1955.[73]

In it, Bickford alleged that a second man, named Desmond Cussen, was involved in the murder and that he, Cussen, had taught Ellis how to use a gun and had driven her to the scene

---

71. Raymond Chandler: A Biography, Tom Hiney, 1997
72. The judge's words in pronouncing her sentence
73. Bickford had first taken the letter to the police and then to the Sunday Times. It was given to me by the then editor of This Week, David Elstein. Laurence Marks, who was later to write Ruth Ellis – A Case of Diminished Responsibility, with Tony Van den Bergh, helped research the Thames documentary and was associate producer of the programme

of the crime. None of this evidence had been produced at the trial. Why Bickford had written the letter, I don't know, but he knew he was dying and I now believe he felt that he had failed properly to represent Ruth Ellis at the trial. He was, as he put it, "trying to put the record straight".

Bickford said when we met that he had taken "the true story" to Scotland Yard some time before but that they had taken no action. So, now he was here to use the media 'to set it all down as it really happened'. John Bickford was hardly cut out to be the defence solicitor in one of the most high-profile trials of the 20th century. Ruth Ellis already had a solicitor, Victor Mishcon, with whom she had made an appointment four days before the murder, to discuss her divorce from her estranged husband, George Ellis, and the welfare of her daughter, Georgina. On the afternoon of the planned meeting, Mishcon had received instead a telephone call from Bickford asking, as a matter of courtesy, if Mishcon minded him defending Ruth Ellis against a charge of murder. Mishcon, primarily a civil lawyer, raised no objections – but would in fact become involved months later in a last-minute attempt to save Ellis from the gallows. Bickford's firm, Messrs Carden, Smith & Ross, were not criminal lawyers either and there are at least two versions of how Bickford became involved at all as a key player in this tragic story.[74] The first is that, as the whole of Fleet Street was elbowing its way towards those who knew Ellis to buy her exclusive life story, the two front-runners were Duncan Webb of *The People* newspaper and Duggie Howell of the *Daily Mirror*. Howell had targeted Ellis' landlady, a Mrs Winstanley, and had persuaded her to sign a draft letter "to a solicitor friend of mine (Howell's)", which would mean that, if Ellis co-operated, all her legal expenses would be covered by the

---

74. Ruth Ellis, Marks & Van den Bergh, Macdonald & Jane's, 1977, p122

Daily Mirror. The solicitor friend was a drinking buddy of Howell's, named John Bickford. Bickford's version is that a friend had called him on the bank holiday weekend to ask him to visit Ellis in HM Prison Holloway because her landlady, a Joan Winstanley, was worried about her. She said: "I refused at first but eventually agreed to go to see her on the Monday, provided I had written instructions. This I did – but Mrs Ellis was under sedation when I arrived at the prison. So, I returned the next day and met her then for the first time."

It would be the first meeting of many, for Bickford would instruct and support a distinguished defence team. It would be, Bickford would say, "an experience I will never forget. It will haunt me for the rest of my life…"

As a result of Bickford's revelatory letter, Thames Television decided to embark on a documentary based on the fresh allegations contained in it – but, because the allegations involved Desmond Cussen, Thames' lawyers advised that the only way the programme could be transmitted safely was if the allegations were put to Cussen. The snag was that, 22 years after the trial, no-one now knew where Cussen was. For weeks, our team searched for him. Then someone said they thought he had emigrated to Australia. *West* Australia, they thought. We explored the Perth telephone directory, looking for 'Cussen', a relatively rare name. And there it was. 'D Cussen, Florist'. If this was Desmond Cussen, we dared not alert him to our interest. We made discreet enquiries locally and learned that this number was indeed listed to a *Desmond* Cussen. We commissioned a photograph. It revealed a small, dark man with a moustache. It could well be the same Desmond Cussen who, we now believed, had given incomplete evidence at Ellis' trial. The next day, we boarded a plane to Perth…

* * *

To the lawyer's mind, the Ruth Ellis case was a bore. It was remarkable only in its simplicity.

A 28-year-old woman, Ruth Ellis, took to herself a lover, David Blakely, who was a racing driver. She sensed he was getting tired of her. Rather than lose him, she went to a public house in Hampstead, London, where he was drinking, waited for him to leave the bar and then emptied a .38 Smith & Wesson revolver into him. Pensioner Gladys Yule witnessed it: "The woman took a shot. The man ran around the car. She shot him again and he collapsed on the pavement. I was petrified. Then he raised himself up on one elbow – and I'll never forget the look of appeal in his eyes ... and she put two more bullets into him, deliberately. Then, very slowly, she put the gun up against her own temple (as if to pull the trigger) – but she couldn't do it. She just couldn't do it. She brought her hand down and the gun went off again. The bullet hit the road and ricocheted through my right hand.

"I was lucky. And it was murder."[75]

If ever there was an open-and-shut case, surely this was it. At the Old Bailey, where she stood trial for her life on June 21st and 22nd 1955, Ruth Ellis made the whole affair even simpler. Mr Christmas Humphreys QC led for the prosecution. For the only time in his distinguished career as advocate and judge, he wrote down the question he wanted to ask the accused prisoner in the dock. It was this:

"Mrs Ellis, when you fired that revolver at close-range into the body of David Blakely, what did you intend to do?"

Ruth Ellis replied: "It is obvious that, when I shot him, I intended to kill him."

The lawyer paused. "Thank you," he said and sat down.

---

75. Conversation with author, 1977. The fact that a passer-by, a member of the public was injured influenced Home Secretary Gwilym Lloyd George in his refusal to grant Ellis a reprieve. He said to Fenton Bresler: "We cannot have people shooting off firearms in the street."

That was the full extent of the cross-examination of the accused woman. The formidable trio of defence counsel – Mr Melford Stevenson QC leading with Mr Sebag Shaw and Mr Peter Rawlinson knew at that moment that, legally, the case was as good as over. As Mr Rawlinson (later, Sir Peter) told me: "Here was a woman admitting, on oath, in front of a judge and jury, that she had committed murder."

Mrs Ellis was an attractive woman, attractive enough to keep a job as a nightclub hostess. There were 10 men in the jury of 12. Yet, midway through the second day of this trial, which had become a formality, they took only 23 minutes to reach their verdict. Guilty. There was no recommendation for mercy. Mr Justice Havers, black-capped and grave, added this as he sentenced her:

"In my view, it was the only verdict possible."

Ruth Ellis was hanged at HM Prison Holloway, London on July 13th 1955. Hangman Albert Pierrepoint later told me: "I have seen some brave men die, but no-one braver than her."

These, then, are the facts. But, the facts don't reveal the whole story. There are three key questions at the heart of the fascination with the Ruth Ellis case.

One: Was her mental state significantly stable to justify her being charged with murder?

Two: Where did Ruth Ellis get the revolver with which she shot David Blakely?

Three: What part did Desmond Cussen play in the last few months of her life?

For there were *two* men in Ruth Ellis' life, not one – Blakely, the man she shot and Desmond Cussen, the man who knew so much more about the background to this case than he was ever asked about in court.

They came into Ellis' life at roughly the same time. It was 1953; Blakely was a fledgling racing driver. He was, at 24, four years younger than Ellis when he died. He was public school-educated; commissioned in the army during his National Service. He had money – at least during the early part of their relationship. His father had left him £7,000 and his stepfather gave him an allowance. He worked in the office of an engineering factory and, with the help of friends, he financed and built his own racing car. He called it the Emperor. He raced at Oulton Park, Brands Hatch, Silverstone and other British circuits and he competed on the Continent. He lived with his mother and stepfather at Old Park, Penn, Buckinghamshire and he had a flat in the West End, which his former nanny looked after for him. To Ellis, it was a fascinating lifestyle, one to which she aspired.

Blakely enjoyed relaxing with a drink at a few favoured clubs in London's West End. He drank with his close friends in the world of motor racing. It was at Carroll's Club in Duke Street, that he had met Ruth Ellis. That was where Desmond Cussen would also meet her, casually over a drink, later that year.

Cussen was 33 when Blakely died, five years older than Ruth. His family owned a chain of retail tobacconist shops in London and South Wales and he was a director of the company. He had joined the RAF at 17, trained as a bomber pilot in South Africa and learned to fly Lancaster bombers. He was demobilized in 1946 and became articled to a firm of chartered accountants. He was comfortably off with a flat at Goodwood Court in the West End. Like Blakely, he was a bachelor.

In November 1953, Blakely's engagement was announced to the daughter of a Huddersfield woollen manufacturer. Blakely was apparently unperturbed about dividing either his loyalty or his energy. For, within a couple of weeks, he began to live with Ruth Ellis.

As for Ellis herself, as Mr Christmas Humphreys was to say at the trial, she took an 'alternative lover' in April 1954.

Desmond Cussen – for he was that lover – would later say that he was "simply trying to provide a home for Ruth and her kiddie".

"You weren't sleeping together?"

"Well, yes, but only when she came home at nights, which wasn't very often. Then occasionally, intimacy took place."

Ellis … Blakely … Cussen. The emotional triangle that was to disintegrate only with Blakely's death, precisely a year after Cussen admitted he had "struck up a relationship" with Ellis.

And what of Ellis herself? The witnesses and the police who saw her after the shooting and watched her at the trial, thought her, without exception cold, hard and unemotional. If she was, it is perhaps not surprising.

She had already built around herself a protective shell against a world she found harsh and unfair. She was born Ruth Hornby, in Rhyl, North Wales. She was pregnant by the time she was 15. The father was a Canadian soldier named Clare. They were going to get married. Clare then flew home to demobilization – and to his wife and three children. On September 15th 1944, Ruth gave birth to a baby boy. She named him Clare Andrea Neilson, for 'Neilson' was the name that Ruth's father and then the family, had adopted during his professional career as a musician.

Her parents moved to London and Ruth took a job, modelling in a camera club. At 19 she was working as a hostess in a Mayfair nightclub. But, though the family appreciated the money she brought home, there were fierce rows with her father. This raged on until Ruth was presented with an opportunity to escape into what she saw as respectability. One of the customers at the club wanted to marry her. And, after a rapid courtship, in November 1950, she married a dental surgeon named George Ellis at Tonbridge Register Office in Kent.

But the marriage didn't work. George Ellis was educated,

cultivated and an alcoholic. Sober, he loved her. Drunk, he often beat her. She became pregnant again, but before her daughter, Georgina Ellis, was born in October 1951, the marriage was as good as over. Ruth walked out. A year after the wedding, the protracted procedure began that would end in divorce four years later.

This was Ruth Ellis' life; a few words to describe a multitude of experiences. By the time she was 25, she was the mother of two children, had been deserted once, petitioned for divorce once and beaten many times. She had the bruises to prove it. They were both physical and psychological.

To support herself, she went back to her old haunts and her old job, working for her former boss, Maury Conley. Conley was later to be described in court as 'one of London's most successful vice bosses'. Ruth was his mistress. He made her manageress of the Little Club, an afternoon-and-evening drinking club in Knightsbridge, London.

Blakely was one of her most regular customers. Initially, he chased Ellis. To her, Blakely was a "poor, little, rich boy" to be indulged and enjoyed sexually. But, as the months passed, the impetus in the relationship changed. Now, it was Ruth Ellis who was concerned – worried she would lose Blakely as his motor-racing friends ridiculed what they saw as a class gap between them and either patronised her or were icily indifferent.

And, as if the mould from which this woman was created was never to be broken, Blakely began to beat her. Savagely. Just as George Ellis had done. They fought at the club and at their flat. They fought over money which Ruth Ellis, by early 1954, was supplying to feed Blakely's appetites in drink and motor-racing. They also fought because Blakely had other women.

And, always in the background – Desmond Cussen. The alternative lover who would be willing to chauffeur her in her pursuit of an errant David Blakely; willing to pay for her to become a model and to learn French; willing to look after her son during the school holiday, to make him breakfast if his mother failed to come home until after he'd gone to school, to hear Ruth's tantrums and maudlin self-pity over the latest slight she felt Blakely had inflicted upon her. Desmond Cussen who was, in short, devoted to her.

In February 1954, Ruth became pregnant again with David Blakely's child. She had an abortion.

In April 1954, Ruth began to sleep with Desmond Cussen. Blakely was furious when he found out after returning from a race meeting at Le Mans. The stage was now set. The players were in place. And, as Ruth Ellis was to confide in the death cell of Holloway prison, just before the final curtain:

"Desmond was jealous of Blakely as, in fact, Blakely was of Desmond. I would say that they hated each other."

* * *

The full entry in the Perth telephone book was 'D Cussen, Florist, Chez Fleur'. The shop was in an arcade, close enough to the Indian Ocean to hear the shouts of the surfers as they rode the great rolling waves. A red mini-van drew up beside the arcade, bearing the legend 'Chez Fleur' and I introduced myself to the driver. Was he Desmond Cussen? He agreed he was and we shook hands. I told him why I'd come – to show him a film, made by director Chris Goddard and myself, for Thames Television on the Ruth Ellis case, in which certain allegations were made. His mouth snapped shut. "I have nothing to say." He said it three or four times. He said it as if he feared that, to enter into *any* form of conversation would mean, almost inevitably, that he would agree to discuss the matter. That evening, however, we shared a few beers.

It is difficult to imagine Desmond Cussen hating anybody.

He's a man who appears so used to the knocks life has inflicted upon him that he has come to expect more. He has been described as a solitary man, a loner when he visited the drinking clubs in London's West End during the 1950s. I got the impression that he hadn't changed, that he had many acquaintances, but I suspect, few friends.

His handshake was warm and firm. I came to believe that he avoided lying if he could possibly do so. By that, I mean he avoided the actual word of the lie passing his lips. If you have the wrong impression, and it suits him that you should remain in ignorance, he will leave the correction unsaid. It's a sin of omission, rather than commission. Like most of us, if it is easier to keep quiet, he will keep quiet. After all, he had kept quiet for the previous 22 years.

His approach to life, like his dress and his language, appeared to be from another era. His moustache traced a thin black line above his upper lip. He wore a light jacket with a dark shirt and a tie that was an explosion of colour. His shoes were white and pointed. Winklepickers. He spoke of "being intimate" with Ruth, in a very proper fashion. Hippies and surfers may live just next-door but, to Cussen, 'pot' was still something in which he stood the flowers he was selling.

He collects the flowers from the wholesalers in his red van early every morning. He is punctilious. He arrives early at his shop, however late he may have been drinking the previous night. He says he is proud of the shop itself and of what he's done to it. On one side is a hamburger stand; on the other, a supermarket. He's built the shelves and planned the layout, including the cold room, which is a large refrigerator crammed into a corner just out of sight of the customers. The shop is neat, almost painfully neat.

That evening, Desmond Cussen talked about life in Australia. He loves the country. He'd sold his share in the family tobacconist business in London in 1964. He'd come to

Australia, he said, to start all over again. He had £10,000 and his hopes were high.

First, he joined a trucking company in Sydney to discover how things worked in the business world. He pulled out because he didn't like some of the deals he saw going on.

He sold second-hand cars. He had his business closed down because the local council said he didn't have the right trading licence.

He set out to drive across Australia in 1967. He saw Perth, liked it, and decided to settle for a while. He began to do feasibility studies for a firm of estate agents. After three years, he left. He couldn't make it pay. He'd lost £3,500.

He tried speculating on stocks and shares. He lost.

He went into the import-export business and discovered that company money appeared to be going into someone else's private account. He left.

Nor has he found it easy being a florist. "There're worms in the carnations this autumn. Now they've sprayed them with a new insecticide and the leaves are turning brown." Desmond Cussen's business is on the verge of bankruptcy.

He tells all this with only a trace of bitterness. Almost as if he expected it. Only once is he moved. Since he's been in Australia he almost married, once. She died of cancer.

He rang my colleague, John Hudson, at TVW Channel 7 in Perth, at 8 am the next day. He wanted to watch our film and together we did so. That evening, in my hotel room in Perth, we discussed the statement Ruth Ellis had made in the death cell, at Holloway Prison, the day before she was due to be hanged:

... it is only with the greatest reluctance that I have decided to tell how it was that I got the gun with which I shot David Blakely. I did not do so before because I was needlessly getting someone into possible trouble.

I had been drinking Pernod (I think that is how it is spelt) in Desmond Cussen's flat and Desmond had been drinking too. This was about 8.30 pm. We had been drinking for some time. I had been telling Desmond of Blakely's treatment of me. I was in a terribly depressed state. All I remember is that Desmond gave me a loaded gun. Desmond was jealous of Blakely as in fact Blakely was of Desmond. I would say that they hated each other. I was in such a dazed state that I cannot remember what was said. I rushed out as soon as he gave me the gun. He stayed in the flat. I rushed back after a second or two and said: "Will you drive me to Hampstead?" He did so, and left me at the top of Tanza Road.

I had never seen the gun before. The only gun I had ever seen there was a small air pistol used as a game with a target.

(Signed)
Ruth Ellis
12.30 pm July 12th 1955.

Though this statement was never read in court, she had given this version of events to two lawyers – Victor Mishcon and, earlier, John Bickford. Was she telling the truth? Desmond Cussen knew what he wanted to say:

"First, let me say quite clearly that I did *not* give Ruth the gun. Nor, on that occasion, did I drive her up to Hampstead...

"Mr Bickford, Ruth's solicitor, says he doesn't want to hurt me, so why is he saying that I told him the same story, only two days after the murder? The statement that Ruth gave is not true in any way.

"There was no question of us drinking Pernod together. To the best of my recollection, it was a gin and tonic I poured her and she said: 'I don't feel like drinking. I'd rather have a cup of tea.' And she went off and made one."

Cussen had admitted to the police that he had spent time with Ellis that day. Now, he added that in her flat they had listened to the radio, played records and entertained her child, Andrea.

How was Ruth?

"She hadn't been her normal sort of cheerful self. In fact, she was exceptionally quiet. She seemed preoccupied, as if she had something on her mind. Didn't really want to talk about anything ... If she'd been doing this drinking, as she claimed, the police couldn't have failed to realise it."

Then, as he told the police 22 years previously, he added that he'd driven Ruth and her son, Andrea, to Egerton Gardens, the home they were sharing with David Blakely – and for which Desmond Cussen was helping to pay the rent. That was at 7.30 pm – two hours before the murder. And that, he said was the last he saw of Ruth, until he visited her in Holloway after the murder.

So, there it was. He hadn't given Ruth the gun at his home at Goodwood Court. He hadn't driven her to Hampstead. And he hadn't then driven away, leaving her near the public house where Blakely was drinking.

And there was one other allegation that he was at pains to deny. He did *not* drive Ruth and the child to Penn in search of Blakely that afternoon, nor did he stop near Gerrards Cross so that Ruth Ellis could get out of his car, walk into the woods and take a practice shot at a tree. That is what Victor Mishcon, Ruth's lawyer in her divorce action, said Ellis told him when she gave the death cell statement the day before she died. That is what John Bickford, her solicitor throughout the trial says, that Desmond Cussen blurted out to him only two days after the murder.

Two solicitors. Two uncannily similar stories. Cussen dismissed them both. Of Bickford's allegations: "I don't know why he's saying this after all these years. Is he trying to make money out of this? Is he writing a book? What other motive could there be?"

I suppose the obvious alternative motive is that he (Bickford) is telling the truth and wants to set the record straight, as it were.

"Well, I just don't see that."

And of the death cell statement that she gave Mr Mishcon? "It could only have been a completely desperate effort to get herself a stay of execution."

But Mr Mishcon says he had the clear impression that she didn't care that she was going to die, that he had to drag that statement out of her for the sake of her family, if for no other reason.

"Well, what he dragged out of her just wasn't the truth."

For about two hours, we talked. Mainly, we explored the implications of Ellis' death cell statement. With his permission, we recorded much of the conversation. I reproduce some of the exchanges, without comment, except when a note of explanation is necessary.

On what he'd been doing on the evening of the murder:

You dropped Andrea and Ruth at Egerton Gardens. What did you do then?

"I went back home."

What did you do for the rest of the evening?

"Oh, good heavens. Probably had a drink. Might have done some office work or something."

You're not sure?

"Well, you know, questions like this after 22 years…"

It was a remarkable day, Mr Cussen.

"I know, but one wouldn't remember exactly what one did

when one went home."

You don't remember where you were when Ruth Ellis shot David Blakely?

"Well, I must have been at home."

You've never, in all these years, said: 'Good heavens, while I was doing so-and-so, she was actually shooting David'?

"Well, I never thought of it that way."

On Ellis' behaviour that day, remembering that she'd been 'stood up' by Blakely that weekend and had been so furious that, only two evenings before, she had sought him out and smashed the windows of his car as it stood parked outside a friend's house:

"She seemed preoccupied … I can only say that the poor damned girl had it, had it on her mind."

Did you sense this (tragedy) coming? I mean, were you worried about this?

"No, I wasn't worried. Although I thought it was odd (pause). I can't really explain."

You weren't perturbed?

"No. No, no, not at the time."

And yet you'd been with her when she'd gone to Tanza Road, smashed in the windows of Blakely's car; the police been called, the Black Maria had arrived – surely, you were concerned about this girl's state of mind?

"It hadn't – hadn't entered my mind at the time."

But didn't you drive her there (that evening)?

"Yes."

And you saw her state of mind.

"Well, she was ... I don't know how, really, to say this. She was highly temperamental at times."

I'm trying to ask you what your observations were on the extraordinary events of that weekend.

(Silence).

I mean, were you simply going along with what this powerful, determined woman was doing?

"Well, I was trying to dissuade her from it."

From what?

"From carrying on – the two of them. I mean, I'd always tried to get them peaceably together. So that they should not be continually fighting."

Did you love her?

"I would say I must have loved her."

It's almost as if you were under her influence that weekend.

"Well, partially. Probably (pause). It could have been. I wanted to help her (pause). Not to the point of giving her a gun, if that's what you're trying to get at. That's ludicrous."

I didn't suggest that.

"I thought that's maybe what you were trying to get at."

When you say 'trying to help them', were you trying to get them to stay together or to part?

"I was trying to get her to stop the futility of tearing off and spying on him. I didn't see what good it was doing. It was getting her more upset ... but I think, now, I was just wasting my time. I think she was so infatuated with him and vice versa, that I realise now that I was wasting my time."

And there you were – in the middle? What was that like for you?

"Well, it wasn't very pleasant. You see, I had my feelings for her (pause). I often wondered whether they were actually in love with one another."

What do you think she was looking for, from you?

"Some sort of guidance – or stability. I think she'd been hurt so much in life by other incidents that she just couldn't find it in herself to trust a man."

She'd been hurt by men?

"Yes."

And what were you looking for in her?

"Oh, it sounds stupid now, I know, but I was probably a bit of a knight in armour … trying to do the right thing by her."

Looking after the child?

"Yes."

Giving him money to go to the zoo?

"Mmmm."

Taking him to the pictures?

"Well…"

Making him breakfast?

"Yes. Trying to make a home for them both, really."

Had you been in love before?

"Not really, I don't suppose."

Why was Ruth Ellis so special?

"I couldn't answer that. Are you married? What's so special about *your* wife?"

That's the way you looked at Ruth?

"Well, whether it was real true love I had for her, or whether I just wanted to help (pause). If you love somebody, you *want* to help."

And yet, with all this, she was sleeping with David Blakely?

(Pause).

That must have been difficult for you.

"Well, it was always a question of whether or not their association would discontinue. And I was, I think, prepared to put up with it at the time, in the hope that it would *dis*continue."

But it wasn't a situation calculated to bring peace of mind to any one of the three of you.

"No – I wouldn't say it was, really."

So – were you never angry?

"Well, I was obviously angry on the occasion when I took him outside and tried to give him a good thrashing."

(*Note:* This was at The Bull public house, Gerrards Cross. Blakely declined the invitation to 'come outside').

But when you wanted to thrash Blakely, that was anger at what he had done to her?

"Yes."

I'm talking about – were you never angry at what they were doing to you?

"No, I wouldn't say I was angry. I wasn't happy about it ... Oh, it seems ridiculous now (pause). Whether I was just hoping in those days that she would be as good as her word and would give him up. But, every time she tried to – one excuse or another and they'd get back together again."

Would you have married her?

"If she'd ... I think I would if she'd made a clean break with him."

When did you realise you'd lost her?

"I suppose, really, when she went and killed him."

All of which brought us to the gun, the murder weapon itself. It was a .38 Smith & Wesson ex-service revolver. Ruth Ellis had held throughout her arrest, her trial, and the days leading up to the eve of her execution, that she had been given the revolver as a security on a debt. A man in the Little Club had given it to her. She was never more specific.

Interestingly, no-one seems to have believed the story. Separately, I have asked the judge, a member of the jury, Ruth's own counsel, the prosecuting counsel and two of the policemen most intimately concerned in the investigation. Each has told me that they thought the story too far-fetched.

But, here again, we come back to the fact that this was an open-and-shut case. The source of the gun seemed to matter very little in the light of the overwhelming weight of evidence against her – that she had indeed committed the murder and was admitting that she'd committed it.

The police, DI Davies and DC Claiden, assembled the evidence diligently and fairly. There is only one small doubt in my mind. And it concerns the evidence of Mrs Marie-Thérèse Harris, who, early in 1955, was giving Ruth Ellis French lessons at Desmond Cussen's flat. Lessons paid for, of course, by Cussen.

Mrs Harris visited the flat one day and Ruth was out. She wasn't the most enthusiastic or punctual student, so Mrs Harris decided to wait. Ruth's son, Andrea, was there. Mrs Harris, as she chatted to the lad, mentioned that they were troubled by pigeons near her home. Andrea said he might be able to help. He went to a drawer in Cussen's living-room – and took two guns out. Mrs Harris was alarmed, naturally enough. "It's all right," assured Andrea, "they're not loaded."

Mrs Harris told the police this story when she heard about the murder. The police went to Cussen's flat and, eventually, Cussen was able to find two guns: a starting pistol (which, incidentally, went off as he and the police handled it!) and a Webley & Scott air pistol.

The police returned to Mrs Harris. They took the firearms with them. She was unable to identify either of them as being those she had seen in the flat, some months earlier.

But did the police take the murder weapon with them, to give Mrs Harris a chance to identify that? There is some doubt that they did. The records indicate that the murder weapon was taken to the Scotland Yard forensic laboratory immediately after the murder and that it stayed there under examination. DC Claiden believes they must have gone to the forensic laboratory and taken the murder weapon from there to court – but cannot be sure.

I took photographs of three weapons to Mrs Harris, admittedly 22 years after the event. They were photographs of a starting pistol and a Webley & Scott air pistol, identical with those taken from Cussen's flat – plus a photograph of a .38 Smith & Wesson. Mrs Harris examined the photographs – and eliminated the starting pistol immediately. Andrea had certainly not taken *that* out of the drawer. Mrs Harris knows nothing about guns. But she is a careful witness.

Of the two remaining photographs, she picked out the

Smith & Wesson revolver as having been the larger gun she'd been shown by Ruth Ellis' son that day early in 1955.

As far as I can tell, this is the only time, when questioned by police, solicitors or journalists, that she ever identified one of the weapons she saw in Cussen's flat. Could it be because it was also the first time she'd ever been shown it since that day?

Mrs Harris was never called to give evidence.

* * *

John Bickford, Ruth Ellis' solicitor from the start of the case, went to see her in Holloway Prison. The only remarkable aspect of their conversation that day was that Ellis wanted a message delivered to Desmond Cussen. She wished him to be informed that she had forgotten to tell him (Cussen) that she had informed the police she had been given the gun by a man in a nightclub, as security on a debt. Bickford had thought the message so peculiar that he had made a note of it in red ink. I asked Cussen about the message:

Do you remember Mr Bickford bringing this message to you?

"Yes. Yes. Something along those lines I think he mentioned to me."

Why did she want to get that message to you?

"Well, I'd been wondering where she'd got the gun (pause). Her parents were."

Why, then, didn't she send the message to her parents?

"Probably because I was closer to her than her parents were, in some ways."

But why should you be wondering where she got the gun? Wouldn't your chief concern be her wellbeing? Wouldn't it have been more likely that she would send a message out to you saying: 'Don't worry, Desmond. I'm all right'?

"No … um … that she, she should send Bickford with that message is … strange. Insofar that she obviously wondered … I, she would have been thinking, I suppose … that I'd want to know where she got it."

Did you then say anything to Mr Bickford?

"Obviously, I would assume, I would have asked if there was any way in which I could have helped her."

In what way? I mean, simple things like sending her a box of chocolates, or..?

"Oh no, it would have been a little bit more than that."

But what did you have in mind?

"Well, possibly, any way I could have helped with the story of the gun."

What do you mean?

"Well, he'd come and told me about this. There was this message; it was quite obvious I'd be interested where she got it … I suppose I was in a state where I could have said anything stupid."

Done anything stupid?

"Well, I suppose there's a possibility. I was very upset about the whole matter."

What sort of stupidity? You say: 'I might have said anything stupid about the gun'. Such as, what?

"I don't really know."

Such as 'I gave her the gun'?

"No, I couldn't have said a thing like that."

I must tell you that Mr Bickford is adamant that you did *say a thing like that.*

"Well, in my upset state … maybe I intimated something like that. There did appear to me that (she was giving) such a lame excuse for having the gun."

So, you might–

"He (Bickford) must have intimated to me that he didn't believe her story about the gun."

So, you might have said to him that you'd given her the gun?

"I might have said it – but I can't believe it, somehow … In an upset state, I might have accidently said it."

* * *

This is not Bickford's memory of the conversation. He remembers Cussen volunteering the information that he had given Ruth Ellis the gun.

I don't know whether Desmond Cussen supplied Ruth Ellis with the gun with which she shot David Blakely. Perhaps no-one will ever know where she obtained the gun. But, of the tragic triangle, Ellis – Blakely – Cussen, only Cussen was still alive and, however far he travelled, he would live in the shadow of the events that shattered the calm of that April evening in Hampstead. He said:

"Looking back on it now, you know these have been difficult questions to answer, because she's gone and why speak evil of the dead? I've had misgivings and thoughts run through my mind since then. In those days I obviously acted like a bloody fool. But what I did, I did with the best of intentions."

She's still on your mind?

"She always will be. I was very fond of her. You just can't cut a person out of your life."

The only woman for you?

"I thought so at the time. I did meet somebody else, who shall be nameless."

What happened?

"She unfortunately died of cancer, over East (in eastern Australia). I was beginning to become very fond of her as well. And there's no doubt she was of me."

Life's hard.

"Some find it easy. Some find it hard."

How about you?

"Well, I wouldn't say I've found it all that easy. 'Specially with things like this cropping up."

Memories, repercussions – they won't go away?

"Oh, there are always times when they go away. Fond memories always come back."

And erase the bad memories?

"Not completely. But I think one likes to remember the niceties and forget the nasty side."

The same with your memories of Ruth Ellis?

"Well, it's natural one would prefer to remember the good times with her. Sitting here now brings back the sadness of the whole thing. It's not been easy to sit here and talk."

I believe that. I believe that.

* * *

The hanging of Ruth Ellis gave impetus to a change in British law. It would be wrong to believe that this single event was responsible for the abolition of capital punishment in Britain but, allied to the executions of 19-year-old Derek Bentley[76] and A6 murderer, James Hanratty[77], in the years that followed, Ruth Ellis' death helped change the minds of politicians and of the general public. Sydney Silverman MP described execution by hanging as a "hangover from medievalism". Silverman was a solicitor. A year after Ellis was hanged, he introduced the Death Penalty (Abolition) Bill, which was passed by the House of Commons but rejected by the House of Lords. It was this Bill that first used the phrase 'diminished responsibility'. Having failed once, Silverman did not give up and in 1965 the death penalty was suspended for an experimental period of five years.[78] Parliament then moved to shorten this experimental period by introducing the Murder (Abolition of Death Penalty) Bill. The rope was put away for good and the gallows dismantled.

Should Ruth Ellis have been executed? As the law stood at the time – probably yes. But that answer has to be seen in the context of her own behaviour. She declared she wanted to die. She said to her lawyer, John Bickford, that she had "taken David's life and … I don't ask you to save mine. I don't want to live".[79] Lawyers on the continent, particularly in France, wondered why Bickford did not argue that Ellis had committed a *crime passionnel* – but British courts do not recognise such a crime.

Leading psychiatrist, Dr William Sargent, was "amazed"

---

76. Derek Bentley and Christopher Craig, then 16, shot policeman Sidney Miles during a burglary in South London in 1952. Craig pulled the trigger but was too young to hang. Bentley (19) was hanged in January 1953 and posthumously pardoned in 1993
77. James Hanratty, hanged in 1962, may have been innocent of the A6 murders
78. Ruth Ellis – A Case of Diminished Responsibility, Laurence Marks and Tony van den Bergh, Macdonald and Jane's, 1977; Penguin Books, 1990
79. Bickford, conversation with author, 1976

that his late partner Dr TP Rees was not called as a witness at the trial because Rees had earlier treated Ruth Ellis for mental illness. Sargent believed that, had he been called, Rees would have argued that on that Easter Sunday in April 1955, Ellis was not responsible for her own actions.[80]

What Bickford *could* and, perhaps, *should* have done was to draw the jury's attention to the allegation that Desmond Cussen had given Ellis the gun and taught her how to shoot it; that, driven to the edge of reason[81] by David Blakely's violence and infidelity, she could have pleaded insanity because she had been abused all her life and had just lost a baby after being beaten by the man she loved. Bickford told me that, after the death sentence, he had wanted to build a vigorous appeal based on these three facts alone – but he didn't because Ruth Ellis refused to appeal.

Ellis fired Bickford on the day before she was due to be hanged. She then asked for solicitor, Victor Mishcon, to represent her – and, prompted by Bickford, Mishcon suggested to Ellis that she should lodge an appeal and "tell the truth". Eventually, she agreed that she would do so – but only if Mishcon promised not to use her statement to save her life. Mishcon avoided that promise and took down her statement, which clearly implicated Desmond Cussen in saying that, after drinking Pernod together, he had given her the gun and driven her to Tanza Road, Hampstead, where she had shot Blakely and killed him. Mishcon took this statement to the police and the Home Office. Throughout the next 18 hours, a hunt for Desmond Cussen was mounted. He could not be found. There was to be no reprieve.

The John Bickford I met in 1976 was a broken man. As a solicitor, he felt he had failed in the most important case

80. William Sargent, conversation with author, 1976
81. Bickford, conversation with author, 1976

of his career. He was drinking heavily. He said: "If I had been stronger, more determined, I might have saved her." I think Bickford was overawed by the unfamiliar, high-profile, intimidating surroundings of the Old Bailey and by the reputations of his colleagues in the defence – Melford Stevenson, Sebag Shaw and Peter Rawlinson. He said: "I should have stood up to them. I had explained to counsel that it was essential to cross-examine the prosecuting witnesses in order to bring out the extenuating circumstances relevant to the case, even though they were outside the law as it was then. It was only as we went into court that my leader told me: 'We are not cross-examining the prosecution witnesses'. I was stunned. I wanted to crawl under the table. I should have said: 'I'm afraid that is unacceptable'. If I had been stronger, or didn't mind making a spectacle of myself, perhaps…"

His eyes are full of tears. "I'm sorry. I should have done it. I'm sorry." Then: "I've worried about this for years…"

* * *

One of Ruth Ellis' close friends was French-born Jacqueline Dyer, who had worked at the same nightclub. When we met in 1977, she asked a series of questions, which lay at the heart of John Bickford's breakdown: "Why, if Bickford knew all this, did he not say something then? It's all very well saying it now, when she's dead. I know she said she loved him (Blakely) and she didn't want to live. But if Bickford had said what he knew in 1955, it could have been so different. Sure, she would have gone to prison for a few years, but to be hanged? To have to go through that? I would tell Mr Bickford: 'It's all too late. When you hang someone you can't dig them up and say, 'sorry, let's start all over again'. It's too late."

* * *

The last conversation I had with Desmond Cussen was in Australia in 1977. It was a clear, bright, new day in this country where Desmond Cussen had tried to find a clear, bright, new life:

"I never thought she would hang, you know. I always thought she'd get a reprieve, right up to the end."

Yet you made no effort to save her life. She wanted to die. And she'd told you that.

"Yes. That's true."

That's what makes the death cell statement so amazing – at the last minute, to change her story. If she'd made that statement even a couple of days earlier that must have led to a stay of execution, so that further inquiries could be made. Inquiries that would have involved you, I'm afraid.

"Well, I could only say what I'd said to the police already, that I'd no idea where she got the gun. And they'd believed me (pause). She was a dreadful liar, you know."

(Pause).

"Mind you, she's got her wish. She used to complain when I visited her in Holloway that they'd cut all the reports of her case out of the newspapers she was given to read. She wanted to know the headlines she was making. She loved the headlines. She always wanted to be a star.

"She achieved that, didn't she...?"

Chapter 5

MISSIONS

The flight to Australia in 1976 to find Ruth Ellis' accomplice and lover was a prime example of what I describe as a 'mission'. Sometimes, a mission begins with an idea of one's own, which develops into an interest, that then threads its way into one's personal and private life. On other occasions, the mission grows from someone else's idea or obsession, into which one is drawn, usually by necessity and often in an emergency, but always because the guidance is issued from behind a desk that is rather bigger than yours. Jeremy Isaacs was often the man sitting behind that bigger desk. Jeremy is one of the grand masters of television.[82] When David Attenborough presented him with his BAFTA award for an Outstanding Contribution to Television, he described Jeremy Isaacs as "both a creator and an inspiration to creative work in others ... his influence in features and current affairs has been felt throughout television".

Jeremy Isaacs was, for many years, my boss, my first national network boss. In 1965, he moved from the BBC, where he had edited *Panorama*, back to ITV with Associated-Rediffusion, as Head of Current Affairs. Cliff Morgan, that prince of Welsh rugby scrum halves, was then editor of *This Week*, a programme Isaacs had produced in a previous stint at the company. It was Morgan who recruited me in 1965

---

82. Philip Purser, 2006

from Southern Television to make a single programme at the Birmingham Accident Hospital, revealing advances in the treatment of head injuries. As a leader, Cliff Morgan had "judgment, enthusiasm, wit and the capacity to inspire".[83] He liked my programme on head injuries and, as Isaacs was later to reflect, "the *This Week* team enjoyed their work … Apart from a few strong documentaries, there wasn't much else to point to with pride in Rediffusion's factual output".[84]

Almost before I had drawn breath, I became involved in my first Mission...

The Search for Space City

Under Morgan, the regular meetings of the *This Week* team were instructive and hilarious. No-one told a story better than Cliff and there were few subjects about which he didn't have a story. As a newcomer, I said little but there was an ongoing debate about how and when the US space programme might be covered by the *This Week* team. On May 25th 1961, President John F Kennedy had set his nation a target – to send an American safely to the moon by the end of the decade. Half that decade had now passed. How far had America's plans advanced in those five years? Were they on schedule? And what sort of people were the astronauts who would sit on top of the rockets that would be blasted into space? The security surrounding these men and their families was understandably tight, limited to official press releases from the National Aeronautics and Space Administration (NASA). But the *This Week* team had been sent a document by a freelance journalist giving a futuristic portrait of 20st century living in Space City USA. The document promised

83. Look Me in the Eye, Jeremy Isaacs, 2006, p120
84. Ibid

access to this unique group of people.

Committing a 10-person[85] film crew to a project was a costly exercise and the research beforehand was usually exhaustive. But, in this case, the author of the document had already completed the research – and I remember thinking that, presumably, meetings had been held to test its veracity. So, a decision was made – and a crew led by producer James Butler,[86] with Ian McFarlane[87] as the director, set off for Houston and the NASA Space Center 40 miles south in Nassau Bay, Texas.

Within four days, it was obvious that all was not well in Nassau Bay. The promised access was not being delivered. During that time, I had read the research document. It was stylish, innovative and exciting. It was written by Anthony Cave Brown. Some basic research revealed a coincidence; this was probably the Anthony Brown who had worked at the *Bristol Evening Post* at the same time as me. Brown's detailed proposal urged that "NOW is the time" to make this exclusive film. But it omitted to mention one vital fact – that all the astronauts were tied exclusively, in print and television, to publishing groups, Time Life and World Books. Cliff Morgan and Jeremy Isaacs also needed to know that, if this indeed *was* the same person, Anthony Brown had in fact left the *Bristol Evening Post* following allegations concerning arson and a curious relationship with the local fire brigade. I told them. The next day, I was on a plane to Nassau Bay, with the mission to confront Brown. As it happened, when I arrived, Anthony had already left. Many years later, Brown's

---

85. In those days, and because of an ancient motion picture agreement, every member of the *This Week* crew always travelled first-class
86. James Butler, son of R A Butler, former Conservative Chancellor of the Exchequer, Home Secretary, Foreign Secretary and Deputy Prime Minister (1962–63)
87. McFarlane had directed my first film for *This Week*

daughter described Anthony Cave Brown as a "brilliant but flawed writer – but a fantasist and a conman".[88]

During the following week, in Texas and New York, I had meetings with those who held the exclusive contracts with the astronauts. We also asked NASA for a meeting with representatives of the astronauts. They arranged it. The astronauts were sympathetic. We had come a long way. But a contract is a contract. By this time, I reckoned Associated-Rediffusion had probably spent £50,000 on the venture.

Every group has its leaders, even among those who have been so carefully selected and screened for their self-sufficiency under pressure. Among the astronauts, Frank Borman[89] was open to our argument that, though the Space Programme was an American affair, Britain was traditionally the USA's closest ally and the British public was both supportive and eager to know more. Among the wives, Joan Aldrin[90] shared that view. But this contract was explicit and binding. Would they co-operate with us, then, if the contract-holders agreed? They said they would.

The crucial contract meeting with a senior legal executive of World Books took place on a sweltering day, in a darkened bar in Nassau Bay, over a few salt-rimmed margaritas.[91] The compromise reached was that we could make a documentary, with Frank Borman and Joan Aldrin as spokespersons for the space team – but only if it was shown solely in the UK and never in the USA. Thus it was, that the first exclusive documentary embracing the US astronauts and their

---

88. Anthony Cave Brown's daughter, the photographer Amanda Eliasch, believes her father was "brilliant but flawed". He was "hugely ambitious but the stories he made up were both irresponsible and irresistible". Conversation with author, 2020
89. Frank Borman commanded Apollo 8, the first US mission safely to fly around the moon
90. Joan Aldrin, wife of Buzz Aldrin, second man to walk on the moon
91. Margarita – a cocktail of tequila, orange cointreau and lime juice, shaken with ice and served in a salt-rimmed glass

families was restricted to the UK's ITV network. It was titled Everyone's Gone to the Moon[92] and it used, as its theme tune, Jonathan King's hit song of the same name. The lyrics of that song[93] are graphic, *"Streets full of people, all alone; Roads full of houses, never home; Church full of singing, out of tune, Everyone's gone to the moon; Eyes full of tears, never wet..."*

On the evening of January 27th 1967, we were close to finishing the shoot and had been invited by some of our (by now) NASA friends to a party at a home in Clear Lake, a community famous for its clams and shrimps and a favourite for astronaut families. It was a happy, convivial time. Texas is a long way from the launch pad at Cape Canaveral in Florida, where rehearsals were going on for the first crewed mission of the Apollo programme. A television set was on in the corner of the room. It was background noise to the barbecue. The programme on the television was urgently interrupted. There had been an explosion on the launch pad in Florida, a flash fire during a launch rehearsal test. The astronauts involved were command pilot, Virgil "Gus" Grissom, senior pilot, Ed White, and pilot, Roger B Chaffee. The atmosphere in the crew's cabin had been pure oxygen, which had helped the flames envelope the capsule – and the plug door hatch through which they might have escaped had jammed. All three astronauts, Grissom, White and Chaffee were dead. The party became a wake. We packed our gear and left. It was an accident so severe that manned Apollo flights were banned for 20 months.

'Eyes full of tears ...'

* * *

---

92. The documentary was transmitted on ITV in 1968
93. See Appendix 4

I never lost touch with Joan Aldrin or Frank Borman. Joan was always honest and outspoken about the stress of being an astronaut's wife. She was one of those wives who, early in the space programme, were photographed holding a banner that declared they were 'PROUD, THRILLED AND HAPPY'. "That wasn't the half of it," she would say. "I married an engineer and here's Buzz, a national hero. Of course, I'm proud of Buzz but I simply wasn't prepared for all the demands. I didn't understand it all and my immediate reaction was to be angry with him. I could have been easier on him."[94]

For her, the risks remained a constant worry.

"I wish Buzz were a carpenter, a truck driver, a scientist – anything but what he is," Mrs Aldrin told *Life* magazine in 1969, recalling her thoughts while waiting to hear if Buzz would be named in the Apollo 11 team bound for the moon.

Weeks later, a photographer captured her expression as the lunar lander touched down on the moon. She is shown turning her face away from the television – in joy, terror or a mixture of both.

The Aldrins divorced in 1974 and Joan – lucid, vital Joan – joined ABC Television as an administrator in Los Angeles. She left in 1998 and died in 2015. She was a great girl.

Frank Borman was a West Pointer (class of 1950) all his life. Proper, controlled, efficient, kindly. Our professional lives crossed once more in 1981. By then, Frank Borman was boss of Eastern Airlines; first as a chief executive, then as chairman of the board. The airline experienced four of its most successful years from 1976, under his guidance. One of his pilots was Kenneth Ulane.

Ken Ulane had flown combat missions in the Vietnam War and had worked for Eastern for two years when, in

---

94. Conversation with author, 2002

1980, he changed gender and became Karen Frances Ulane. Eastern's then vice-president dismissed her by letter because 'the operations you have undergone will … prevent any flight crew from operating in the integrated, co-ordinated fashion … necessary … for safety'.[95] Other Eastern pilots, continued the letter, would refuse to fly with her. The case raised fundamental issues, both of civil rights and unfair dismissal. On film, Frank Borman publicly defended his company's decision – but I know he would have preferred to settle out of court without the hurt and pain that emerged during the high-profile litigation. Ulane won her case against Eastern, then the judgment was overturned on appeal. Karen died when a DC3 she was piloting crashed in May 1989.

I am no judge of whether or not the gender change affected Karen Ulane's ability as a pilot. What I *do* know is that her coolness under pressure probably saved my life. Years later, we were filming her story[96] and my cameraman John Brennan and I were aboard her Cessna when the controls indicated a problem with the landing gear. As we came in to land, lights were indicating that the undercarriage was not locked down. Ulane aborted the landing and initiated the emergency procedures. The fault continued to blink its warning. Ulane said: "I've got a feeling that the undercarriage may, in fact, be down. We'll ask the control tower to see if the wheels are down as we fly past." We flew past the control tower – and then we flew past again. And again. The tower's occupants reported: "It looks as if the wheels are down." But, as Ulane observed, no-one actually knew if they were *locked* down and in place for a safe landing.

She was calm and professional. "Our best shot is to take her down gently and see how it goes." I remember thinking it

95. Ulane's dismissal letter, seen by author
96. For The Human Factor, an ITV series I was then editing

was our *only* shot. We couldn't stay up there for ever. Ulane brought the Cessna down in a shallow descent and the wheels reached for the tarmac as tenderly as a mother. The moment of contact was a caress. The wheels bore the weight of the aircraft. The undercarriage *was* locked down. The fault had been in the computer all the time. Ulane taxied towards a parking stand. There was applause from the control tower. She switched off the power and, in the deafening silence, she said: "Sorry about the hiccup…"

* * *

I was on holiday with my family in a remote part of Portugal in the summer of 1968. A message was left at our hotel: would I please call London, Jeremy Isaacs' office? He said: "It looks as if 'Everyone's Gone to the Moon' may win an award at the Berlin Film Festival. If that's the case, can you go there to receive it?" Which was good of him. I set out the next day on an ancient train with wooden-slatted seats, which wound its way slowly along the coast towards Lisbon. Then, by plane to Berlin, and to an outfitters to hire a dinner jacket, as a black tie had not been part of my holiday wardrobe, I attended the award evening the next day, which was sumptuous and entertaining.

We won nothing.

I handed in my dinner jacket, boarded the next plane for Lisbon and took my place again on the wooden-slatted seats as if I'd never left them. That's the thing about Missions; you win some, you lose some. And sometimes it's a mixture of the two…

The Pursuit of Marlon Brando

Marlon Brando is one of the *Most Important People of the*

20th Century, as named by *Time* magazine in 1999. A double Oscar winner, he was also named Actor of the Century. In 1968 when he was at the height of his fame, I was despatched; firstly, to find him and secondly, to ask him to work for Thames Television.

No pressure then.

This Mission, because that is what it became, was divided into two parts. First, we had to find Brando. This entailed calling agents, friends and acquaintances, none of whom wished to expedite a meeting with a powerful and unpredictable man who might resent an intrusion and who would remember for ever the person who was the enabler of that intrusion. Thames' objective was to ask Brando to narrate a film that director, Ross Devenish, had made on the Native American entitled *Now That the Buffalo's Gone*. Brando's support for the Native American Indian was well-known. He had Native American blood in his veins. This was going to be Thames' first documentary shot in colour – a groundbreaking and expensive project.

The search for Brando took months. He was either on location, in Hawaii or going to North Africa or simply in business meetings. But I knew one thing for certain – he lived in Los Angeles and, through a series of coincidences, I discovered when he would be there for a full week. I flew to Los Angeles, equipped with Brando's home telephone number. I checked into a hotel in Beverly Hills and called the number straight away. It rang and rang. No reply. I called regularly throughout the day and tried frequently the next day. And the day after. The week sped by. I drove to Brando's home. It was like a fortress, impenetrable. I eventually called London and Isaacs said: "Come home".

I packed and went to bed. At 3 am, my sleep was disturbed by the hotel's bedside phone ringing. I lifted the receiver. "Marlon Brando here. Is that Peter Williams..?"

The next morning I drove again to his home. It was large and comfortable in a Hollywood kind of way and Marlon Brando gave me an hour of his time. In that hour, I noted that scattered around his many-roomed living area on the ground floor, were a number of telephones all silent, but each equipped with a small, red light. They were all winking all the time. In a break in our conversation, Marlon Brando picked one of them up and made a note of the message. As far as I know, the remaining dozen telephones may still be winking away in Beverly Hills.

I believe it was the purest chance that it was my call, my message that he picked up that early morning in Los Angeles. The result was that he agreed that he would come to London to work on the film – provided he liked it and thought it fair. I flew back to London and a month or so later, Brando appeared at Heathrow and booked into the Hilton Hotel. I'm told that his first question on arrival was, unsurprisingly, "Where's Peter Williams?" But, with little notice of his arrival, I was out of the country on location. I didn't meet Brando in London, but he narrated the three-part series on the Native Americans – and asked for no fee. "No fee ... just expenses – a room at the Hilton for a week." This turned out to be two rooms, one on another floor for his girlfriend. Charges also appeared for flowers and for jewellery. As Isaacs says,[97] "It might have been cheaper to settle on a fee".

So, I didn't see Brando in London but 50 years later, I bumped into him in the market town of Faversham in Kent. This is almost literally the case. As he got older, Marlon Brando frequently had problems with his weight. He liked to take gentle exercise. Faversham's main street narrows and bends at the Guildhall and, as I walked towards the town

---

97. Look Me in the Eye, Jeremy Isaacs, 2006, p136. Isaacs omits my part in achieving this agreement with Brando, crediting my colleague, Ian Martin

centre, virtually without warning we almost collided. He was in a hurry. But he said he recalled our meeting and responded generously to my memories of it and of the programmes.

Brando seldom sought the spotlight and he was in Kent to avoid it. He found tranquillity there; he said that it was one of the least publicised periods of his turbulent life. His link with Kent was through Belinda Frixou who, in American parlance was Brando's English attorney for nearly 30 years. Frixou is a London lawyer and she met Brando soon after she qualified. One of her clients, film director Terence Young, recommended her and she advised Brando about the process of becoming godfather to a friend's child. Belinda Frixou lived in Kent, worked internationally and the partnership lasted till Brando died. Her only child is called Christian, just as was Brando's eldest son. She was often photographed at his side all over the world and it was rumoured that they were romantically linked. I think it unlikely; Brando once claimed he had "bedded every woman I've met" but this was a warm, sometimes stormy, professional relationship, which suited both parties. Frixou gave him advice before meetings with businessmen, giants of the film world and leading politicians. She was with him when he met France's President Chirac to negotiate over the atoll Teti'aroa that Brando had bought near Tahiti and where he lived for several years. She spent weeks at his Beverly Hills home, much to the delight of her son Christian, who told Brando before one visit that he would 'love to see an elephant'. When they arrived, there it was – a baby elephant on the lawn. A real one.

Brando spent his time in Kent trying to be as ordinary as possible. Perhaps he knew that the 17th century Native American princess, Pocahontas, was buried at the appropriately named Gravesend in Kent. He stayed for months in an apartment at Sheldwich, near Faversham. Belinda Frixou then lived in Lees Court, former home of the

Sondes family; a long, impressive white building, created in 1652 on the site of a former stately home in an ornate garden designed by Inigo Jones. It has its own ballroom – now part of an apartment owned by Peter Harris – and it was here that I last saw Brando one summer evening at a musical soiree – in that ballroom. He drifted in late, did not sit down, stayed at the back of the room near the door – and the next time I looked, he had gone. Belinda Frixou remembers that Brando "always wanted to get out of London when he could. He hated the limelight. He would wander into Faversham for a haircut, often unrecognised. He asked one young hairdresser how much the trim had cost. 'Five pounds', she said. He gave her a £20 tip; she still didn't recognise him and that was the way he liked it.

"I remember he had a long filming stint in London and was booked into the Kensington Park Hotel for three months. I had a flat in De Vere Gardens nearby and, after three days, he knocked on my door. 'I can't stand it, Belinda. Everywhere I go someone wants a piece of me. Can I stay the night, please?'" Belinda gave up her bedroom and slept on a bunk bed. That became the arrangement for the next three months.[98]

Brando spent months in Kent, year after year. Frixou remembers: "He was a skilled craftsman. I had a Habitat chair that was a bit rickety. It probably cost me £20. Marlon offered one day to mend it for me. He took Christian off to the do-it-yourself shop in Faversham and came back with every conceivable tool he would need. It must have cost a thousand pounds. He and Christian had a great time mending the chair. I've still got it."

For Brando, the interludes in Kent were idyllic, a therapy. His favourite walks in and around Sheldwich and on the Kent

---

98. Frixou conversation with author, 2020

Downs, were 'a relaxation', he said, that he found nowhere else. He cared about the Kent environment and his name is among the objectors when a developer sought to build a large, cold store in a rural setting near Faversham. Belinda Frixou's single regret is that someone "tipped off the press to these arrangements. That was the end of it. I think someone in Shelley's coffee shop recognised him, a customer perhaps. Anyway, that week, the lawns at Lees Court were covered with cameras and reporters".

Marlon Brando died in 2004. "My last conversation with him was early one morning. He had been ill for some time and I was trying to find a moment to get out there and see him. But I didn't and I deeply regret that. His last words to me were 'I really miss Kent, you know...'"

Two weeks later, he was dead.

Charlie Chaplin takes no prisoners

Marlon Brando and Charles Chaplin were not bosom friends. Each admired the other's talents but their methods of working could hardly have been more different. Brando brought a Stanislavski approach to acting, an ambition to be 'natural' that led to his being labelled a Method actor. Chaplin's success, even in his most crazy, knockabout moments, was based on structure. The two men worked together once in 1967, on the film *A Countess from Hong Kong*. Chaplin directed. Brando was appalled at Chaplin's "didactic style ... and his strict authoritarianism ... he was a fearsomely cruel man ... a genius ... but as a human being, a mixed bag".[99] The film, involving these two giants of the cinema was underwhelming. In the 1970s, Thames decided to make two series on the cinema; one called *Hollywood*, inspired by film

---

99. Brando: Songs my Mother Taught Me, Robert Lindsey, pp316–319

historian Kevin Brownlow, partnered by my friend director/ editor, David Gill, which transmitted on ITV in Britain in January 1980; the other, *The Unknown Chaplin*, a three-part documentary which aired in 1983. I'm not too sure for which of these two series Jeremy Isaacs needed Charles Chaplin but I was tasked to find him. An official approach from Thames had failed. Now, the usual round of enquiries proved a waste of time – but I *did* discover that Charles, Oona and the family were fond of going to a particular hotel on the west coast of Ireland for a summer holiday. I arrived at the hotel on the same day as the Chaplin family.

Given his earlier rebuff, there was little point in asking for an audience with the great man. A 'chance meeting' was needed to replace it. On the third day, Charles Chaplin took a stroll towards the rocky coast. I happened to be strolling in the opposite direction. We fell into conversation and I outlined the detail of the Thames' plan and how important this conversation could be. He was both interested and polite. Then he said: "It sounds a good project (pause), but don't you think that television diminishes everything it touches?"

Duly dismissed, I left on the Tuesday flight to London. Curiously, Jeremy, on being told Chaplin's reaction, recalled that, during his initial discussions with cineaste Kevin Brownlow, the doyen of early silent movies, Brownlow had said to him that he was "not sure television was a serious medium, or that its cramped screen could do justice to the cinematic qualities that we love".[100]

It can't, of course.

* * *

---

100. Ibid, Look Me in the Eye, Jeremy Isaacs, p239

But What About the Gun?

Missions can be brutal and short. On other occasions they can become an important thread in one's life. On January 30th 1972, for instance, in the Bogside area of Derry, or Londonderry, in Northern Ireland, British soldiers shot 26 civilians during a protest march against internment without trial. The march had been organised by the Civil Rights Association. In London, faced with how best to cover the tragedy, *This Week* decided to send two teams to produce a programme for the following Thursday. Peter Taylor interviewed the civil rights protestors. My job was to find and interview the British troops involved. Four days after what became known as 'The Bogside Massacre', *This Week*, on the advice of its lawyers, restricted itself to broadcasting two unedited 10-minute rolls of film of our interviews; one with the protesters, one with the troops. Both sets of interviews, Peter's and mine, became important evidence to the Widgery Tribunal, which produced its report three months later. Thirty-eight years later, on June 15th 2010, The Saville Report discredited the Widgery findings, 38 years during which the first-hand evidence assembled on 16 mm film on a rainy night in Belfast in January 1972, was examined and argued over in a search for justice, never far from the headlines.

From a personal point of view, the most traumatic Mission developed from a desire in Thames, who held the ITV weekday franchise, to reflect that crime was becoming so violent in London in the 1960s that it was necessary to explore the underworld to assess the extent to which the citizens of the capital could rest easily in their beds. A national newspaper headline declared that an assassin could be hired in London for as little as a few thousand pounds and this was what gave the project impetus. At that time, the Kray twins, Reggie and Ronnie, led a gang which was engaged in a turf war with another ambitious group of criminals, the Richardsons – Charlie and Eddie. The exchanges between the two were fierce; the injuries suffered by both sides were grievous and often crippling. The Richardsons were also known as the 'Torture Gang'. Ronnie Kray, it was alleged, had shot and killed George Cornell, an associate of the Richardsons. There were other, smaller groups of criminals who worked together – 'The Watney Streeters', of which Cornell had once been a member, and 'The Nash Family', who operated for years south of the River Thames.

I got to know Derek Nash. How accurate were the lurid headlines that appeared almost daily, in both the tabloids and the broadsheets? How much of what was written was the creation of imaginative journalists? Derek Nash said: "I'm pretty sure I know someone who would top anyone for money." I said I would be eager to meet him.

And so it was, on a Thursday afternoon, in the front room of a terraced house in South London, a Thames film crew set up its camera and lights and waited. There were two chairs on 'set'. I occupied one, the other was empty. Derek Nash was with us. We waited. "Don't worry, he said he would come and I think he will." After more than an hour, the back door opened and a grey man, average in height, entered the room. He acknowledged Derek Nash and said: "Right. Let's get on with it." We filmed him anonymously in deep shadow. He was softly-spoken in contrast to the violence he chronicled as we took him through his life of crime. It was, frankly, both chilling and fascinating. The going price for killing, he said, was £2,000. Finally, I asked him why we should believe a single word he was saying. He paused, then reached into his inside pocket and took out a revolver. I heard an intake of breath. It was mine. I had completed my National Service in the Army in Schleswig-Holstein, Germany, some years before. I automatically leaned forward to get a better view of the weapon. He gave it to me and I took it. This was not a fake. It was a German Luger pistol. I returned the pistol to him. The interview concluded and the grey man left the house the same way he had entered. We struck our filming gear, reflected on what had happened and went back to the studio.

If the aim of this Mission was to indicate there was substance to the allegation that there were gunmen for hire in London in the 1960s, then the interview was an important piece of evidence. It was also dangerous, both legally and personally. Legally, we immediately consulted the Thames lawyers, who advised taking the opinion of a leading silk. They appointed Victor Durand QC, who, in a distinguished career had defended, among others, Christine Keeler and the Russian spy couple, the Krogers. An appointment was made for the great advocate to see the interview. Thus it was that Jeremy Isaacs, Victor Durand and I crouched together over a Steenbeck editing machine in a small, darkened room in the Euston Road. It emerged that their concern centred on contempt of court. Trial by television was, at that moment, very much a matter for public debate following David Frost's interview with fraudster, Emil Savundra. There was outrage in Fleet Street, partly, I think, because Frost had manoeuvred the confrontational scoop with Savundra and entered the territory that national newspaper crime reporters felt should be *their* bailiwick. Our interview, said Durand, would attract considerable publicity. Contempt was the danger. Isaacs agreed – and, of course, so did I. But my concern was also that I had taken and handled, the Luger pistol and given it back to the gunman. I remember, rather plaintively, asking: "But what about the gun..?" The advice was: Don't worry about the pistol. That's not the major problem.

The programme was later transmitted, entitled '*You Only Do Life*'.

In the days that followed, I was twice interviewed by detectives from Scotland Yard and asked the name of the man I had interviewed. I genuinely did not know it. I was called to appear at Bow Street Magistrates' Court. I was accused of inducing a person to appear in public with an offensive weapon, that could have occasioned a breach of the peace.

By this time, Durand and I were well acquainted and he said he thought that Scotland Yard had framed a clever charge. He analysed it for me. It was not so serious that it would go to a jury trial, which was a pity because he was of the opinion that I would 'stand a better chance in front of a jury'. The charge I would now face in court would be dealt with by a stipendiary magistrate[101] who would, of course, be fair but "was more likely to be closer to the prosecution". This did not fill me with confidence, as Durand also said that I "could go to prison if found guilty but a heavy fine was more likely". As I stood in the dock, it transpired that the prosecution case hinged on the allegation that I had met the gunman beforehand and that I had asked him to bring a pistol with him to the interview.

This was encouraging because I knew that it wasn't true. I had never previously met him, nor did I know his name. None the less, the prosecution assembled its case and, as I listened, I wondered how credible an independent mind would find it. The accusations were clear. If the magistrate believed the prosecution, I was in trouble. During a break for lunch, Phillip Whitehead, then editor of *This Week* said, sympathetically: "That this should be happening to you of *all* people, is shocking." It was friendly and supportive but it didn't increase my confidence in the outcome.

Salvation appeared from a completely unexpected source. We received a message that morning; we had an extra witness

---

101. A stipendiary magistrate is a salaried and professional lawyer

for the defence. His name: Derek Nash, member of the Nash family gang – my contact in London's underworld and my informant. He had seen the way the trial was going and had, he said, something to contribute.

Durand took Nash through his evidence. He was nervous but on one aspect of his evidence he was absolutely certain. I had never met the gunman before the filmed interview and had certainly not asked for a pistol to be part of the arrangement. He echoed the evidence I had given from the witness box and, at one stage during cross-examination, he said to the prosecuting lawyer: "You're not listening to me. Peter knew nothing about who he was going to meet."

The stipendiary magistrate recorded a 'not guilty' verdict.

I said earlier that there was personal danger involved in this Mission. Derek Nash had shown considerable bravery in coming forward, publicly, to talk of his involvement in the affair. It caused a stir in those circles in which he moved, rubbing shoulders with the Krays and the Richardsons. I was, and still am, grateful for his intervention. But, after the court hearing, the Metropolitan Police and the Kent Constabulary put a 24-hour guard on my home in Kent. "Just in case," they said.

Some Missions produce a quite unexpected outcome…

* * *

Two months after the interview, a man was arrested and charged. The interview was used as part of the evidence against him. His name was Lawrence.

Chapter 6

UNCLEAR (anagram of NUCLEAR):
Dounreay and the Pursuit of Truth

It was a thunderous rush of water in the coastal town of Lynmouth in North Devon in 1952 that convinced me of the power of nature. I had been a journalist for nearly three years and, now 18, was continuing my training in the Taunton office of the *Bristol Evening Post*. I was a very junior, junior. My boss, Robert Moore, an experienced reporter, was out of town. It was a Friday afternoon. The week was winding down when we took a message in the office. There was an incident in Lynmouth and the caller thought people were injured.

Lynmouth is nearly 50 miles from Taunton, reached through narrow, winding country roads that criss-cross Exmoor. The only other person in the office that day was Eric Wood, the *Post's* local photographer. Should we take a look at this which may, after all, be nothing? I couldn't yet drive. But Eric could. Which was why, on an early morning still heavy with storm clouds, at 3 am we found ourselves stationary jammed together into a Ford Popular high on Exmoor, on the outskirts of Lynmouth. We slept for two hours and then crept through the rain towards a now roaring river on the outskirts of town. In the dim light, we could see that the road bridge had collapsed. A log had fallen across the turbulent water and that is how we crawled into Lynmouth.

We found that a village had been washed away. It was

Saturday August 16th 1952. Thirty-four people had died as a thunderstorm and a cloudburst had caused a flood that had swept down the funnel formed by the convergence of two rivers. Twenty-eight of the 31 bridges over the rivers had been demolished and 165 buildings destroyed or severely damaged.[102] Miraculously, a single red telephone box, just off the main street of the village, was still standing. There was a dialling tone and I telephoned the office, who sent a grown-up reporter to Lynmouth to cover the story properly.

The locals mourned their dead and agreed that nothing could resist nature in that mood. But years before, there had been those who had warned that because of its geographical position, Lynmouth could be vulnerable to flash floods.

As long ago as 1769, the fishermen and almost every inhabitant had petitioned their lord and landowner with their concerns after 'the river at Lynmouth by the late rain rose to such a degree as was never known by the memory of any man now living'. The flood was a "foaming torrent, rolling great boulders along and destroying all in its course".[103]

There were further floods in 1859,[104] in 1875 when the town's bridge was swept away,[105] in 1910 when there was also a high tide,[106] in 1924 when both the East and West rivers were "madly raging ... having waves like an angry sea ... a sight never to be forgotten. Trunks of trees were tossed around like feathers...";[107] and in 1935 when "Lynmouth Hill resembled one huge waterfall".[108] In all these carefully chronicled floods, there was considerable damage to property in the

---

102. Lynmouth Flood: 40 Years On, WB Harris, 1992. (See also Appendix 8)
103. A History of the Parishes of Lynton and Countisbury, John Frederick Chanter, Commins, Exeter, 1907
104. North Devon Journal, November 3rd 1859, p8
105. Ibid, November 18th 1875, p8
106. Ibid, December 22nd 1910
107. Ibid, September 25th 1924, p8
108. Ibid, June 27th 1935, p8

twin towns. Despite this recurring threat, reaction, both regional and national, had been negligible. The view in the 20th century appeared to be that there had been a settlement in Lynton and Lynmouth for more than 400 years and there had been no major disasters during that time. Why should it happen now? Well, there is a possible reason. Fifty years later, declassified documents from the Public Record Office (PRO) showed that the RAF had carried out cloud-seeding experiments[109] in the area and in the weeks leading up to the disaster. These artificial rainmaking experiments, known as Project Cumulus, had been conducted between August 4th–15th 1952 over Southern England. They stopped abruptly on the day of the Lynmouth disaster. They had been carried out sporadically and with government approval since 1949.[110]

Whether or not the RAF's rainmaking activity had made any impact on the Lynmouth disaster, we will never know. But from that day in August 1952, there was one young reporter who was in no doubt, first about the inherent power of natural energy and, subsequently, that the right hand of government may not necessarily know what the left hand is doing – and if it does, it may not wish to admit it.

* * *

For centuries, the source of power for Britain's homes and factories has been at the heart of political debate. Coal drove the Industrial Revolution and fed the warships that protected Britain's imperial interests around the world. The ability to provide power also produced political influence for trade unions that grew to protect the interests of the workers in the

---

109. "We poured dry ice down into the cloud. We flew down to see if any rain came out of the cloud. And it did about 30 minutes later." Group Captain John Hart, Guardian, August 2001
110. BBC Radio 4, August 2001

mines, the shipyards and the factories. The power the trade unions wielded in Westminster increased with the election of the reforming Labour Government at the end of World War II. Coal was still king and, with oil from the Middle East, would provide the motive power for UK plc. Then, the words 'pollution' and 'climate change' were seldom heard. Winters of impenetrable fog continued to obliterate British cities; trams and buses continued to carry the notices 'No spitting' in a vain effort to reduce the deadly annual toll of chest infections and tuberculosis.

The oil crisis of 1973–74 when Britain was reduced to working a Three-Day Week, was a turning point, however. In its agony, the Edward Heath government seemed at the mercy, both of the Middle Eastern sheiks who were controlling the price per barrel of crude oil and of Britain's trade unions, particularly the National Union of Mineworkers (NUM), who were striking for higher wages and better working conditions. Britain discovered its own oil and gas in the North Sea in the 1960s. Yet, only in the 1970s, in the context of the international crisis in which oil tripled its price, did the offshore production of Britain's own oil become economically enviable. In 1975, the Ardmore Field, the Forties Field and the Beatrice Field began to produce oil – and Britain's Chancellor of the Exchequer, Denis Healey, was jubilant. Total revenue for the year 1975–76 from UK oil and gas production was £25,000,000. Five years later, the figure was £2,313,000,000. Ten years later, in 1984–85, UK oil and gas revenues would total £12,035,000,000 and in the following year, £11,348,000,000.

All this was duly reflected in the media, where television was still something of a novelty. TV sets now stood firmly in the centre of the nation's living-room, demanding attention and getting it from up to 15 million people each evening. Among its daily offerings, TV inspired the heyday of what were known as current affairs programmes. Every week, BBC's *Panorama* opened its window on the world and every ITV station was mandated to carry two half-hour current affairs programmes at peak time each week – Granada's *World in Action* on a Monday and *This Week* from Thames Television on a Thursday. These programmes were the focus of national political debate and they examined the issues at the heart of that debate.[111]

I worked for *This Week* for 14 years up till 1980 as a reporter/producer and, in that time, we made a number of programmes that explored the alternative energies of wind and wave power and solar energy. We also argued that a small percentage of the North Sea oil might profitably be devoted to 'green' research. That argument gained little purchase in Westminster, for energy was a political as well as a financial issue.

During World War I, the atom had been split in Manchester by New Zealander, Ernest Rutherford. The discovery of nuclear fission had followed during the late 1930s. Fission is the process that releases the energy stored in a nucleus, which make it possible to generate considerable quantities of heat and power. This can either be harnessed to produce electricity or it can be used to create a huge explosion that could, and would, devastate cities and slaughter thousands.

With Hiroshima and Nagasaki fresh in the collective memory of the 1950s, East and West became involved in a nuclear arms race with the apt acronym, MAD.[112] Nuclear power also had an obvious domestic and industrial potential, but from the outset, there were those with misgivings about an energy policy that relied too heavily on it. The United Kingdom Atomic Energy Authority had been set up in 1954

111. See Appendix 2, Thirty-five Years of This Week, Thames Television, 1991
112. MAD – Mutually Assured Destruction

to pioneer the development of nuclear power and, in August 1956, Britain's first nuclear station, Calder Hall, was opened and connected to the National Grid – though its equally important task was to produce weapons-grade plutonium. The first prototype Fast Breeder Test Reactor (FBTR) at Dounreay in Scotland – of which, more later[113] – opened in 1966 to produce weapons-grade plutonium from uranium and thus, British Nuclear Fuels Ltd (BNFL) was established in 1971.[114] Newly-elected Prime Minister, Edward Heath, set up a group called the Central Policy Review Staff (CPRS). Its job would be to advise on a range of national and international issues and CPRS would have privileged access to the Prime Minister's office and the heart of the government. Heath had used a similar committee while in opposition and felt that it liberated debate, lessened factionalism and produced fresh ideas. Its nickname was the 'Think Tank'. It was a high-profile, high priority group of decision-makers and scientists and energy policy was to be part of its brief. By September 1972, the CPRS warned: "We have spread our bets too widely in the development of nuclear energy and have wasted money … looking ahead, the dominance of the Middle East in proven oil reserves looks capable of imposing a stranglehold over energy supply … There are high stakes in getting our national energy policy right."[115]

The oil crisis that this committee predicted in 1971 occurred within two years, in 1973.

Britain had also been examining alternative energies as it sought to make the country less dependent on coal. As an island nation with an estimated 20,000 kilometres of coastline, the UK was well placed to harness energy from

---

113. See pages 141-146
114. In 1984, BNFL became a public limited company, wholly owned by the UK government
115. National Archives, Cabinet, Government Strategy, September 1971

its oceans. Yet despite the first patent for wave power being filed in France back in 1799, it wasn't until the mid-1970s that the British Government began seriously exploring the potential for coastal and offshore energy generation. By that time, a strong lobby believed that the energy contained in the movement of the sea could be harnessed commercially to help solve the oil crisis. The rise and fall of tides and the lapping of water on the seashore all involved the creation of energy, which could be converted into electricity. Professor Stephen Salter at the University of Edinburgh championed his invention known as Salter's duck or by its official name, the Edinburgh duck which, with curved cam-like bodies, could extract up to 90% of the energy contained in the circular motion of waves. On a small scale, the experiments were more than promising, but the proposed development of wave energy presented complex and expensive technical challenges. Salter envisaged, for instance, "a long line of ducks from the Hebrides down the west coast of Ireland, with a break to allow shipping through … plus a line from the west of Scotland, past the Faroes and perhaps as far as Iceland…" It would be "a really enormous resource … which could power continents".[116] All this required imagination from politicians and a huge, long-term capital investment. In our country where short-term thinking from politicians is a continual and besetting sin, Salter built a unique multidirectional wave tank in Edinburgh. He was, by nature, an optimist, driven by the long-term need to ameliorate the effects of climate change. "We are in a massive state of denial about this," he said. "We simply have to do something about it."[117] But high costs killed Salter's ducks, promising though the test results were. The Wave Energy Programme was abruptly closed down early

116. Conversation in Edinburgh, 1977
117. Ibid

in the 1970s and it would take many years for this fledgling industry to recover any momentum. Salter later put forward an additional theory for the closure of his programme. He said: "We were close to becoming economically viable. They killed the project because it was going to threaten the expansion and the supremacy of the nuclear industry."[118]

Whether or not he was correct, Salter had good grounds for expressing this view. The energy technology unit had been moved to the nuclear power station at Harwell. Dr Walter Marshall, a brilliant physicist who had begun his career in the United Kingdom Atomic Energy Authority (UKAEA) in 1954 and was now Deputy Director, was invited in 1974 to become Chief Scientist to the newly-formed Department of Energy. He remained Director at Harwell, where the entire energy research would be based, including the exploration of the alternative energies. Marshall would become, between 1974 and 1977, chair of the government body known as the Association for Cooperative Operations Research and Development (ACORD) and the UKAEA's Board member for research. He was also the Department of Energy's Chief Scientist. Thus, at a crucial moment, one of the nuclear industry's leading figures became the government's top scientific adviser on energy policy. One of his first priorities was to assume the chairmanship of the new Off-shore Energy Technology Board that included wave, wind and solar power.[119] He was knighted in 1982.

It is hard to overestimate Marshall's influence over Britain's energy policy in the 30 years between 1960 and 1990. He was a formidable Welshman, with a peculiarly guttural voice that made some believe he was from Eastern Europe. He was weighty in thought and figure. The youngest

118. Ibid
119. JC Wilson, A History of the UK Renewable Energy Programme, 1974–88, University of Glasgow, 2012

child of three and a grammar school boy,[120] he had become the Welsh junior chess champion at the age of 15. He gained a major scholarship to the University of Birmingham to study mathematical physics and, after taking his first degree, he found time to write a thesis on 'Antiferromagnetism and Neutron Scattering from Ferromagnets', which won him a PhD at the early age of 22. By the age of 30, he was spending a sabbatical year at the Oak Ridge National Laboratory in Tennessee, where the director, Alvin Weinberg, was heard to reflect that "if Walter had stayed any longer, he would have taken over the laboratory". He worked on the science he loved "during his leave, at home, in airport lounges and other unlikely places … all recorded in his neat handwriting in a number of notebooks".[121] After he was recruited by the UKAEA, the success and international reputation of Harwell's Theoretical Physics Division under his leadership confirmed Marshall's ability to lead scientific programmes and to motivate others. Then came a significant switch in his career, from pure science to the administration of applied science and technology, with his promotion to deputy director of Harwell in 1966 and then to director in 1968. His priorities, he said, were to improve industrial performance across the UK and to respond and fulfil the government's energy needs.

Marshall was not against alternative energies. He re-launched a modified wave power programme in 1975. He recommended several increases in the funding of renewables. But he was a nuclear man, through and through. Going forward, nuclear energy would be the strongest plank in the platform of Britain's energy policy. He did not agree with the earlier CPRS' judgment that Britain had "spread her bets too widely in the development of nuclear power". He had

---

120. St Illtyd's College, Cardiff
121. Royal Society biography 44, pp299–312. Marshall was its youngest Fellow in 1971

glimpsed the future and the future was nuclear.

Nonetheless, with the rebirth of the Wave Energy Committee, the research into and development of green energy continued in a limited way. Surprisingly, the potential of wind power had been virtually ignored for years. It wasn't until 1978 that a Wind Power Steering Committee was set up, with this backhanded and less than enthusiastic endorsement:

"...the potential contribution from this source has a significance too large to ignore."[122]

This was the first detailed consideration of the potential of wind energy in the UK.[123] Marshall's view was clear. Nuclear power worked. It could be properly controlled and developed "provided that senior people ... strive constantly to ensure that they have enough time to think about problems beyond that day and that week".[124]

The fact is, however, that the development of alternative energies and the potential for them to assume a major role in Britain's energy policy, had been constrained by the government's concentration of effort and money into nuclear power. The Green lobby was dismissed as both impractical and eccentric.

* * *

The decision to give nuclear power priority was taken in the knowledge that it was not without risk. Those who doubted the risk were urged to look back to the previous decade. Governance of the nuclear industry had been questioned most critically in October 1957. On October 10th that year,

---

122. National Audit, Energy Paper 21, June 1972
123. Ibid
124. Walter C Marshall, David Fishlock and LEJ Roberts, Royal Society, November 1998

at Windscale (now Sellafield), a fire broke out in Unit One of the two-reactor facility. It burned for three days. It spread radioactivity across the UK and throughout Europe. No-one was evacuated from the villages around the nuclear station but milk produced in a 500 sq-kilometre area of Cumbria was destroyed. The radioactive isotope iodine-131, which is associated with thyroid cancer, is now estimated to have caused 240 cases in the local population.

The Windscale fire of 1957 was the worst nuclear accident in the UK's history. It reached level 5 on the International Nuclear Event Scale – the top disaster level is 8.

Windscale was built not to produce electricity but to create plutonium for Britain's first atomic bombs, scheduled to be ready by 1952. An inquiry was set up by the UKAEA, chaired by William Penney, Lord Penney, 'father' of the British atomic bomb. The committee sat in the 10 days following the Windscale disaster. Its findings were criticised as a whitewash. The management's reactions to the fire, it said, had been "prompt and efficient" and they had shown "considerable devotion to duty" as the fire raged. Penney added that there was "no immediate danger to the health of any of the public or workers ... and (it is) most unlikely that any harmful effects will develop".[125] Penney's report *did*, however, question the governance of the plant. He said: "The evidence that we received revealed deficiencies and inadequacies of organisation," and he recommended greater liaison between the different sections of Britain's nuclear industry. "Windscale's organisation," he continued, "is not strong enough for the responsibility that it carried." Twenty-three years later, in 1980, the Nuclear Inspectorate published a much more detailed report on the leak of radioactivity that

---

125. Report on the Accident at Windscale No 1 Pile on October 10th 1957, Penney, Schonland, Kay, Diamond and Peirson

had occurred at Windscale. It inspired a leading article in *The Guardian* of August 1ˢᵗ 1980, which described the leak as having been 'discovered more or less by accident'. It criticised the inspectors for treating Windscale 'as though it were an old-established family brewery of interest only to local historians'. It declared:

'Windscale is not like any other factory. It is potentially one of the most dangerous places in Europe. On the whole its record is good, but 'on the whole' is too low a criterion … There are too many loose ends at Windscale, too little safety consciousness.

'In the film *The China Syndrome,* the panic was caused by a gauge which stuck, giving a wrong reading. At Windscale, the rise in the level of radioactive liquor in the tank that overflowed, was not detected because the circular gauge measuring from 0 to 50 cm was on its *second*[126] journey round. It measured 30 when it should have measured 80. But worse, it appears that the management did not know whether the stuff in the tank was radioactive or not. It rather thought not.

'Radioactivity can outlive many generations of management and the sins of the 1950s' intake can be visited upon the 1980s. British Nuclear Fuels (Ltd) is not going to discipline anybody, presumably because the old-timers have retired. Nor will there be prosecutions of the company: to what end, since the fine would be a transfer of public funds from one account to another? But after this sharp rap from the inspectorate, BNFL should expect an even sharper public eye on its workings. It has unlimited funds only because the public needs maximum safety. That has not been provided.'[127]

That August in 1980, I spent several sun-drenched weeks

126. Author's italics
127. The Guardian, August 1ˢᵗ 1980

at Wick in the north of Scotland, at the Dounreay Nuclear Power Station.

* * *

There are moments when the relationship between the media and government descend into black farce. So it was at Dounreay, home of the experimental fast- breeder nuclear reactor, in the summer of 1980. One afternoon in May, I sat in the living-room of Mrs Jackie Swanson, in the village of Thurso, beside Dounreay, discussing why her 23-year-old husband, Alan, had been digging around in a waste pit at the nuclear power station, searching for 'lost' plutonium and uranium.

Alan Swanson has been deaf and mute since he was born.

The reason why Alan had spent three working days in the cab of his JCB delving into Waste Pit No 4 was logical, if you were working for the government's UKAEA, for, twice in three years, most recently in 1977, Dounreay had 'lost' a number of uranium/plutonium fuel pins. And if they were lost, they had to be found.

For journalists, getting answers from the authorities at Dounreay was not easy.[128] It was from both Mrs Swanson and from workers at Dounreay, who wished to remain anonymous, that Ted Harrison and I pieced together the security problem that had beset this experimental nuclear reactor. In the previous years, there had been:

- an error in accounting for a quantity of plutonium waste,
- an explosion in the deep underground silo where the most dangerous solid waste was stored, and

---

128. My colleague, Ted Harrison – now an artist and author – had moved to Orkney in 1979. It was because of rumours 'leaked' from Dounreay that we began our investigation for BBC's Panorama

- a loss of plutonium-enriched uranium pins, which lie at the core of the fast reactor and of a nuclear bomb.

At the end of 1977, an anonymous informant spoke of "an almighty flap when they discovered they (Dounreay) had lost some plutonium fuel pins". He said that "clerical staff had worked overtime, till 2 am, night after night. Things were frantic. I don't think they ever found the plutonium". One senior scientist had said in his hearing: "Well, that's another Dounreay cock-up."

Routine security governs the use and movement of fuel pins in the nuclear industry. Each is identified with a number. When moved from the core for renewal, they are replaced by dummy pins, which are then removed when the 'live' plutonium/uranium pins are restored. Dounreay later admitted that the amounts of uranium/plutonium 'lost', with these 'missing' fuel pins, were 10 grams in 1973, 25 grams of plutonium and, in 1977, 140 grams of uranium. On the one hand, there was no evidence that any of this fissile material was stolen, according to a member of the Dounreay security force. But, on the other hand, there is no evidence that it *wasn't* because none of this material was ever found. Our informant said that, in 1977, three fuel pins and "well over a kilo of plutonium went missing".

In August 1980, we discussed these matters with the then Director of Dounreay, Clifford Blumfield, who put the 'loss' of the nuclear fuel down to accounting errors and/or confusion between a dummy pin and a 'live' fuel pin. It became apparent that, if the latter were the case amid this confusion, the 'live' uranium/plutonium fuel pins might well have ended up in Dounreay's Low Waste Pit No 4, yards from the seashore. Someone would have to find out if this had happened.

Pit No 4 is the pit into which young Alan Swanson manoeuvred his JCB in 1978. Young Alan, remember, has been deaf and mute since birth. Two thousand five hundred people worked at Dounreay in the 1970s and looking after them safely was a serious business. What was UKAEA's motivation in allowing Alan, deaf and mute, to take on the job to try to find the missing fuel pin? The JCB he drove had no independent air supply in its cab. Alan, working for his father, was told in writing not to leave his cab and he wore, Mr Blumfield declared, "adequate protective clothing". But did Alan Swanson understand the potential danger of what he was being asked to do, particularly if he unearthed a fuel pin? At the time, his brother, Donald, thought not. Donald worked at Dounreay for 2½ years. He said: "Radiation and contamination are pretty difficult to understand. You can't see it. I can't say I really understand everything about it. I doubt if Alan understood it any better."

Dounreay's Director Clifford Blumfield thought he did. "We have a responsibility to make sure (people working here) are safe and that's exactly what we did." Professor Joseph Rotblat (later, Sir) commented that, if "even 35 milligrams of plutonium settled in the lungs from dust, it would mean he (Alan) had a 50 per cent chance of dying of cancer".[129] Alan Swanson was searching for a total of 175 grams of plutonium/uranium.

The second issue we raised with Mr Blumfield involved an explosion in 1977 in the high-active waste silo at Dounreay, the shaft where the most dangerous radioactive material is stored, in effect, for ever. It wrecked a reactor control panel just after an employee had left it, cracked the huge concrete top of the silo and hurled a 5-ton concrete plug against the boundary fence. Dounreay issued a statement describing the explosion as a minor incident, for no debris had travelled

129. Professor Joseph Rotblat, a physicist who worked on the Manhattan Project atomic bomb project in World War II; conversation with author

beyond the boundary fence, it declared. The crack in the plug could have been caused by a structural weakness and the explosion had taken place because some sodium had 'inadvertently' got into that shaft.

The explosion had been loud and large enough to be heard by every resident within five miles. And it caused Dounreay to change its safety procedures. We asked Clifford Blumfield if, following these 'incidents', any disciplinary action had been taken against any employees?[130] He replied:

"We didn't … nobody was put over anyone's knee and spanked, but there was disciplinary action and no-one was left in any doubt that safety is a serious business; the level of risk is very small.

"I mean, you took a risk coming here (to Dounreay) to talk to me. Plutonium is one of those materials which create certain problems for people. But it's all relative…

"I mean, we measured the radiation from a (camera) lens very similar to yours. There's far greater radioactivity coming from your camera lens than is here today. Do your cameramen know they should take precautions? When they get rid of the camera, what do they do with it? Isn't the television industry, in using such cameras, endangering mankind?"

Q: Mr Blumfield, you're not seriously comparing the lens of a television camera and the problems of working with that, to a nuclear power station fast breeder reactor and the problems of working with that?

A: "I'm just showing you that people get things out of perspective."

Q: I know that the nuclear industry is proud of its safety standards, but this is disturbing. If fuel pins can go missing, Mr

---

130. BBC's Panorama, December 1980

Blumfield, what else CAN'T go wrong?

A: "If it *has* gone wrong, we shall find out *what* has gone wrong and put it right…"

I concluded my report for *Panorama* with the observation: "If nuclear power is to improve its image, it must convince the public that it has a system that can control its dangerous materials and that it is being frank about its problems – *all* its problems."

The UKAEA made representation to the BBC to try to stop *Panorama* being transmitted. Forty years later, despite the protests they had made at the time in 1980, Cabinet papers released under the 30-year rule revealed that, firstly, plutonium and uranium fuel rods *had* been lost at Dounreay and, secondly, on May 10th 1977, there *had* been an explosion that could have been life-threatening.

The papers revealed that the UKAEA had dumped at least two kilograms of sodium and potassium down a 65-metre shaft packed with radioactive waste and flooded with sea water. The sodium and potassium had reacted violently with the water. The explosion blew off the shaft's huge concrete lid, threw its steel top plate 12 metres to one side, badly damaged the 5-ton concrete blocks at the mouth of the shaft and blasted scaffold poles up to 40 metres away. An eyewitness reported a plume of white smoke blowing out to sea. And, as government papers revealed for the first time, the ground around the shaft was littered with radioactive particles hot enough to injure and kill.

Over the years, almost 150 such particles have been found on Dounreay's beaches. The Committee of the Medical Aspects of Radiation in the Environment (COMARE) and the Radioactive Waste Management's Advisory Committee revealed in 1995 that no comprehensive monitoring of these particles on the beaches had been carried out for the seven years after the explosion and thus, the presence of particles such as these could explain the excess of cases of childhood leukaemia in the area. It was, they said, "a horrifying scenario".[131]

The management at Dounreay will have known most of these damning facts when they gave us their defensive interview in 1980.

* * *

Walter Marshall had always been aware of the risks involved in the development of nuclear energy. Throughout the 1970s, he vigorously defended the safety of fast reactors such as Dounreay. Nuclear energy to produce electricity was, he said, for Britain, "a moral imperative". He was convinced that a larger nuclear power programme was essential to meet the energy requirements of an expanding world population and that a gradual change to fast reactors and an efficient, closed fuel cycle would therefore be necessary. He thought the fears expressed about fast reactors were exaggerated. He saw fast reactors as a means of controlling the total stocks of plutonium in the world, since they could be designed to consume plutonium or to 'breed' plutonium slowly. He disliked the regime of storing spent fuel indefinitely, as advocated by the United States, fearing that the stores could become plutonium sources of increased accessibility and thus "a target for diversion or theft".[132]

In 1983, Energy Secretary, Nigel Lawson, summoned Marshall to inform him: "The Prime Minister and I have decided that, in the national interest, you should be the

131. New Scientist, June 1995
132. Royal Society, David Fishlock, LEJ Roberts, pp299–312, National Academy of Sciences

next chairman of the Central Electricity Generating Board (CEGB)." Margaret Thatcher, having been in No 10 Downing Street since 1979, was preparing for a political and strategic battle with the miners' unions that would come to a head the following year. For the moment, then, she simply hoisted the nuclear flag firmly to the top of Britain's energy masthead.

Marshall, said Lawson privately, was "Mr Nuclear". As such, Marshall set out to be seen as its champion. Radioactive fuel, he said, must be able to be moved openly between Britain's nuclear sites. Anti-nuclear critics charged that the spent nuclear fuel shipping casks in use by the CEGB and the UKAEA would not survive a serious transportation accident. Marshall agreed to a dramatic public demonstration of casks' integrity. An empty cask was placed on a railway siding and a locomotive was driven into it at full-speed. The event was well attended and accompanied by racecourse-style commentary. The cask bounced up in the air and came down intact. The locomotive did not fare so well. The event was a remarkably successful public relations exercise.[133]

Three years later, however, in 1986, the confidence of the nuclear industry was profoundly shaken when a Soviet-designed reactor exploded at Chernobyl. Officially, 31 people were killed. The United Nations (UN) estimated that a further 4,000 people might die from radiation exposure. Thousands of animals were slaughtered and 200,000 people evacuated. Unofficially, more than 12,000 members of the clean-up teams have since died and the death toll has been estimated to top 90,000.[134] Former Premier Mikhail Gorbachev has since cited Chernobyl as the chief reason for the collapse of the Soviet Union. Walter Marshall acknowledged that the reputation of nuclear energy could not "survive another accident as

---

133. See photograph, page 234
134. BBC Future, Richard Gray, July 2019

severe as Chernobyl" and helped the Soviets modify their reactors to rectify the design weaknesses that had led to the accident. Marshall stepped down as chairman of the CEGB in 1989. He was immediately appointed chair of the World Association of Nuclear Operators (WANO), a post he held until 1993. A year before he retired from that position, he was asked to become an independent advisor to the newly-formed Institute of Nuclear Safety Systems Inc in Japan. The aim of the Institute was to reinforce public confidence in the safety of nuclear power in Japan. Marshall accepted and built "an unusually warm and productive relationship with the Japanese".[135]

* * *

In the second week of March 2011, at Okuma, in the Fukushima Prefecture of Japan, nuclear energy and the irresistible power of nature combined to bring about one of the world's greatest nuclear disasters. It began with an earthquake, which caused a tsunami, which flooded the Fukushima Daiichi Nuclear Power Plant. The tsunami generated by the earthquake was 14 metres (46 ft) high, as high as the second floor of a high-rise building. It surged over the nuclear plant's sea wall, flooding the reactor buildings. The emergency generators were knocked out and the reactors were thus robbed of their coolant. There were three nuclear meltdowns, three hydrogen explosions and a huge release of radioactive contamination. More than 150,000 residents within a 50 kilometre radius of the nuclear station had to be evacuated. The toll of radioactive-based cancer and other serious illnesses resulting from the Fukushima disaster is still being calculated to this day.

---

135. Royal Society, Ibid

The aftermath was causing deep concern even 10 years after the disaster, when the Japanese Government announced plans to release more than one million tons of contaminated water into the Pacific Ocean. The water had been stored in huge tanks on the site ever since the explosion.[136] The decision caused uproar among Japan's neighbours and the beleaguered Japanese fishing industry urged ministers not to allow the release of the contaminated water, saying it would undo years of work to restore their reputation. South Korea banned imports of seafood from the Fukushima area.

Close monitoring of the pollution and adherence to scientific advice on the impact of the radioactive contaminants would be "key", according to Simon Boxall at the University of Southampton. Given local rainfall and, without this discharge, the 1,000 tanks at the former nuclear power station would soon be full.[137]

In July 2012, an investigation found that the causes of the accident had been 'foreseeable'. A report in *The Economist* said: 'The operating company (the Tokyo Electric Power Company, TEPCO) was poorly regulated and did not know what was going on. The operators made mistakes. The representatives of the safety inspectorate fled. Some of the equipment failed. The establishment repeatedly played down the risks...'[138] The official interim report criticised 'poor communication and delays in releasing data on dangerous radiation leaks at the facility'. The authorities had 'grossly underestimated the tsunami risks', for the wave that had struck the plant was twice as high as the most pessimistic of the planners' forecasts of what *could* happen in the event of a tsunami.

Japan's politicians were, or should have been, aware of

136. The i newspaper, October 17th 2020
137. New Scientist, October 31st 2020
138. The Economist, March 10th 2012

much of this. A government committee in Japan's Cabinet Office in 2004 forecast that tsunamis were possible and could be higher than the maximum being forecast (5.6 metres, 18 feet) by TEPCO and the government.[139]

In 2007, TEPCO set up an in-house department to supervise its nuclear facilities and in 2008 they produced a report identifying an immediate need to protect the Fukushima Daiichi facility from sea water flooding. The report forecast the possibility of waves up to 10 metres – three years before the disaster. The forecast was dismissed as "unrealistic".[140] Earthquake researchers warned at that time that TEPCO needed urgently to revise its assumptions on the impact of earthquakes and subsequent tsunamis[141] and in 2008, the International Atomic Energy Agency (IAEA) told a meeting of the G8's Nuclear Safety and Security Group in Tokyo that a "strong" earthquake could pose a "serious problem" for Japan's nuclear power stations. The issue had engendered a lively debate in 1995 with the publication of an article by seismologist, Katsuhiko Ishibashi, in the *International Herald Tribune* in which he coined the phrase 'nuclear earthquake disaster'. The article warned of an accident similar to that which was to happen at Fukushima in 2011, when the tsunami wave was 46 feet high.

As a direct result of the disaster in 2013, 60,000 people marched in Tokyo against the use of nuclear power; they carried a petition supporting their demonstration, which was signed by more than 8 million people.[142] The debate raged on so fiercely that Japan switched its energy priorities to coal-fired power stations. Coal would once again be burned, with

139. Martin Finckler, The New York Times, March 19th 2012
140. The Mainichi Shimbon, October 2018; Jagadees Wordpress.com, February 13th 2012
141. Yukinobu Okamura, Yomiuri newspaper, March 11th 2011
142. United Press International, June 2nd 2013

the attendant negative impact on the world's pollution and on Japan's declared intention of cutting greenhouse gases by 80%, by 2050.

The lessons of the Japanese disaster pointed directly at a failure of governance. The government, who were customers as well as regulators, had been too close to TEPCO, the operating company. The investigating committee[143] declared there had been "a culture of complacency about nuclear safety and poor crisis management". TEPCO had given jobs to many of the most senior government regulators on their retirement.[144] It was all too cosy. There had been a climate of mismanagement and corruption. The Fukushima disaster killed 18,500 people.

The Japanese considered the structural imperfections of the design of the nuclear station and its situation so close to the sea. Among the recommendations was to re-build the sea wall, separating the nuclear station from the ocean. Having previously miscalculated by a scale of at least 50 per cent on the height of the wall needed to protect the Fukushima station, the government declared that the wall would have to be high enough to repel the ocean and keep it out.

But how high is 'high enough'?

* * *

The disaster in Japan was the one which Walter Marshall had feared. The Japanese Government had failed to heed the repeated warnings of a forthcoming disaster. No-one should expect governments to be infallible, but some governments are more fallible than others...

Most nuclear power stations are built near the sea whose

---

143. Investigating Committee on the Accident at the Fukushima Nuclear Power Station, October 29th 2011
144. The New York Times, April 27th 2011

water is needed as a coolant. So, the question: 'How high is high enough?' is, or should be, taxing governments around the world. It is a question significant not only to nuclear power stations but for civilisation itself. The evidence that climate change is driving up the world's sea levels is worryingly widespread. Holland has long battled the sea for its survival and it is salutary to hear how the man who leads the country's long-term flood management summarises what he observes as a "serious situation":

"The rise in the level of the North Sea may accelerate sharply from 2015, potentially by two metres (6½ feet) by 2100 ... entailing far-reaching consequences," he told the FLOODEX 2020 International Conference in Peterborough, UK.

According to the *New Scientist*,[145] 'we already know that we are heading for a one-metre rise (3½ feet) by 2100 ... with estimates of a 5-metre rise ... in a couple of centuries, possibly even sooner ... there is hardly any doubt that this rise is inevitable'.

That the sea will become a killer is a given, says David Wallace-Wells, as he considers climate change in his book The Uninhabitable Earth.[146] 'Barring a reduction of emissions, we could see at least four feet of sea-level rise and possibly eight by the end of the century. A radical reduction, of the scale that could make the Paris (Climate Change Conference) 2°C goal a conceivably attainable target, could still produce a rise of as much as 2 metres (6½ feet) by 2100.'

The rise in sea level is linked to global warming. The Intergovernmental Panel on Climate Change (IPCC) calculates a 2.3 metre (7 feet) rise for every 1°C increase in temperature. A 2°C increase would mean a five-metre rise

145. New Scientist, June 13th 2015
146. Published by Tim Duggan, New York, 2019

(17½ feet) in the water level.

The potential threat from our weather, our rivers and our oceans has the fundamental ability to change our entire way of life. Late in 2020, UN Secretary General Antonio Guterres berated world leaders on the "suicidal war" being waged on nature. This, he said was "the moment of truth for the world" if the disaster were to be avoided. Prince Charles, the Prince of Wales, warned that climate crisis could "dwarf" the impact of the coronavirus pandemic. The environmental crisis had been evident for "far too many years – decried, denigrated and denied. It is now becoming a comprehensive catastrophe".[147]

Nearly two-thirds of the world's major cities are built on the coast, close to large stretches of water; so too are fisheries, power stations, farms, rice paddies and marshland, all making key contributions to national economies. Twelve of Britain's 19 nuclear power sites could be at risk. The areas of flooding linked to weather change, have quadrupled since 1980 and doubled since 2004.[148] The potential impact on the world's population is already dramatic. Without immediate and strategic forward thinking, large swathes of Northern Europe and the eastern half of North America could be subject to 10 times as many floods as they now experience. No continent will escape.

Jeff Goodell envisages[149] a shattering image of a drowning world: "Monuments, in some cases, whole cultures – will be transformed into underwater relics, like sunken ships, this century: Facebook's headquarters, the Kennedy Space Center, the entire nations of the Maldives and the Marshall Islands; most of Bangladesh, including all of the mangrove forests that have been the kingdom of Bengal tigers for millennia; much of the South Florida paradise engineered

147. The i newspaper, September 21st 2020
148. European Academies Science Advisory Council, 2010
149. The Water Will Come, Jeff Goodell, Hachette

out of marsh and swamp and sandbar; Saint Mark's basilica in Venice, the White House at 1600 Pennsylvania Avenue, as well as Trump's 'Winter White House' at Mar-a-Lago…

"By 2100, if we do not halt emissions, as much as 5% of the world's population will be flooded every single year. Jakarta is one of the world's fastest growing cities; today home to 10 million: thanks to flooding, it could be entirely underwater as soon as 2050. Already, China is evacuating hundreds of thousands every summer to keep them out of the range of flooding in the Pearl River Delta."[150]

In Britain, the Town and Country Planning Association (TCPA)'s Policy Director, Hugh Ellis, told Prime Minister, Boris Johnson, that "the government doesn't understand the climate debate", which requires "you to think long-term". The UK's approach to climate change and flooding, he said, was "flawed". The anticipated collapse of two glaciers in the Antarctic – the Thwaites and the nearby Pine Island Glacier – could alone cause the sea level to rise by 1 metre (3½ feet). If this triggered the melting of the West Antarctic Ice Sheet (WAIS), the rise could be 3 metres (10½ feet). A rise of more than two metres could cause major permanent changes to Britain's coastline at Scarborough, Hull, Peterborough, Portsmouth, parts of East Kent and East London and the Thames Estuary, where thousands of acres would be submerged. The collapse of the Thwaites Glacier, once begun, could be "irreversible". Humanity "cannot afford to wait".[151] There were signs that the British Government was at least beginning to listen, as in 2020 Prime Minister Johnson heralded a Green Revolution.

On the other side of the world in March 2020, the World Meteorological Organization (WMO) reported that the depletion of the ozone level over the Arctic "reached an

150. The Uninhabitable Earth, David Wallace-Wells, 2019, p60
151. Scott Borg, US National Science Foundation, May 2018

unprecedented level".[152] At the same time, a six-month heatwave in Siberia produced a record temperature of 38°C.

* * *

Some governments and companies have read the writing on the wall more clearly than others. In July 2020, German politicians finalised the country's long-awaited plan to phase out coal as an energy source. The last coal-fired power plant will be closed by 2038. British Petroleum (BP) announced in the same month that they would halve their oil and gas production. Instead, they pledged as they moved into "a green future" that they would build enough wind and solar power plants around the world "that would meet peak UK energy demand".[153] World-wide, in 2020 BP was responsible for 45 million tons of carbon emissions – more than the entire UK economy. Significantly, BP boss, Bernard Looney, revealed that this was not simply a commercial decision. He said: "Oil and carbon fuels are increasingly becoming socially challenged."[154]

Yet we currently confront the possibility that the story of the human race may end in disaster caused by human incompetence. Recent history shows that commitment to nuclear energy inevitably carries risk.

In 2020 the British Government announced they were still considering another nuclear power station on the Sizewell site in Suffolk operated by the French company EDF and costing around £20 billion. The work force would come fresh from constructing a similar nuclear station at Hinkley Point in Somerset. Part of the Government's reasoning was that 10,000 skilled jobs would be lost if Sizewell C weren't

---

152. The Independent, May 2nd 2020
153. The i newspaper, July 2020
154. The Sunday Times, August 9th 2020

built. Jonathan Marshall, head of Britain's Energy & Climate Intelligence Unit, commented that a renewable energy 'green' alternative to Sizewell C would offer a cheaper and more flexible solution to close the gap in Britain's energy needs which the Government forecast. Marshall said: "If you look at the amount of money involved and the highly-likely overspend, it's pretty easy to come up with a green alternative."

Clearly, the future no longer looks too bright for the oil producers. They possessed research in the 1970s that showed their products were changing the climate, but they did nothing. Climate change activist, Sir Jonathon Porritt, believes that the oil companies have invested "next to nothing in Green alternatives to fossil fuel – 2.3 per cent of total capital spending in the case of BP".[155]

There is hope, however. Crucially, the market has turned against fossil-powered energy generation. The costs of solar and wind power have plummeted and Porritt believes that renewable energy generation, which was, in 2020, 23 per cent of global electricity supply, could rise to 75 per cent by 2035. The obstacle to achieving this target is now political rather than scientific. Porritt, for years a persuasive but peaceful leader of the Green lobby, now believes it is time to change tactics. He says:

"I've come to the conclusion that we have no choice. Without mass civil disobedience, at this very late stage, I cannot see any other way of avoiding the threat of runaway climate change … what we all know now, irrefutably, is that this is literally the last decade in which authentic, grounded hope will be available to anchor everything we can do to save our families, friends and future generations."[156]

---

155. Hope in Hell, Jonathon Porritt, Simon & Schuster, 2020
156. Ibid

* * *

There are companies staking their future prosperity on assessing our ability to negotiate a way through the current threats to the future of the planet. Lloyd's of London and the Bank of England agree that insurers "stand exposed ... by emerging vulnerabilities ... and longer-term risks that could have severe impacts on the financial and insurance sectors". They have discussed the impact of longer and stronger heatwaves, the intensification of droughts, a greater number of severe storms and severe flooding caused by "at least a 10% increase in rainfall". This is, they record, "a prospect guaranteed to dampen the spirits and the shoes of those who don't equate climate change with global warming". At one meeting, Lloyd's discussed the 20 cm rise in the sea level, which has occurred "at the top of Manhattan since the 1950s". This had "increased insured losses ... by 30% in New York alone".

For the insurer, this is a time of 'unprecedented levels of risk'.[157] The publication, Natural Catastrophe Risk Management, admitted in 2017 that there was low confidence in detailed regional projections of the likelihood of disasters but that 'many studies propose natural, multi-decadal, climate-driven variability in the genesis and the impact of some perils ... such as hurricanes, cyclones ... and heavy precipitation'. In other words, from the folk who judge the impact of disaster in dollars, pounds, euros and yen: It's going to be rough out there and you'd better believe it.

* * *

---

157. Natural Catastrophe Risk Management, Mitchell-Wallace, Jones, Hillier and Foote, John Wiley & Sons, 2017

In Britain, in the last 50 years, it is the height of the headlines, the persistence of the critics, that can influence those who make global decisions. In 1968, we produced a documentary that foresaw the Thames Estuary being inundated. It was called *If London Floods...*[158] It caused a stir both in print and in politics. The Government and the (then) London County Council (LCC) had been discussing the construction of a Thames Barrier for years. No decision had been reached. In 1953, flood water had risen to within half an inch of the top of London's flood defences – half an inch from a major disaster in Britain's capital. We discussed this, standing beside a bucket of 'puddle clay' that, in London's low-level tube stations, was going to be patted into the gaps between boards that would be slotted into place in an attempt to prevent the River Thames flooding the underground tube network. The entrances to the underground stations at Temple, Charing Cross, Waterloo and Westminster were all up to three feet below the level of the Thames Embankment. The boards and the puddle clay didn't seem too convincing. 'Heath' and 'Robinson' came to mind.

Later that month, we received a private letter from Toby Jessel, then the member for Richmond on the Greater London Council (GLC) and later, for 30 years, Member of Parliament for Richmond. He wrote: 'I hope and believe that your programme will have done something to stir waters up at Government level.' It still took a further four years for the construction of the Thames Barrier to be authorised.

Currently in Britain, a second Thames Barrier is being discussed. The target date for the construction was originally 2100, then 2050 – now the earlier date of 2030. Optimistically, it confirms a degree of urgency argued by some government

---

158. If London Floods … This Week, Rediffusion Television, February 8th 1968. It was based on original research work by Brian Haynes who is also responsible for much of the research in this chapter

advisers on climate change. The agency at the heart of the discussions puts it quite simply:

"Hard choices need to be taken. We must either invest more in sustainable approaches to flooding and coastal management – or (we must) learn to live with increased flooding."[159]

But, if that's the choice, and if we have to build more walls to keep out the sea, the question remains: how high is high enough? And what will be the cost, in both financial and human terms if the right strategic, long-term decisions are not made?

To the interested layman, it all seems so obvious: amid climate change, to invest in nuclear power will increase the risk of catastrophic disaster. To invest in the natural elements of sun, wind and water, to explore the potential of hydrogen as a source of power, will reduce carbon emissions, remove the world's dependence on oil, coal and gas and allow the world to breathe again.

But, surely, it can't be as simple as that…

---

159. David Wardle, Executive Manager, Thames Estuary Programme, 2019 correspondence with Brian Haynes

Chapter 7

THE SURGEON:
The Guinea Pigs of East Grinstead

*"We are trustees of each other. We do well to
remember that the privilege of dying for one's
country is not equal to the privilege
of living for it."*

Archibald McIndoe, 1944

Archibald McIndoe

The sole benefit of war, they say, is
that science makes advances amid
the terror and the human carnage.
I am not a war reporter, a member
of that freemasonry of journalists
who specialise in the important
job of professionally bringing us
to conflict, its implications and its
agony. But I have reported war and
riot in the Middle East as an 'Arab'
reporter[160] during the Six-Day War
and after, and in Israel when I was chosen from the *This
Week* team to cover the peace conference in Tel Aviv, called

---

160. In the Middle East in the 1960s and 70s, journalists were divided into those
who covered the conflict from the Arab side, or from the Israeli side. A stamp
from an Arab country in your passport meant that you could not enter Israel and
vice-versa

by President Carter. Curiously, amid the struggles I have tried to reflect and contextualise, the closest I came to being killed was in the West Indies when, in 1976, Edward Seaga of the Jamaica Labour Party (JLP) was running against the then president Michael Manley of the People's National Party (PNP). It was a bloody struggle punctuated by gunfire and death on both sides. We were on the back of a high-sided open lorry, part of a Seaga election cavalcade. Around us, a boisterous crowd of Seaga supporters. These rallies drew huge crowds. Shots rang out and our truck stopped. As the shots rained in, the instinct to jump and run was irresistible, but impossible. Someone tried to release the exit boards at the back of the lorry. They wouldn't budge. We were trapped and everyone threw themselves flat. The body of the next man became your best cover. Two Seaga supporters died in that lorry before the shooting stopped.

I remember thinking that if I were to be killed or injured, 'how much would it hurt?' I recalled reading somewhere that being shot is so traumatic that the body produces its own defensive painkiller, the endorphins. I wasn't too convinced. But what surprised me was that I feared being badly deformed more than I feared dying. What follows, then, is the story of a group of men in World War II who almost died in the most appalling agony, but who survived though severely handicapped and re-built their lives through advances in the most public of all medical procedures – plastic surgery. They are a group of men who also illustrate in their being, the triumph of the human spirit.

The Guinea Pig Club was formed on July 20ᵗʰ 1941, at the Queen Victoria Hospital, East Grinstead, Sussex. Its members fell into three categories; one, fliers mutilated by burns suffered in challenging and repelling Hitler's *Luftwaffe*; two, a surgeon called Sir Archibald McIndoe and the doctors and medical staff who were treating the airmen and three, a number of friends and benefactors whose objective was to make the life of the 'Guinea Pigs' a happy one and who came up with the title The Royal Society for the Prevention of Cruelty to Guinea Pigs.[161]

Tom Gleave

Each Guinea Pig has his own vivid story to tell of how he was 'fried', to use the description favoured by the Chief Guinea Pig, Tom Gleave. Gleave was shot down in 1940 during the Battle of Britain. He remembered his struggle to open the hood of his burning aircraft and the explosion which hurled him out through a sheet of flames. He remembered pulling the ripcord of his parachute and floating down to earth. He remembered his face and body "blowing up like a Michelin man". He remembered the pain, being given a lift by a passing motorist and then being taken into hospital in a wheelbarrow. He was hurt, but he was also angry. He wanted to get back to flying again. Under bright lights in the operating theatre, he asked a nurse:

"How long will I be here? Six weeks?"

She replied: "Yes, something like that." It was eleven-and-a-half months before Tom Gleave could fly again, with a new nose and a huge scar on his forehead that never disappeared.

It is fascinating to identify the corner in which a damaged, sometimes broken man, finds hope – hope that may grow into confidence and, ultimately, into a determination to

---

161. The author is an honorary Friend of the Guinea Pigs. The ITV documentary The Guinea Pig Club, produced by the author and Robert Fleming was broadcast in June 1979

continue living.

He may find it in religion, or in the love of others, or in a realisation that life, with all it has to offer, is simply too good to let go by default. In this very special club, hope springs from one harsh, realistic sentence: 'There's always someone worse off than yourself...'

It is the credo of the Guinea Pig Club; even though the members themselves may not realise it because, if it is anything, it is a club that exists on, and for, mutual support. There is no room for any more hurt, least of all, dwelling on the specific details of the misfortunes of another member of the club. Yet, time and again, when asked to recall how they climbed out of the lowest troughs in their lives, the moments when they were tempted to cry "Enough!", that sentence bursts into the conversation: 'There's always someone worse off than yourself...'

For the Guinea Pigs, scarred and handicapped, it is a fundamental truth. Of course, no-one identifies who the Guinea Pig *is* who has been most disfigured by his injuries. In any case, it is very much a matter of opinion. It's enough to believe this Fundamental Truth, to take comfort in it, to wrap around the knowledge that, however difficult it is for you to cope with problems, others always have greater injuries. These were vigorous, bright and, usually, handsome young men transformed in an instant into A Problem – a problem for others but, most importantly, to themselves. It was Guinea Pig Edward 'Blackie' Blacksell, who tried to resolve their situation. Blacksell was assigned to Queen Victoria Hospital as an RAF physical training instructor[162] and became the Guinea Pigs' unofficial welfare officer. He summed up the challenge:

---

162. In itself, an odd appointment to patients who were incapable of anything but carefully monitored movements, particularly during lengthy treatments

"How were these men going to cope? Most of them had never even *seen* the faces or the hands of a badly burned man, let alone thought about what it would be like to be one.

"How were they going to work? To eat? How were they going to attract a pretty girl? How were they going to manage courtship, making love? We picked, incidentally, the prettiest nurses we could find to work at East Grinstead – and I didn't hear too many complaints either from the patients or the nurses.

"We tried to place the men in jobs and, though many of the firms were sympathetic, they hadn't the faintest idea of what these young men needed. After all, they were fit young men who'd simply been disfigured. One firm offered a number of jobs as lift men. Now, how could you ask a squadron leader to become a lift man? And one very famous retail store in London expressed an eager interest in placing the Guinea Pigs in proper employment – but once they'd met just one of the Guinea Pigs they contacted us and asked:

'*We'd love to help. But could you please arrange for the men to wear some kind of a mask?*'

"Now, how can you begin to convince a man that he may once more take his place in society if his employer will give him a job only if he hides his face?

"Right from the early days, we've been certain that the most important task for the club has been to see that every member recognises and retains his own essential dignity. We've been determined that no member of the Guinea Pig Club shall, as it were, be seen selling matches from a tray on the street corner."[163]

On June 9th 2014, a statue was unveiled in the heart of the Sussex town of East Grinstead that had embraced the Guinea Pigs as their numbers grew. It was of the man who

---

163. Conversation with author, 1978

was the inspiration for the club, Archibald McIndoe. He is immortalised in bronze, his hands on the shoulders of one of his Guinea Pig patients – supporting, encouraging.

Plastic surgery is not new. The father of European plastic surgery lived in Shakespeare's day in Italy. He was a professor at Bologna, Gaspare Tagliacozzi. Shortly before his death, he published a textbook of plastic surgery describing how to raise a flap of skin from the arm with which to rebuild the patient's nose or ear. It must have taken great courage on the patient's part to submit to such an operation. Not only were there no anaesthetics but Tagliacozzi also insisted the patient be kept in a rigid harness, akin to a straitjacket, for 40 days after the operation. Along with all branches of surgery, plastic surgery made its greatest strides as a result of two 19th century developments: anaesthesia and antiseptics. The notion that surgical implements, operating theatres and the surgeon's hands have to be clean, has saved thousands of lives.

In 1939, when Archibald McIndoe arrived at Queen Victoria Hospital, the pattern of plastic surgery was established. It was a branch of surgery with three strands; first, the treatment of injury, specialising in burns; second, the repair of congenital deformities and third, cosmetic for those who could afford it.

McIndoe was born in Otago, New Zealand, in May 1900 and graduated from the University of Otago Dunedin School of Medicine in 1923.

Every New Zealander, it seems, is genetically driven to travel and, through a colleague and admirer, McIndoe was offered a five-year fellowship at the prestigious Mayo Clinic in San Francisco. Soon, he was demonstrating his skills elsewhere and in 1930, in Chicago,[164] he was approached

---

164. PMFA journal, Jacquie Pinney and Anthony D Metcalfe, 2020

to operate on a patient suffering from chronic liver disease. The patient's only requirement was that he should remain anonymous. The patient was 'Mr Mancini' and he was also willing to pay five times the normal fee for his abdominal surgery. Mr Mancini arrived in a fleet of Cadillacs. After the successful procedure, a member of the entourage sidled up to McIndoe, gave him an envelope (which contained $1,000) and whispered: "Al says thank you for operating on his kid brother." The patient was the younger brother of the notorious gangster, Al Capone, later gaoled not for any of the killings with which he was associated, but for financial gain through tax fraud. It is recorded that McIndoe was relieved to have been rewarded in cash, rather than cheque.

The medical dignitaries watching the Chicago demonstration included the president of Britain's Royal College of Surgeons, Lord Moynihan, who took McIndoe aside afterwards and remarked: "You have hands like a ploughboy, but they behave like an artist's hands." He suggested McIndoe pursue a career in Britain, where he would help him find a job. Thus encouraged, McIndoe and his family arrived in Liverpool during the winter of 1931 and travelled to London to take up the offer. His welcome was less than effusive. He had difficulty contacting Lord Moynihan, whose memory of their conversation differed from McIndoe's. There *was* no job. Moynihan commented incredulously: "Bless my soul, but the hospital isn't even built yet. I can hardly give you a job if the place doesn't exist, can I?"[165] He suggested McIndoe apply for a Fellowship of the Royal College of Surgeons. McIndoe and his family found themselves thousands of miles from home and security, with no job and no income. He did, however, have a distant cousin in London, Sir Harold Gillies, a plastic surgeon highly regarded because of his work

---

165. Ibid

on the wounded in World War I. Gillies found McIndoe a job at St Bartholomew's Hospital in London and, working beside this experienced surgeon from 1932 until 1939, McIndoe refined his surgical skills and set up his own practice. By the outbreak of World War II, McIndoe's medical papers indicated that he still felt the textbook treatment of burns, in particular, was 'primitive'. It involved the application of tannic acid and gentian violet, which 'healed' the skin in a most unsightly manner and caused damage to the more delicate areas, especially eyelids. If McIndoe made one major breakthrough in burns treatment, it was to convince the medical profession and military authorities to replace their standard treatment with the saline bath. He believed that the task of the plastic surgeon was to ameliorate the results of burns and not simply to be called upon to cover or remove ugly scars after the damaged tissue had healed. Incidentally, it is part of Guinea Pig folklore that McIndoe invented the saline bath after watching the unexpectedly good progress made by burned airmen who had fallen into the sea as they defended Britain against the *Luftwaffe*. They healed more quickly than those who fell on dry land. Medically, however, this is unlikely. To be of any value, the saline bath has to be kept at blood heat, much warmer than the English Channel, and the salinity of the water has to remain at a constant level, which simply does not naturally occur in the waters around the British Isles.

In 1940, McIndoe was advocating that the best protection for exposed tissue caused by burns or wounds was skin. This is the principle behind the Gillies[166] tube pedicle; if a flap of skin is raised, the flap can be turned in on itself to form

---

166. The Gillies tube pedicle, a flap of skin and soft tissue from a patient is formed into a tube from source to target area by anchoring it at both ends, periodically severing it an one end and then anchoring it closer to the target site (i.e., from armpit to nose)

a tube, which may be transferred to the damaged area of a body. It cannot, however, be *any* skin. As in all transplant surgery, rejection is the problem. McIndoe solved it by taking the graft from the patient's own skin.

The father of plastic surgery, Tagliacozzi, had failed to recognise the problem of rejection in the 19th century. He had tried to cover burns with a sheep's skin. The graft had failed but the 'foreign' skin provided a useful temporary cover, foreshadowing a modern technique – the use of pigskin as short-term protection.

During World War II, the treatment of burns advanced through a better understanding of shock, post-operative infection and the effects of anaesthesia. McIndoe devised a two-pronged programme of treatment. He would first

Geoffrey Page

reconstruct a patient physically, each operation producing a marginal improvement. But he was also preparing the patient psychologically for a life in which some degree of disability or disfigurement was inescapable. The treatment phase ended when the patient himself decided that he was happy to try to cope with life with what he had – to quote one Guinea Pig: "You get to a stage, perhaps after 10, 20 or 30 operations, when you decide the next operation isn't worth it. You've had enough. You decide to live with the face you've got." As another Guinea Pig, Geoffrey Page, once wearily said: [167]

"Each of us has a bank of courage. Every time you go to the operating table, you spend a little more. Eventually there's

---

167. Conversation with author, 1979

no more left."

Some of the Guinea Pigs lived through 80 operations.

Today, the burns unit at the Queen Victoria Hospital tackles the traditional killers with great success. Fewer people, if they even survive a burn, will die either from shock, dehydration, infection or the metabolic changes that can reduce a healthy man to almost half his weight. Nowadays, with the availability of plasma, artificial feeding and antibiotics, more patients survive the early traumatic weeks than would have done in McIndoe's day.

Over the years, there were 649 Guinea Pigs. Each had his own story of the way life can be re-built. We will consider four of them. The words that follow will not illustrate adequately the experiences they attempt to portray...

If Archibald McIndoe ever had a favourite during his Guinea Pigs – and he swore that he didn't – it was probably Geoffrey Page. Early members of the club report that they were like father and son. The Boss, as Page always addressed McIndoe, had a special relationship with all the Guinea Pigs but with Geoffrey, it seemed very special. More accurately, they behaved like brothers, elder and younger. Page, debonair, determined, witty, came to East Grinstead almost from the outset. He was one of the early casualties of the Battle of Britain and when he was shot down again he returned there in 1942.

He initially became a Guinea Pig one sunny August day in 1940. Ten British planes took off to defend Manston Airfield in Kent. A phalanx of 90 German aircraft, Dornier bombers and escorting Messerschmitt fighters, were heading up the Thames Estuary towards London. Page and the Hurricane squadrons intercepted them. Climbing to attack, the British aircraft were vulnerable. They were caught in crossfire from the bombers. Then, the German fighters dived on them. Page said he remembered "things like electric light bulbs flashing past me". Suddenly, there was a great explosion. The smaller fuel tank, the only one of the three tanks which was not self-sealing, was hit. Through an ill-advised quirk of design, it was positioned almost in the lap of the pilot.

"I was in the middle of a blazing inferno. The whole episode is instantly memorable. It was a crossroads in my life. The beautiful thing about it is that your basic RAF training stands you in good stead.

"Initially, you record absolute terror. I'm not ashamed to say it. You're screaming with fear. Secondly, the thing is happening so quickly; if you don't get out within a few seconds, you're dead. You can see your hands burning in front of you. The life is just draining out of you.

"They say the temperature goes from 5° to 350° centigrade, which is like a cooking oven, in about seven seconds. But you do the RAF lifesaving drill instinctively. You pull the split pin out of the sub-harness, disentangle your oxygen and radio communication and roll the aeroplane. You do it as if it were second nature. And, after that, you're tumbling head over heels through the air. I remember starting to fumble with the ripcord of the parachute but my hands were so badly burned that I couldn't pull the ripcord. But the instinct for survival is enormous – so, despite the pain, the ripcord was pulled..."

Geoffrey Page had his first saline bath where the Thames Estuary meets the North Sea. He was taken to a Margate hospital[168] and, later, to the Royal Masonic Hospital in Hammersmith, where McIndoe found him. Page remembers:

"In came this man who looked like a young Harold Lloyd;[169] squat, wearing spectacles. He was a delightful person and he sat on my bed and asked me various questions. I did not know that he was a doctor. He asked nothing medical at all.

---

168. Ironically, it was the Royal Sea Bathing Hospital, Margate, designed as an open-air hospital for tuberculosis sufferers
169. Harold Lloyd, a zany comedian, star of silent Hollywood movies in the 1930s

He wanted to know the type of aircraft I was flying, whether I had been wearing goggles and practical things like that. He said, 'Were you wearing gloves?' I said, 'No'. He said, 'Clot'. I'll always remember that answer. Gloves would have saved my hands. Then he said, 'I'll be seeing you again', and he did, at East Grinstead."

The realisation that he was going to be badly disfigured came slowly to Page. When he was first in hospital, he imagined getting back to his squadron "within a week". He was there two years. He was sustained by two things: what he describes as his "stupid mania to get back to flying", and his hatred for the Germans. "I made a resolution that, for every operation I had, I would shoot down one German plane when I got back to flying. After all, those operations weren't too much fun, you know."

He had fifteen operations over two years. Then he went back to operational flying. He shot down 17 enemy aircraft. His peers said that, in his obsession, Page was fearless. But the bedrock of youth is that young men believe themselves to be immortal. "That's why youngsters drive their cars at high speeds. We just happened to fly aeroplanes rather than cars and motorbikes – and someone gave us a medal instead of burying us in a graveyard."

Back in the cockpit in October 1942, Page admits he was driven by hatred. He wanted to shoot down and kill as many Germans as he could. He became more and more experienced and was promoted Wing Commander, with his own fighter wing. "Then suddenly, I was tired of it all. The lust for revenge burnt itself out. I was not liking myself. I was full of hate and it was damaging me. I felt myself drained of energy. Mind you, I was exhausted by my operational flying – but, in the end, how long can you carry on a vendetta? What is the point of it?"

On the second occasion Page was shot down, he was

protecting Allied gliders during the airborne landings on Arnhem after D-Day. He returned to East Grinstead for further treatment. He was one of only two Guinea Pigs to qualify twice, the other being Frankie Truhlar, who was killed in a flying accident after the war.

Page found that Ward Three, the Nissen hut, which had housed the early Guinea Pigs, was still there but it was now part of a more institutionalised hospital. What had been experimental was now routine. Page was pleased to note that a keg of beer still had its place at the centre of the ward.

When Page returned again to flying, after another series of operations, it took a while to adjust. His hands were tender. He admits he was tentative. His first 50 hours of flying were non-operational. He went to an air training calibration unit and spent tedious hours "getting bored to tears". He had doubts about flying in bad weather but "it was like riding a bike – you don't forget".

Did he fear that he might be shot down again? "It never entirely left me. But I coped with it, being a little older and a little wiser."

As the war came to an end, Geoffrey Page toured the United States, talking of his experiences as a Guinea Pig. There, he met British actor, Nigel Bruce. "One day," Bruce said to Page, "you must come back when the war's finished and marry our daughter who's in the (Royal) Canadian Air Force." Geoffrey Page returned to Britain and began working as a test pilot with Vickers-Armstrongs Limited. He wrote to Nigel Bruce's daughter, whom he had never met and said:

"Behave yourself or I'll come back and marry you one day."

He *did* go back. They *did* get married. McIndoe became godfather to one of their children.

Geoffrey Page became a successful businessman in Switzerland. Though he had nothing to prove, he was determined to take his place again as a useful member of society. He died on August 3ʳᵈ 2000.

* * *

Sam Gallop, RAF pilot, sharp of mind and feature, has devoted much of his energy in the last 50 years convincing the rest of the world that they should not forget the needs of the disabled. He became a Guinea Pig on Easter Sunday 1943. He was coming in to land in the south of England in bad weather when another aircraft "flew up my backside". His aircraft hit the ground and blew up. Despite the flames, a corporal and a jeep-load of Americans managed to drag him out

Sam Gallop

and saved his life. When an RAF doctor arrived, Sam Gallop was lying beside the aircraft, his eyes wide open but totally unconscious. He had suffered minor brain damage, fractured upper and lower jaws, teeth loss (most of them), an injury to his left arm, a lost left hand finger and extensive burns on his body. Both his legs were badly broken below the knee and required amputation. He had also injured his back.

The next 18 months Sam Gallop remembers as a succession of operations. He remembers too, the moment when it would have been easier to die than to fight on. "I was lying in bed, looking out of the window at the stars. I felt I could have wafted gently away. It was a curious feeling of being outside myself, looking down at myself and feeling that, if it weren't for the people walking up and down outside in the corridor, keeping the world turning, I could easily have made my excuses and left."

Sam Gallop had 17 operations altogether. As the weeks

became months, Sam Gallop accepted the challenge of living on. Between operations, he won a place at Oxford University. He learned about being disabled. He resisted sympathy.

"Excessive concern can undermine a Guinea Pig's self-confidence. He may become dependent, whereas the aim is to make him *in*dependent." One of the secrets of the Guinea Pig Club's success, says Gallop, has been that by their irreverent attitude towards each other's disabilities, they have helped each other. "All our injuries are matter-of-fact, to be overcome. There is a real sense in which you have to be disabled fully to understand what being disabled is about."

Becoming disabled means that life is riddled with unnecessary frustrations – steps where they are not required and doors that are an inch too narrow to accommodate a wheelchair. Early in his life as a Guinea Pig, Gallop determined to work to improve the lives of the disabled. He spent years voluntarily vetting the City of London's facilities for the disabled. He was encouraged by his three years' study at Oxford. Though the university may not have been designed for the disabled, the college staff were eager to accommodate his special needs. The authorities did not discuss his disability. They did not suggest *how* he was going to get into the college. They left it entirely to this sorely disabled airman to work out himself how to get in and out of the buildings, assuming that he would tell them if a change were necessary. He did. He received special dispensation to go to hospital for treatment, as part of his Guinea Pig's normal life. Having gained his degree, he had to find a job. By coincidence, when he applied for a post in the Central Electricity Generating Board, he found himself being interviewed by another limbless person. Instead of discussing the job, they talked of the difficulties of driving a car without hand controls. And, at the end of it all, Gallop got the job. "Perhaps the other people on the interview board were fascinated by the conversation …"

It is part of the philosophy of the club that all Guinea Pigs should attempt anything if they want to. Hard as they try, the Guinea Pigs may not always succeed. Excellence, says Gallop, is sometimes unattainable. "You may be disabled and learn to play golf, but you're never going to become a scratch golfer. The quicker you recognise that, the less anguish for everyone."

Sam Gallop, a man with no legs, learned to ride a horse.

He believes that three factors enabled him to come to terms with his disabilities. First, there was the professional help and support of McIndoe and the staff at East Grinstead; second, there was the supportive and sympathetic attitude from the town of East Grinstead that the stricken airmen experienced whenever they left the hospital grounds bound for pub, restaurant or cinema. Encouraged by McIndoe, many East Grinstead citizens visited the ward to take patients out. It was as if East Grinstead itself had taken a corporate decision to help the men as part of their war effort. The Guinea Pigs described East Grinstead, in a phrase borrowed from some long-forgotten newspaper article, as the 'town that never stared'. Finally, the third factor was what every Guinea Pig experienced every single day – the example set by his fellow Guinea Pigs. The newcomer to this elite club quickly learned that its members felt they were "special ... people who mattered", says Gallop:

"They feel that they were given the best treatment in the world, that they had a unique experience and that they have 'enjoyed' that experience. They believe, too, that everybody else who is disabled ought to be made to feel special. Unfortunately, I think, this is not always the case. We in the Guinea Pig Club were, and are, very lucky.

"The club gave us an identity. It gave us back our self-respect."

* * *

They forecast, for Jimmy Wright, a promising career in the film industry. That was before he joined up. In 1942, he became an aerial photographer and film cameraman in the RAF. As a result of a plane crash in Italy the following year, he was blinded. Despite this and the fact that he was injured to the point of death, he pursued his chosen career and became a much-respected film producer.

In a nutshell, the story of Jimmy Wright is remarkable.

Jimmy Wright

Told at greater length, the story is less improbable as the character of the man emerges.

The Guinea Pig Club is proud of Jimmy Wright. Talk to any club member about their own collective achievements and, before long, you will be asked: 'Have you met Jimmy Wright yet?' One of the unofficial rules of membership of the club is that you do not boast of your own achievements. It is quite permitted, however, to boast about the achievements of fellow Guinea Pigs.

Wright joined the RAF at the age of 19. For the previous two years, he had worked for Technicolor in the camera department. He started as clapper boy but, with a flair for photography and a father who was a respected cameraman, he flourished.

If Jimmy Wright had to go to war, he was keen to get into the RAF film unit. He took the photographic course. He started operational flying in Britain, based in Norfolk, and flew frequently over the Low Countries mapping enemy movements. In 1943, he was posted to the Mediterranean.

He went from North Africa to Malta to Sicily and eventually to Italy, as the Allies pushed north through Europe. He flew 43 missions.

His active service as a cameraman ended suddenly. His aircraft caught fire on take-off. The fire in the engine was not spotted until the aircraft was airborne. It was too late to stop and there was insufficient height for the crew to bale out. The plane crashed and exploded. Jimmy was amidships and he and another crew member, in the tail of the plane, were the only two survivors. Wright believes he was trapped and eventually dragged out by an American who saved his life. But as he was unconscious he has no memory of it.

The registrar at the hospital in Taranto, Italy, was so convinced that Jimmy Wright would not survive that he had posted him as dead along with other crew members. Jimmy's mother received a telegram informing her that her son was dead. At that moment, Jimmy Wright was fighting for his life in an Italian hospital.

"I didn't know where I was. I was drifting, only partly conscious. I was in a totally different world; in fact, I thought I was being tortured in a prisoner of war camp."

Because of the pain?

"Yes. And because of the foreign voices, the Italian voices as the stretcher-bearers took me to and from the theatre for treatment. I imagined I'd been captured and they were trying to make me talk…"

His father, by coincidence, was also in Italy at the time as a war correspondent. He heard about the accident and raced to the hospital. He asked for the morphine doses to be relaxed so that he could talk to his son, perhaps for the last time. On the second day after the accident, Jimmy Wright briefly regained consciousness. His eyes were heavily bandaged. He considered with his father that he might lose his sight. Three months after the crash, Jimmy Wright came back to England

and to East Grinstead. McIndoe gave him his assessment: that he would need four years of extensive plastic surgery to re-build his face and eyelids. Then, there was a good chance of being able to give him corneal grafts.

The plastic surgery went according to plan. But treating Wright's eyes proved difficult. In the summer of 1944, Jimmy Wright was registered as a blind person. But he was still sure, in his own mind, that his sight would be restored. Seven attempts were made to give Jimmy Wright a new cornea in the left eye. Each time, there were complications. It was eventually decided to give it a rest as Wright had already undergone dozens of operations.

"I kept a count in the early days. Now, I can only estimate that it must have been 70 and 80 operations altogether…"

While he waited, Jimmy Wright began to learn the skills to enable him to cope with being blind. He was taught braille and he built a braille filing system in his office at home, so extensive that anyone phoning him who did not know him would have no idea he was handicapped. Welfare Officer 'Blackie' Blacksell considered that "the realisation that you are blind is greater than coming to terms with any other disability. In a situation like that, there must be a temptation to end one's life. I know that thought has occurred to more than one Guinea Pig, because so much of what you previously relied on has been taken from you, through no fault of your own. But it's at these times when the bonds of friendship and brotherhood are all-important. Thank God, as far as I know, no Guinea Pig has deliberately taken his own life".

Jimmy Wright was ambitious. But now that he couldn't see it was surely impossible for a blinded man to build a career in the film industry. None the less, this is exactly what Jimmy Wright set out to do. When he finally left hospital in 1951, a friend who had been with him in the RAF film unit asked if he would like to help form a small film production company.

He didn't hesitate and began work at Shepperton Studios. He had to learn a completely new job. He had known about filmmaking from behind the camera; now, he had to learn production administration. He doubted if he would be able to pull his weight in the business, but he wanted to try. He *needed* to try.

He joined the company as a producer. Much of his work was done on the telephone and, until production was under way, few clients realised that they had been dealing with a blind man.

Whether or not you're blind, making a film is a complex job. Jimmy Wright had to trust his director and cameraman to advise him. His strength was in co-ordination and production administration and, as well as being involved in making commercials, he produced documentaries both for business clients and for more general release. Closer to home, he worked on two films about aspects of disablement.

From the moment a film idea was hatched, Wright became the backbone of the production team. He visited the client and discussed the project in detail. He advised on the type of film, style, proposed length and number of locations and once he had a clear idea of the film's content, he called in a scriptwriter. Next, he gave the client a draft treatment and a costing and, on agreement, he went ahead and produced the script. He then assembled the film crew and saw the post-production through to the screen. He kept meticulous notes on his braille shorthand machine. His most important and valuable piece of equipment, however, was always his own memory.

Jimmy Wright also had a second job, a voluntary one. Early in 1978, he became involved in producing a local talking newspaper for the blind. He became chairman of *The Talking News*, a weekly sound recording for the blind and partially sighted. I am sure Jimmy Wright surpassed even what *he* hoped to achieve. He said to me once:

"Archie McIndoe instilled that confidence in us. He used to say nothing was impossible – it simply takes a little bit longer."

The life of Jimmy Wright proved that point precisely.

He died on February 12th 1993.

* * *

It is 1975. The man in green crouches over the operating table. His hands are short and square and quick. The surgeon's mask covers only his mouth, leaving his nose free, because that is the way he prefers it. The face bears the savage scars of war, for Bertram Owen Smith is a Guinea Pig.

Bertram Owen Smith

The harsh white light concentrates on a black hand that Owen Smith is reconstructing. For this is Salisbury, Rhodesia[170] and, if he ever pauses to reflect on the situation, life for Owen Smith has come full circle. More than 30 years after he was himself shattered by injury, he operates on the victims of the conflict between black and black, and white and black, as Rhodesia becomes Zimbabwe. He is a plastic surgeon, just as McIndoe was before him. He fights to restore others, just as McIndoe used his skills to restore him. Of his life, Owen Smith said in 1975:

"We spend at least a third of all our time in the operating theatre working on war casualties. You don't see as many burns as there were at East Grinstead. After all, it's less of

---

170. Now Harare, Zimbabwe

an aerial war than it was in 1940 and, in any case, they've learned a little about aircraft design. You're no longer sitting on the fuel tank, I guess!

"But the injuries caused by missiles are devastating. And there are the usual refinements of war, such as land mines and bullets and shrapnel and rocket fragments, all of which keep us busy."

Owen Smith lived in a well-heeled suburb of Salisbury,[171] amid the swimming pools and tennis clubs. As a white man, he was philosophical about the transition to majority rule, though he joined the campaign to prevent it. For a while, he was an MP, a member of the former Premier Ian Smith's Rhodesian Front Party. He didn't relish the experience. "Politics weren't for me. But, after UDI [Ian Smith's declaration of independence from Britain] I felt the British Prime Minister, Harold Wilson, had sold us down the river and I wanted to do what I could to help my country through what I knew was going to be a difficult period."

Owen Smith was softly spoken. There was hardly a trace of the accent of South Wales, where he was born. He was not self-conscious about using words like 'patriotism' for, as he said: "I fought for my country in 1940 and, right or wrong, I feel my cause over the past few years here in Africa was equally just…"

He volunteered for that first battle, the Battle of Britain. He was 17 and was badly burned when the Whitley bomber he was piloting crash-landed and caught fire. He and his crew members, Freddie Whitehorn and French-Canadian, Gerry Duport, all became Guinea Pigs. Overall, Owen Smith had 26 operations on his face and hands. While he was a patient at East Grinstead, 'Blackie' Blacksell remembers:

"Owen Smith began to show an amazing interest in the

---

171. Ibid

complexities of the surgery that was going to be used to save his face. He wanted to know about the techniques. He talked to anyone and everyone about it. And he let it be known that he wanted to become a doctor.

"Now, there seemed no way that he would achieve this. He was a young lad with a background in insurance who, as far as I know, hadn't even got his School Certificate [the school-leaving examination]. We talked about him and his ambitions and we just didn't believe he'd ever achieve what he wanted to do, we *knew* he wouldn't achieve it. But we supplied him with the books and encouraged him in his studies. Because, from our point of view, at that time, the important thing was that he wanted to achieve something. He wanted to help himself. If he failed, well, that was something to cope with later on."

It is a matter of record that Bertram Owen Smith proved wrong those who had doubted him. He matriculated, he qualified as a doctor and became a Fellow of the Royal College of Surgeons. He was at The Royal Marsden Hospital in London, working mainly on what he described as "repairs following major surgery on malignancies" when he suggested that many of the techniques he'd seen McIndoe employ at the Queen Victoria Hospital might profitably be used in his current speciality. The hospital agreed. A year later, Owen Smith returned to East Grinstead, this time as a surgeon. Owen Smith recalled:[172]

"After a few months, the Boss very kindly said: 'Why don't you take up plastic surgery, become a specialist? I think you have a bent for it. I think it's the work you'll enjoy doing for the rest of your life as a surgeon.' And I agreed. So I became a senior registrar at Queen Victoria Hospital and, from him, I learned the business from top to bottom. It was a tremendous privilege."

---

172. Conversation with author

Many of the Guinea Pigs had a close relationship with McIndoe like Page, Gleave and Richard Hillary,[173] but Owen Smith's relationship differed from all the others in one respect. Certainly, there was the gratitude that all the Guinea Pigs felt and still feel. After all, he owed McIndoe his face. But there was more – the feeling a pupil has for his master. He was always deferential about McIndoe:

"I don't think one ever had the presumption to think that one would emulate the Boss; it was enough to try to follow his example … you couldn't give up on anything, not with a chap like the Boss. It was a matter of pride that you didn't let him down. I've never, truly never, met a man like him; he didn't tolerate fools gladly, nor incompetence, but I'll never forget the patience he showed me in those early days, when I became almost a permanent resident of the operating theatre, watching how he worked, asking him all the questions; trying to understand his explanations. Whether he believed I'd ever become a surgeon, I'll never know."

Owen Smith experienced despair in those early months at East Grinstead. He recognised it and saw it among his peers:

"There were some men at the hospital who just couldn't cope with the whole business. They just seemed emotionally incapable of coming to terms with everything that had happened to them in such a short space of time. They were the ones who'd say very little and, psychologically, would go away and hide in a corner. I felt sorry for them and I'm glad to say that, among the Guinea Pigs, they were in a minority. But they helped me; I was even more determined not to give in."

And as he tended his patients later, he remembered this.

"It's what goes on *inside* a man's head that matters, more than anything else. I know this from being disabled myself, as much as anything I have observed in others.

---

173. See page 185

"Very early on, while he's still grieving over what's happened to him, he's got to make a decision. Do I want a life, or don't I?

"Now, no-one pretends this is an easy decision. But I believe that disabled people can be divided into these two clearly defined groups – those who try to achieve their maximum potential and those who give in to self-pity for the rest of their lives. Being suddenly disabled makes you look at yourself pretty clearly. You like some of the things you see and you're not too keen on some of the other aspects of your own character. But the self-assessment involved in making the decision is bound to be of benefit.

"Provided you make the right decision, that is…"

Would Owen Smith, the young insurance clerk from South Wales, have become a plastic surgeon without the disasters of 1941? Could he have done so, without the injuries and disfigurement that led him to East Grinstead and Archibald McIndoe? Owen Smith said that to speculate isn't necessarily profitable but he believed "I wouldn't have achieved half of it without the experience and the support I received at East Grinstead. I've been very lucky…"

Of course, there are those who believe that a man largely makes his own luck.

Owen Smith died on June 6th 2008, on the anniversary of D-Day.

* * *

Of the 649 Guinea Pigs in McIndoe's legion of wounded airmen, as I write, seven are still alive – John Black, Sam Gallop, Len Knott, Jim Marshall, Doug Vince, 'Red' Wolff in the UK and three overseas – Ted Edwards in Greece, in Canada, Henri Marceau in Quebec and Eric Lacasse in Ontario. One of the most high-profile members of the

Guinea Pig Club was Richard Hillary, a Spitfire 'ace' who survived hideous burns when shot down during the Battle of Britain on September 3rd 1940, only to die in 1943 when his Bristol Blenheim bomber crashed during a night flight. Hillary left this poem, which today still speaks for all the Guinea Pigs who are proud to have lived, rather than died, for their country.

Up, up the long, delirious burning blue,
I topped the windswept heights
where neither lark nor even eagle flew
And whilst with high uplifting mind, I trod,
The high untrespassed sanctity of space,
I've put out my hand and touched the face
Of God.[174]

---

174. McIndoe's Guinea Pigs Memorial Trust has funded medical research in Britain into reconstructive surgery at the Queen Victoria Hospital in East Grinstead and is developing a similar partnership with the Royal College of Surgeons.

Chapter 8

THE TORTURERS:
The Guinea Pigs of Unit 731

The elderly man with the rheumy eyes sat upright in his wing chair and the white Persian cat, declawed to avoid spoiling the leather furnishings, sat on his knees purring gently. Though in his seventies, this man's speech and bearing were clipped, even military, which befitted a physician who had spent a significant part of his life in the US Army. His office was part of his long, low ranch-style home near the ocean at Delray Beach, Florida. He reflected:

"Both the Americans and the Japanese used me as a pawn, you know. They both knew how high the stakes were."

His name is Murray Sanders, once a colonel in the US Medical Corps, thrust into the heart of one of the most Top Secret negotiations of World War II. In 1945, he was part of General Douglas MacArthur's staff as the American Occupation forces moved into a defeated Japan. His assignment was to investigate allegations that the Imperial Japanese Army had been guilty of war crimes.

What Sanders uncovered would lead to the discovery of crimes against humanity as despicable as any carried out by Nazi Germany on the other side of the world and which, in Europe, resulted in the German perpetrators being sentenced to execution or imprisonment at the Nuremberg trials.

The deal which Sanders set up resulted in a morally questionable trade-off that prevented hundreds of Japanese scientists being prosecuted and brought to justice, unlike their Nazi counterparts. Murray Sanders said:

"Sure, I suggested the deal to MacArthur – giving immunity for prosecution in exchange for information. But my Japanese informant[175] had assured me that no human beings had been involved in the experiments. When the deal was struck, I believed him. Only weeks later did I discover he had duped me. Thousands of human 'guinea pigs' had been killed by the Japanese scientists, over many years. I did tell MacArthur when I found out. But no-one wanted to know."

To the soldiers and politicians, the deal itself was more important. It was this: If the United States was given access to the records of the biological warfare (BW) experiments carried out by Unit 731 of the Japanese Army, the United States promised not to prosecute the Japanese scientists involved. MacArthur was delighted, his advice to Sanders quite clear:

"Keep quiet about any human experiments..."

On the wall in Sanders' office is a handwritten document, framed and glass-fronted, given pride of place among the 76 research papers he presented during his working life.

It is signed by Lt Col Ryoichi Naito, an officer in Unit 731 and Sanders' Japanese informant in 1945. It sets out in detail the command structure of Unit 731 and outlines the Unit's biological warfare objectives. Nowhere does it mention experiments on human beings. Naito denied to Sanders that human experiments had ever been carried out. Did Sanders believe him? "For a very short time. But I needed that document. It opened the gate and showed me where to go and who to see." He paused. "And thank God I thought to ask him that question about human experiments before I went with the document to MacArthur." Sanders' question to

---

175. Lt Colonel Ryoichi Naito, member of Unit 731

Naito is written in Sanders' own hand at the end of the deal document. It reads:

'I have asked Dr Naito whether prisoners were ever used as experimental guinea pigs. He vows that this has not been the case. (Signed) M Sanders, Lt Col.'

Nothing, of course, could have been further from the truth. On May 6th 1947, Douglas MacArthur, Supreme Commander of Allied Forces in the Pacific, wrote to Washington. He said: 'Additional data (on BW[176] experiments) can probably be obtained by informing (the) Japanese involved that information will be retained in intelligence channels and will not be employed as 'War Crimes' evidence.'

He named the officer commanding Unit 731 as General Shiro Ishii.

* * *

The story of what the Japanese military described as their 'Secret of Secrets' raises at least two issues – first, the horrific nature of the torture these men inflicted on thousands of prisoners; and second, the moral validity of the attitude taken by the United States in gaining access to the results of the Japanese scientists' work.

Unit 731 operated in the guise of the Epidemic Prevention and Water Purification Department of the Kwantung Army. It was based in the Pingfan District of Harbin in Manchuria and its hideous skills in BW had already been employed during the invasion of China in the 1930s, killing thousands of Chinese – and sometimes their own troops – by spraying bubonic plague manufactured at Unit 731 from low flying aircraft. In Nanking, typhoid and paratyphoid germs were dropped into wells and waterways. At least 12 large field trials

---

176. BW – Biological warfare

of biological weapons were carried out and, in 1941 in the city of Changde, there were an estimated 10,000 casualties, 1,700 of whom died. Farmland and reservoirs were infected; anthrax, plague-carrying fleas, typhoid, dysentery and cholera were regularly used.

Unit 731, under the command of General Shiro Ishii, pursued a determined experimental programme for 20 years from its headquarters at Harbin, or in its other four satellite laboratories. In the interests of science, these men tortured men, women and children in a multitude of ways, without anaesthetic and to the brink of death and beyond. They were starved, frozen, raped, pressurised, infected with syphilis, burned, electrocuted, spun in centrifuges, tested for resistance to various poison gases, staked out for days to assess the survivability of the human body and given lethal doses of X-rays. Unit 731 gassed them, drilled into their skulls, used flame throwers on them and performed live vivisections. It is estimated that the Imperial Japanese Army killed 580,000 people with its germ warfare and human experiments.[177] At least 3,000 men, women and children – 600 every year – underwent experiments by Unit 731. In an attempt to dehumanise their victims, the Japanese referred to them as 'marutas', literally, logs of wood. If a Unit 731 scientist wanted another human being to experiment upon, he simply filled in a form for the required number of marutas. In their scientific papers, they referred to them as 'Manchurian monkeys'. Most of the victims were Chinese, Mongolian, Korean or Russian. They were alleged criminals, political opponents of the government and the mentally handicapped. A smaller number of marutas were prisoners of war from Europe, America, India, the Philippines, Australia and New Zealand. Major Robert Peaty of the Royal Army Ordnance

177. International Symposium on Causes of Biological Warfare, 2002

Corps (RAOC) was senior British officer in the Mukden prisoner of war camp for 3½ years, responsible for the British and Commonwealth troops.

Peaty – organised, direct, precise in his language – came from the very English cathedral city of Winchester and kept a daily diary of life in the prison camp at Mukden. Amid the record of his battles over the need for more soap, food or bedpans, there runs a thread of medical inspections and care that is not apparent in many other Japanese prison camps. Peaty decided early on that, for his men, the job of survival was all-important. Culled from the pages of his daily diary (recorded on scraps of paper torn from exercise books or saved from the daily ration of a single sheet of toilet paper) he logged a story of consistent medical surveillance by the Japanese in stark contrast to their other Japanese prisoner of war camps. The extracts, written in a secret code to confuse the Japanese, read:

25 Jan 43 – Today there was an inspection by a general of the Japanese Army Medical Corps.

30 Jan 43 – Everyone received a 5 cc Typhoid-paratyphoid A inoculation.

13 Feb 43 – About ten Japanese medical officers and twenty other ranks arrived today to investigate the cause of the large number of deaths.

14 Feb 43 – Vaccination for smallpox.

15 Feb 43 – Two Americans died in hospital, autopsies being performed on the corpses by visiting Japanese. Owing to the frozen ground we have been unable to dig graves for some time, and all the bodies have been kept in rough board coffins in 'cold storage'.

18 Feb 43 – The medical investigation is still in progress.

Inspection by a Lt-General of the Japanese Army Medical Corps. Many high-ranking officers have inspected us since our arrival.

19 Feb 43 – Several officers have been questioned about dysentery and diarrhoea.

20 Feb 43 – Factory work was suspended, while everyone was tested to find carriers and sufferers from dysentery and diarrhoea.

21 Feb 43 – Graves for eighty-five coffins are being dug today, but ground is still frozen and progress is slow.

23 Feb 43 – Funeral service for 142 dead. One hundred and eighty-six have died in 105 days, all Americans.

24 Feb 43 – The medical investigation is completed.

19 Apr 43 – Another Japanese medical investigation started today, as apparently the findings of the first did not meet with approval.

24 May 43 – Diarrhoea is increasing.

25 May 43 – While waiting for medicine for diarrhoea (which was not forthcoming) men were ordered to exercise by playing baseball. The ball could not be found!

26 May 43 – Diagnosis of diarrhoea consists of running the men around the parade ground (I saw some of them with bare feet). Those who do not mess their pants, or drop from exhaustion, are reckoned to be liars, and are told to "go back".

4 June 43 – Third Japanese medical investigation started.

5 June 43 – Anti-dysentery inoculation ½ cc.

8 June 43 – Diarrhoea still steadily increasing.

13 June 43 – Second anti-dysentery shot, 1 cc.

6 Aug 43 – There are now 208 dead.

29 Aug 43 – 1 cc TAB[178] inoculation, and anti-dysentery.

19 Sep 43 – Everyone was subjected to Mantoux test. Each man also had about 40 cc of blood drawn off supposedly for a sedimentation test.

9 Oct 43 – Everyone X-rayed for TB.

10 Oct 43 – Anti-cholera 1 cc inoculation.

21 Nov 43 – There are now over 230 dead.

5 Feb 44 – Vaccination of the whole camp.

7 Mar 44 – Everyone is being stool-tested for round-worms.

12 Mar 44 – The stool-tests show that 41 per cent of us have worms. The Japanese say no remedy is available at present and we can't expect it to be forthcoming.

14 Apr 44 – The stool-tests showed: worms, assorted, 500 men; amoebic dysentery: 3 men; trichinosis: 10 men. We can obtain no information as to when medicine may be expected.

18 Apr 44 – Inspection by the Surgeon-General of the Japanese Medical Corps.

28 Jan 45 – Everyone was vaccinated today.

27 Feb 45 – Everyone was given 2 cc TAB injection.

6 May 45 – We all had 1 cc TAB inoculation.

At his home in Winchester, many years after he had survived his experiences in the camp, Major Peaty said: "I welcomed some of this extraordinary medical attention. But, much of this work must have been done by the scientists of Unit 731 – though we didn't know as much at the time."

---

178. TAB – Tetanus anti-bacillus

Arthur Christie was a private in the Loyal Regiment (North Lancashire), one of the men for whom Major Peaty was responsible. He was in no doubt about what was happening inside the camp. "The injections were supposed to be beneficial but we had no idea what was in them. Blood samples were regularly taken – but we never seemed to receive treatment. I understand now. We were guinea pigs…"

Jack Roberts from Bedford was a sergeant in the Royal Army Medical Corps (RAMC). He worked as an orderly in the camp hospital, where conditions were no better than in any of the other huts. He said: "It was pretty obvious to me that we were being used as guinea pigs for some reasons that we were not aware of and that we hadn't been told about." He remembered prisoners being measured with callipers and a series of injections and inoculations he was ordered to give on the grounds that it would 'do the prisoners good'. "This group of strangers appeared in the camp from time to time. I don't know where they came from. We were never given any information. They were dressed differently from the normal camp staff. They carried out these duties and after this series of visits they disappeared and we never saw or heard of them again…"

Among the hundreds of American prisoners of war in Mukden was Warren W Whelchel, known more familiarly as 'Pappy'. He came from Tulsa, Oklahoma, and was a master sergeant with the US 200th Coast Artillery Regiment (Antiaircraft). On April 9th 1942, Bataan fell. On May 6th so did Corregidor Island. Pappy Whelchel and 88,000 Americans and Filipinos were captured. Pappy remembers: "It was the beginning of one of the most dehumanising experiences ever perpetrated on humans…"

Whelchel and his fellow prisoners had to endure the familiar ill-treatment the Japanese meted out to prisoners of war, an abuse that grew from the Japanese belief that to die in battle is honourable but to surrender is to be shamed. Whelchel spent three years of his life herded into the special prison camp at Mukden. Pappy Welchel remembers:

"A group of five or six Japanese medical personnel entered our barracks and called out various prisoner of war numbers that we'd been assigned. They gave us various shots; not all the prisoners were given the same shots. Then, some were tested through oral or rectal smears. Later, some were inspected for the welts the injections had caused and more rectal and oral smears were taken. At that time we were the only ones to be given this particular treatment and the Japs were keeping accurate records of every one of us in this one barracks. All the time, men were dying in their scores."

Greg Rodriquez, from Oklahoma, was a private in 59th Coast Artillery Corps, US Army. For him, one of the oddest incidents took place when he was too sick to leave the barracks.

"A Japanese came in and looked me over and then placed a mirror in front of my nostrils. At the time, I thought: 'Well, he's just checking to see if I'm still breathing'. But, after a little bit, he came back again with a feather. He ran that feather up and down under my nostrils – and, later on, I discovered this was one of the methods used to get prisoners to ingest bacteria."

After his capture by the Japanese, Dr BJ Brennan from Croydon, New South Wales, was taken with other Australians to Mukden where he became one of the doctors in the camp hospital. Like Major Peaty, he kept a diary that he protected from discovery by concealing it under the mattress of those prisoners stricken most severely with tuberculosis – and near whom the Japanese refused to go. Dr Brennan remembers three specific visits by 'strangers' who came to the camp. The first group, under a doctor named Tanaguchi, behaved, he recalls, perfectly properly. They carried out dissections of those who had died and they took samples, clearly labelled. They were highly critical, both of conditions in the camp and of the inhuman travel conditions that had killed so many – an attitude that was not shown by the white-coated scientists in either the second or third parties to visit the camp. Dr Brennan recalls:[179] "They rubbished Tanaguchi and the work he had done, but, if the Japanese were experimenting on the men, they will have used the samples Tanaguchi had taken at the end of that first winter and which I believe were removed to the laboratories at the local university."

One other memory has always puzzled and disturbed Brennan. "The camp guards made a great fuss one day and singled out about 150 American prisoners. They then partly dressed them in British and American uniforms, lined them up and marched them out of the camp. They never came back and I never heard of any of them again…"

The testimony of these men who survived the Mukden experience must necessarily be subjective. But in 1985, we obtained in Japan detailed first-hand evidence to support the feelings and impressions they held. It came from a man who worked for Unit 731 in the headquarters at Harbin, 350 miles from the prisoner of war camp at Mukden. Naoji Uezono was a member of Unit 731 for four years. He was the Unit's printer and, as such, he had the opportunity to read all the most secret documents as he printed them. By now, a dignified 70-year-old with a flowing white beard, we met in a cemetery near his home in Tokyo. He said:

"As regards the white prisoners at Hōten [Mukden], many of our scientific teams went there. Whenever important experiments or assessments were carried out in the Unit, at least 15 or 16 copies of a report had to be prepared for circulation to senior officers.

179. Interviews in this chapter carried out by author, 1985

"Unit 731 was also working in the military hospital at Mukden. So the fact that it was necessary for our scientists also to visit the prisoner of war camp indicates that some type of work was going on there."

Through Uezono, we contacted Tsuneji Shimada, who had worked in the dysentery group of Unit 731. Shimada, then 74 and waiting to go into hospital "for observation because of hypertrophy of the heart", lived in Osaka, in a small house tucked away between river and railway line. We telephoned him and recorded the conversation. He declined an interview. But he confirmed that he had, for seven years, "been attached to the Minato group of Unit 731, the dysentery group from early 1939 until the end of the war".

Yes, he said, blood samples *were* taken from the American and British prisoners. And he believed there was a balloon bomb factory at Mukden.[180]

What had Unit 731 put into balloon bombs?

"Epidemic germs. They used cholera and typhus."

But what about the prisoners of war, the Americans, Australians and British?

"We studied whether dysentery could be used as a weapon. Now the cholera group constantly required serum and other things."

That is, blood samples from the prisoners?

"Yes, they required them for their research."

Research records?

"This becomes a long story. We did not experiment on soldiers, but we carried out dissections. Normally, we gave

---

180. See also page 211

them infected materials to drink and carried out autopsies to ascertain the symptoms. We had to observe the progress [of the diseases] and we had to ascertain the potency of the various viruses."

So, are you saying they made the Americans drink various infected liquids?

"Yes, because we also carried out the same experiments at the headquarters of Unit 731 [at Mukden]."

So, the American prisoners were made to drink–

"Yes, of course…"

Eventually, Shimada agreed to meet us, in order to let us have a photograph that he didn't mind us reproducing. He was a little wizened man on a bicycle…

* * *

The scientists and researchers of Unit 731 never paid for their crimes against humanity, except for a small group of Japanese captured in 1945 by the Russian forces, striking south into Manchuria. On Christmas Day 1949, in the Soviet Union's industrial city of Khabarovsk, 12 members of the Japanese Kwantung Army and Unit 731 were tried as war criminals for manufacturing and using biological weapons during World War II. All 12 accused were found guilty and sentenced to up to 25 years in prison. The records of the Khabarovsk War Crime Trials were published in 1950 in Moscow[181] – and virtually ignored in the West. In 2002, however, US historian,

---

181. Material on the Trial of Former Servicemen of the Japanese Army – Biological Weapons, Foreign Languages Publishing House, 1950. Supplementing the excellent research for our film on Unit 731 by David Wallace, director David C Rea found a second-hand copy of this book, which was invaluable in its record of Unit 731's activities

Sheldon Harris, described the trial thus:

"Evidence introduced during the hearings was based on 18 volumes of interrogations and documentary material gathered during investigations over the previous four years. Some of the volumes included more than 400 pages of depositions ... Unlike the Moscow Trials of the 1930s, the Japanese confessions made in the Khabarovsk Trials were based on fact and not fantasy."

In contrast to the fate of Nazi war criminals such as Josef Mengele, most of the scientists of Unit 731 prospered after the war. Immune from prosecution, they returned to an untroubled civilian life – their past, if anything, aiding their future careers. On a personal note, once the iniquity of what these Japanese scientists had done was established, a major motivation of mine in investigating and publishing the results of our research, was to reveal not only the extent of the Japanese war crimes but the names of those who had carried out these experiments. The Nazi war criminals were identified and shamed in the transcripts of the Nuremberg Trials and in the headlines of newspapers around the world. The names of these Japanese war criminals were not even known in Japan. We set out to name them and challenge them to dispute what we alleged. Many of the perpetrators are now dead, but I do so again today:[182]

Dr Kiyoshi Asanuma, who visited Harbin in 1942–43 and identified the tick insect vector of epidemic haemorrhagic fever, went on to work at Japan's Research Institute for Natural Resources. His companion on the entomological trip, **Dr Asahina,** became chief of the Entomology Section of the Health and Welfare Ministry's Preventative Health Research Laboratories.

---

182. Unit 731: The Japanese Army's Secret of Secrets, by Williams and David Wallace, Hodder & Stoughton, 1989

Dr Ken'ichi Kanazawa, who performed tests on the Songo ticks, became chief of the research section of the Takeda Pharmaceutical Company Limited.

Dr Kōji Andō, who once headed Unit 731's vaccine-producing detachment at Dairen, became a professor of Tokyo University's Infectious Diseases Research Institute.

Dr Tsunesaburō Fujino, formerly a member of Unit 731's Singapore Unit, became a professor at the Biological Research Unit of Osaka University.

Dr Tachiomaru Ishikawa, once a pathologist at Unit 731 who had brought home with him thousands of human pathological samples, became a professor at Kanazawa University in 1944, a position he held throughout the 1960s and 1970s. He eventually became President of the university's medical school. The local newspaper, the *Hokuriku Shinbun*, once planned to award him a medal for his contribution to society, but after students discovered his wartime record, the award was cancelled.

Professor Rem Kimura, the bacteriologist at Kyoto University under whom Ishii had gained his doctorate and who was jointly responsible for drawing up the *makimono* (scroll) of young medical graduates to go to Unit 731, became director of the university's medical school for four years beginning in 1944. Afterwards, he became dean of the Nagoya Municipal Medical School, holder of the Japan Academic Institute Prize and a member of the New York Academy of Sciences.

Dr Mas Kusami, leader of Unit 731's pharmacology squad, became professor of the Showa University of Pharmacology.

Dr Tōru Ogawa, a researcher at Unit 731's Nanking Department working on typhoid and paratyphoid organisms for poisoning food and drinking water, went on to work with his brother, Jirō, at the Nagoya Prefecture Medical University.

Dr Kōzō Okamoto, pathology squad leader at Harbin

between 1938 and 1945 who carried out human vivisection experiments, became a professor at Kyoto University and director of the university's medical department. He went on to become an emeritus professor of the university and then medical director of Osaka's Kinki University.

Dr Kazu Tabei, researched dysentery, typhoid and paratyphoid at Harbin between 1938 and 1943 and was involved in feeding typhoid germs in milk to human experimentees to increase germs' virulence by cultivating them in man. He also tested a buckshot-type germ bomb on one *maruta*. Subsequently, he became professor of bacteriology at Kyoto University.

Dr Takeo Tamiya, Unit 731's talent scout at Tokyo Imperial University, became dean of the university's medical school in April 1945 and later achieved worldwide fame for his research into contagious diseases caused by rickettsia, notably scrub typhus. He went on to become the first general director of Japan's National Cancer Centre and president of the Japan Medical Association.

Dr Hideo Tanaka, Unit 731's expert on the mass production of fleas, later became director of Osaka Municipal University's School of Medicine. For his research work he received an Order of the Rising Sun in March 1978.

Dr Yoshi Tsuchiya, leader of the diagnostic group at the Nanking sub-unit, became an honorary professor of Juntendo University.

Dr Toshikazu Yamada, once a director of Unit 731's first bacteriological unit, became a professor at Kumamoto University and then temporarily became Director of Hygiene for the city of Yokohama.

Dr Taboku Yamanaka, from February 1940 a civilian technician attached to the Nanking Unit, became dean of Osaka Medical School and in 1974, director of the Japanese Bacteriological Association.

Dr Hisato Yoshimura, who directed Unit 731's frostbite experiments, literally freezing people to death, became a faculty member of Kyoto Prefectural Medical College in the 1950s and later its president. He became an adviser to the Japanese Antarctic Expedition and in 1973 was appointed the first president of the Japanese Meteorological Society. He was expelled five years later when there were rumours about his wartime experiments. Yoshimura, however, stated that he left the society because he was suffering from tuberculosis. He received one of Japan's highest accolades: on April 29th 1978, the Emperor's birthday, the Order of the Rising Sun – Third Class.[183] He subsequently became president of Kobe Women's University and was a consultant to an association that advises frozen food and fishery companies.

Yoshimura did not deny that freezing experiments took place. But he claimed that the "maruta were paid for their services". A baby used in one test belonged to a female Japanese member of Unit 731 and was "volunteered", he claimed.[184]

Many former members of Unit 731 joined the Japanese National Institute of Health (NIH) after the war. They included **Dr Shinpei Ejima**, a dysentery researcher at Unit 731 and the Unit's former bomb expert, **Jun'ichi Kaneko**, who went on to study Sendai virus (SeV) infection in laboratory mice.[185]

Professor Suburō Kojima, once a director of a Unit 731 research department, worked in the Health and Welfare Ministry's National Preventative Health Research Centre after the war, becoming its director in 1954.

Yujirō Wakamatsu, was active in the NIH studying streptococcal infections in primary school children.[186]

---

183. US backed Japanese Germ Tests. The Observer, August 21st 1983
184. Ibid
185. Document Fort Detrick, ref 007
186. Ibid

Dr Yukimasa Yagizawa, Unit 731's plant disease expert for a decade, became secretary of the Japanese Penicillin Association, joined the Society of Antibiotics and worked at the NIH.

Many other former members of Unit 731 went into general practice or succeeded in business.

Dr Kiyoshi Hayakawa, a member of Unit 731's Singapore Detachment, went on to become manager of the Hayakawa Medical Company and used vaccine-producing techniques that he had acquired during his wartime work.

Ishii's protégé and deputy, **Tomosada Masuda**, took up practice in Chiba Prefecture after the war. Travelling by motorcycle on his doctor's rounds one day, Masuda was in collision with a truck, suffered head injuries and died in 1952.

Dr Hideo Futaki, who headed Unit 731's tuberculosis research squad, became president of SJ Company Ltd.

Dr Kiyoshi Ota, one of Unit 731's original military surgeons and the man who headed the BW raid on Changteh town, returned to the old castle town of Hagi in Yamaguchi Prefecture and entered general medical practice.

Dr Masahika Takahashi, Pingfan's leading plague researcher, became a general practitioner, managing a clinic in Mobara, Chiba Prefecture.

Dr Zen Kawakami, a compatriot of Ishii's from Kyoto Imperial University who initiated Unit 731 research on the different susceptibilities of races to infectious disease, died while in Manchuria.[187]

Dr Sueo Akimoto, the young serologist, wrote a book on the ethics of medicine, but abandoned his academic career as a result of the traumas at Unit 731. "I will regret it to my death," he admitted. "I was silent for 30 years and nothing can change that. I admit ... these people (in Unit 731) were

---

187. Soviet record of Khabarovsk trials, p103

my friends and I did not have the courage to condemn them."

Shunichi Suzuki, became Governor of Tokyo and a leading member of Japan's then ruling Liberal Democratic Party. Also an accountant, he worked for Unit 731 and knew of the human experiments, though he was "not involved in them".[188]

Seiichi Niizuma, the man who censored and prevented most of Unit 731's scientific information from reaching the Americans during the Sanders' investigation, entered the Tokyo Research Institute of the Japan Self-Defence Force.

Prince Tsuneyoshi Takeda,[189] ran a stock farm in Chiba Prefecture after the war, under the pseudonym Miyata. Prince Takeda had been the central link between Kwantung Army Headquarters and Unit 731. Takeda, a grandson of the Emperor Meiji, was stripped of his royal title. But in October 1951, the Japanese government officially 'depurged' nearly 2,000 former military officers at and below the rank of colonel, including Takeda. He became managing director of the Japan Amateur Sports Association and in October 1962, he was appointed president of the Japanese Olympic Committee and president of the Japan Skating Union.

After the war, Unit 731's second in command, **Masaji Kitano**, formed a company to produce vaccine. He worked with former Unit 731 colleague, **Takeo Tamiya**. The company went bankrupt. However, Murray Sanders' one-time interpreter, **Ryōichi Naitō**, formed the Japan Blood Bank and asked Kitano to join him. Kitano became chief of its Tokyo branch.

Naitō, who had opened his own surgery before forming

---

188. Horohito approved Germ Warfare Unit, The Guardian, September 17th 1982
189. Ibid. Members of the Japanese royal family were involved in Unit 731's activities. Our documentary posed the question in its title: Unit 731 – Did the Emperor Know? There is evidence that he did know but did nothing to stop the war crimes

the Japan Blood Bank, went on to transform the blood bank into the highly successful and multinational Green Cross Corporation. The Osaka-based international pharmaceutical giant, which employed many former Unit 731 members, specialised in the manufacture of interferon, plasma and artificial blood. Naitō became vice-president of the company. Kitano was also a board member. Naitō became the company's president in 1973 and its chairman in 1978. The company's projected profits for 1985 were 6,000 million yen. The company had subsidiaries, the Alpha Therapeutic Corporation, with large research laboratories in Los Angeles, California and Alpha Therapeutic UK Ltd in Norfolk, England.[190] As a member of the New York Academy of Sciences, Naitō received an award in 1963 from the Japanese Science Society for his pioneering work in artificial blood. At Unit 731, researchers had once pumped human guinea pigs full of horse blood in primitive attempts to find a substitute for human blood.

Green Cross' artificial blood had a chequered record. In April 1977, Naitō received an Order of the Rising Sun. He died in July 1982. The Green Cross Corporation there had plans for a huge new complex in Los Angeles. It would be named after Dr Naitō.[191]

Even 40 years after the war, the scientists were less than eager to discuss their links with Unit 731: **Naeo Ikeda**, ran a clinic specialising in blood diseases in a suburb of Osaka. In 1968, Ikeda felt secure enough to publish in a Japanese scientific journal the results of a human experiment that had been carried out in Manchuria with epidemic haemorrhagic fever. Extraordinary as it may seem, Ikeda wrote:

'The author examined infectivity of fleas and lice isolated

---

190. Alpha Pharma prospectus and Who's Who
191. Ibid

from patients, and acquisition of infectivity on the artificially incubated unsustained louse line, by stinging the patients with EHF. Thus, it was confirmed that the healthy persons would develop the disease by stinging of poisoned louse.'[192]

When we tracked him down and asked him in 1968 about the documentary evidence that indicated he had supervised injections of tetanus into the heels of prisoners of war, he declined to comment. We pressed him to find out why he had done these things and he muttered that he was "too old … and it was a long time ago". He shuffled away out of sight, into a back room of his dingy clinic.

Some scientists would speak only anonymously. In a Japanese hotel bedroom, we discussed with a stocky chemist, once a member of Unit 100 – a sister unit of Unit 731 – killings, deadly virus and bomb manufacture. Then he left the hotel, walking back into the warmth of the afternoon – a pillar of society, the sunlight glinting on the Rotary Club badge on his lapel.

Shirō Kasahara, who researched Songo fever at Pingfan, published medical papers undoubtedly based on his experiments on human beings at Pingfan. He became emeritus vice-president of the Kitasato Hospital and Research Unit in Tokyo where he agreed to see us, to discuss his published papers. A small man with expressive hands and a fixed smile, he was gradually drawn into a discussion of horrors far removed from the white-coated world in which he now moved.

"… I could submit a form to the administration section … to get *maruta* for my experiments …

"… Maybe I could check the blood to see whether the blood would carry the virus to the next one …

" … we tested on a Chinese spy using the blood and liver

---

192. Ikeda, Naeo – 'Infection experiments with the flea and lice of epidemic'

and kidney of the other dead body."

A secretary and several laboratory assistants floated deferentially in and out of the great man's laboratory. The final dialogue:

To experiment on, let alone kill even **one** *prisoner of war is against the Geneva Convention, never mind medical ethics.*

Kashara: "Yes. I think it was a contravention. They were soldiers, prisoners of war, and I think the Japanese Army was wrong."

But what about **your** *part in the work of Unit 731? Do you have any conscience about that?*

Kashara: "I feel very guilty about what I have done ... I think I did wrong."

How did Ishii and yourself escape prosecution?

Kashara: "I don't know much but I've heard there was a deal between General Ishii and the American Occupation Army..."

* * *

The Japanese government's efforts to cover up the Unit 731 affair have been considerably aided by the self-censorship of most of the detachment's former members. In 1945, Ishii had sworn all junior members to take the Unit's secret to the grave and instructed them never to contact each other, or to hold public office. It was an oath that they all, for many years, took extremely seriously. Many junior members lived out the rest of their lives in fear. So seriously did some take their secrecy oath, that in order to hide their past they did not register for military pensions and ended their lives destitute.

Gradually, however, junior members began to contact

their former companions. Old comrades' societies sprang up with regular and clandestine meetings. Memorial services were regularly held and congratulatory telegrams read out. On September 5th 1981, these societies met together for the first time. The inaugural Kwantung Army Unit 731 reunion was held at a hotel in Sinchu Matsumoto village in Yamabe. The Kwantung Army song was sung:

"Looking into the distance under the dawn clouds, the mornings, the evenings, the mountains and rivers eternal; our power and efficiency is our authority and our force, our allies are content.

"Our Army is glorious ..."

Sutras[193] were chanted for the Unit's founder, 'War God', the Honourable Shirō Ishii, and for all former members of the Unit. A memorial to the Unit, called the Seikon Tower, has been erected in Tama cemetery, in a suburb of Tokyo. Around two metres high, it is inscribed with a few Sanskrit characters. Otherwise, it is anonymous, undated and has no other identifying marks. The detachment's printer, Naoji Uezono, was among those who tended the memorial. During the early years of the American occupation, Uezono hid in Kagoshima in the south of Kyūshū Island, but he later returned to continue his printing trade in Tokyo. For two or three years after the war, he suffered nightmares. Unlike most former members, he said he felt it was his duty to talk about Unit 731 "so that young people know what happened".

In the Soviet Union, scientists sentenced at the Khabarovsk Trial in 1949 served their sentences in prison and labour camps – but on December 13th 1956, the Soviet government decided to commute the sentences passed on the Japanese war criminals. A proclamation was issued stating that because the state of war had ended between the two countries, and

---

193. Sutra – a Buddhist chant

acting on the basis of humanity, the Supreme Soviet had decided that all Japanese citizens would be freed and allowed to return home.

The Kwantung Army's former Commander-in-Chief, **Otozo Yamada**, died in Japan in 1965. He was 83.

Bacteria factory chief, **Tomio Karasawa**, died aboard ship during his homeward passage. His predecessor at Unit 731, former **Maj-Gen Kiyoshi Kawashima**, survived to attend the detachment's reunions.

But what of Unit 731's leader, **General Shirō Ishii**? We visited Kamo village, Ishii's home. The people avoided answering questions about the war and what had happened in Manchuria. "I have nothing to say concerning the military secrets of the Honourable Shirō Ishii," was the customary reply.

We know that while the investigations were in progress at the end of World War II, American officers regularly frequented Ishii's house in Wakamatsu-chō. After the end of 1947, however, his movements became more difficult to trace. In June 1948, the City's Metropolitan Bureau interviewed Ishii in Tokyo and he advised the authorities semi-officially about the investigation of a mysterious Imperial Bank poisoning case.[194]

On August 17th 1958, 13 years after the end of the war, in the back room of a stonemason's shop called Iwaki-ya near Tama Cemetery, Tokyo, Ishii made his first and only post-war appearance before assembled junior members of his former unit. He made his farewell speech to 20 former youth trainee technicians who had come from all parts of Japan for the inaugural meeting of this Boyu-kai society of old comrades. He reminisced about the early days of Unit 731.

---

194. Triplett, William: *Flowering of the Bamboo*, Woodbine House, Maryland 1985, pp145–151

In a speech reportedly still rich in xenophobia and elitism, Ishii described how his unit was to have been the salvation of Japan, a country then encircled by the West, scientifically impoverished yet spiritually rich. He apologised for the sufferings since the end of the war but urged his audience to remain proud of the memory of Unit 731.

Ishii died of cancer on October 9th 1959. Part of one of his bones is buried beneath the Unit 731 memorial in Tokyo's Tama Cemetery.

* * *

The contrast between the way that, at the end of World War II, the Allies pursued Nazi war criminals – such as Mengele, Barbie and Bormann – and the leniency and acceptance shown to Ishii, Naito and the scores of Japanese scientists named in this chapter, is distinct and worthy of exploration. In 1945–46, the United States made similar discoveries in both Germany and Japan – unethical experiments had been carried out on human beings that constituted war crimes. In Germany, those war criminals were brought to justice and their actions were given maximum publicity around the world. In Japan, however, information about the scientists' actions was supressed and the perpetrators were encouraged to continue their lives scot-free. More than this, the United States, without, it seems, consultation with its Allies – Britain, the Commonwealth, France and China – played a key role in bestowing immunity on these Japanese war criminals.

The guinea pigs who had survived but suffered at the hands of the Germans, at the very least, had their day in court at Nuremberg. The *marutas* who had been tortured by the Japanese had no such day of reckoning.

If there is a scale of comparison in the magnitude of the horror inflicted by the two sets of scientists, German and

Japanese, it is:

The Germans, in their concentration camps and laboratories, carried out between 10,000–25,000 experiments on human beings. About five per cent of the 'guinea pigs' died, though many thousands were badly mutilated.[195]

The Japanese, in Unit 731 alone, in Manchuria, where 600 prisoners at a time could be held for experimental use, killed as many as 580,000 human guinea pigs. There were other centres of biological warfare in Japan and it is unlikely that accurate totals of those maimed and killed will ever be known. For instance, hundreds of Chinese were deliberately infected with typhus, cholera, the plague and other viruses. Most of those who did *not* die from the infection were killed to be studied at autopsy. In the last days of the war, the Japanese killed any survivors among the guinea pigs to conceal evidence of these experiments.

There was a racial thread in both programmes. The Germans' victims were primarily Jews, gypsies, people of colour, the handicapped, Russian prisoners of war and people who the Nazis believed to be inferior to the 'master race' of German-Aryan stock. Hitler, through the 1930s, set out to create in the German public's mindset, an attitude that there were racially inferior human beings, who could be sacrificed to aid the war effort.

The Japanese felt that the Chinese and Koreans were also racially inferior. They were interested in testing different racial reactions to disease; they valued Caucasian guinea pigs for comparison with the average *maruta*. They also argued that the subversives and criminals used in experiments would have been executed anyway.

But there the similarities end. The crucial difference

---

195. Psychiatrist in the Shadow of the Holocaust, Paul Weindling, Oxford Brookes University, 2010

between the Allied response to the litany of war crimes carried out by the two nations was the intervention of the United States in the judicial process to protect the Japanese scientists in order to obtain the results of their human experimentation, this catalogue of excess which is still unique in scientific history.

It came about because, at its simplest, the Japanese were cleverer than the Germans. In Germany, the Nazis kept records of the abuses, filed and photographed, and these were discovered by the Allies and used at Nuremberg to prosecute the perpetrators. In Japan, scientists and military worked together with two objectives – to convince the US Forces that firstly, no human beings had been involved in the BW experiments and, secondly, that this work was purely defensive. Biological warfare, they said, was "clearly against humanity ... but we had to be ready to repel and deal with it".

Murray Sanders certainly knew in 1945 that Japanese BW ambitions were anything but defensive. He knew that they had been experimenting with balloons to transport germs from Japan to the West Coast of the USA using the prevailing transoceanic winds. He knew because, in 1944 and early 1945, he had been asked to examine a number of balloons, 91 feet round and 30 feet in diameter, that had appeared without warning in Hawaii, California, Michigan, Canada and Alaska. They were made of rice paper, cleverly-designed[196] and Sanders had warned his superiors in his report that, if the Japanese had used the balloons to carry anthrax or encephalitis B "we have no defence. We would be in real trouble. If they had sent encephalitis, in particular, four out of five people who contracted it would have died". This series of balloons despatched by the Japanese fortunately carried

---

196. Conversation with Murray Sanders, 1984. The balloons were controlled in flight automatically, releasing a little helium if flying too high, or jettisoning a sandbag of ballast if flying too low

no deadly viruses. Sanders believed they were part of a trial, to see whether the Japanese could devastate and paralyse the population of the US west coast.

None the less, General Douglas MacArthur accepted the soothing Japanese arguments that the BW experiments were defensive and had not involved human beings. When presented with evidence that both statements were untrue, he and his intelligence staff chose to ignore it. He also knew that the Japanese had lied when they said the entire records of Unit 731 had been destroyed. Those records had, in fact, been carefully preserved. MacArthur judged that the United States needed those records. He was also aware that some scientists from Unit 731 had been captured by the Russians. They could well, at that moment, be offering the same unique records and conclusions to Russian interrogators – and the chill of the Cold War was already being felt in the post-war relationships between the two former Allies.

The decision to protect the Japanese from prosecution was approved in the US at the highest level. It was set out, in a Top Secret report by Dr Norbert H Fell, a scientist and investigator from Camp Detrick. It was dated June 24th 1947 and read:

At a conference yesterday at which the Chief of the Chemical Corps and representatives of the War, State and Justice Departments were present, it was formally agreed that the recommendations of the C.inC., FEC [Commander-in-Chief, Far East Command – General Douglas MacArthur], and the Chief, Chemical Corps would be accepted, i.e. **that all information obtained in this investigation would be held in intelligence channels and not used for 'War Crimes' programs.**[197]

This report confirmed that the Japanese experiments would

---

197. Report by Robert H Fell, June 24th 1947, p2; author's emphasis

remain secret, rather than be disseminated to the lawyers and the wider public, which would have happened if they had been deemed war crimes. Scientific and military considerations took precedence over ethical and criminal accountability. Six months later, a final report by Camp Detrick scientists, Dr Edwin V Hill and Dr Joseph Victor, contained detailed reports on Unit 731's experimental programme, including a listing of 8,000 pathological slides and hundreds of colour drawings. Hill and Victor summarised the Japanese data:

"Such information could not be obtained in our own laboratories because of scruples attached to human experimentation ... It is hoped that the individuals who voluntarily contributed this information will be spared embarrassment because of it and that every effort will be taken to prevent this information from falling into other hands."

The avoidance of potential embarrassment to these Japanese scientists was regrettably high on the US scientists' agenda.

The report added a further argument. It was based on cost-effectiveness. The US had so far spent approximately 250,000 yen in its investigations of the Japanese biological warfare programme. By contrast, Ishii's research in Unit 731 had cost "many millions of dollars and years of work". In short, the US had paid proportionally a "mere pittance" compared to the cost of generating these data.[198] There was no mention of the human cost in terms of lives and misery.

The debate rumbled on in US intelligence circles. A task force of the State-War-Navy Coordinating Committee (SWNCC), a high-level group overseeing the military occupation, indirectly admitted on August 1st 1947 that the US ethical position was questionable. They acknowledged

---

198. Kondo S, editor, Unit 731 and Biological Warfare, Tokyo, 2003

that Unit 731 "violate[d] the rules of land warfare",[199] and that the Japanese experiments were similar to those for which Germans had been tried for war crimes.[200]

The US now sought justification for refusing to prosecute. First, the SWNCC task force concluded that the evidence available was insufficient to document legal guilt, which was obviously incorrect. They then fell back on the reasoning[201] contained in the Hill and Victor scientific report: 'The value to the US of Japanese [biological warfare] data is of such importance to national security as to far outweigh the value accruing from 'war crimes' prosecution.' Even in this context, money talks.

The Allies' ethical decisions differed sharply in Germany and Japan. The divergence can be explained partly by Japanese ruthlessness. The women of Ravensbrück, who survived the experiments and displayed the scars of their wounds in the courtroom, were among the most effective prosecution witnesses at Nuremberg. The Japanese simply eliminated all potential witnesses.[202]

The Americans reached and justified their decision to give the Japanese scientists immunity very much in anticipation of an imminent Cold War. The Japanese work was unique and the advantages outweighed any moral considerations. Yet the framing of the US agreement with the Japanese not only ensured that the Unit 731 scientists escaped prosecution, but *all* Japanese scientists, whatever their activities during World War II, would not be accused of war crimes. The US effectively granted immunity to the entire Japanese medical

---

199. Ibid
200. Ibid
201. The author is grateful for permission to quote from the paper, United States Responses to Japanese Wartime Human Experimentation, Howard Brady, Sarah E Leonard, Jing-Bao Lee, Paul Weindling, 2020
202. The Nazi Doctors and Nuremberg, ED Pellegrino, Annals of Internal Medicine, 1997

profession.

It is fair to criticise the Japanese for the crimes committed and the Americans who covered up their crimes. Similarly, it is also ethically right to consider if the human cost of the nuclear bombing of Hiroshima and Nagasaki was necessary and justified as a dramatic way of ending Word War II. But it would be scandalous if, as part of that debate, we ignore the question asked from beyond the grave by the thousands of human guinea pigs who were secretly tortured and killed by pitiless Japanese scientists:

How is it that man's inhumanity to man can be so ruthlessly overlooked?

* * *

At the end of World War II, Dr Murray Sanders returned to his Columbia University in New York as an associate professor, once he had convalesced from tuberculosis. He continued his microbiological research and, for his work on the investigation of viruses and degenerative diseases of the central nervous system, he was nominated for a Nobel Prize in 1967. In latter years, he suffered both cancer and Parkinson's disease and fought both cheerfully and bravely.

Towards the end of his life, Murray Sanders' eyesight began to fail. He lost the sight in his right eye because of a decision he took in 1942, when he was seeking to help beat an outbreak of kerato conjunctivitis, an eye complaint that was then causing absenteeism and threatening the US war effort. Sanders, helped by RC Alexander and, later, by Phillips Thygeson,[203] had isolated the virus. He needed to prove that the suggested remedy could be safely and effectively used.

---

203. Sanders M and Alexander RC. Epidemic Kerato Conjunctivitus, Journal of Experimental Medicine, Vol 77, No 1943, pp71–96

The only sure method was to take the virus and "complete the circle" by attempting to reproduce the disease. He needed a volunteer, a human guinea pig. He chose himself. He took a virus that had been passed through six laboratory mice and introduced it into his own eye. "On the sixth day, I was on the way to get a pizza and my eye felt as if I had grains of sand in it – I had caught the disease."

Sanders proved his point – and, gradually, lost the sight of that eye. Because, once the virus was introduced into the eye's reservoir, it never left. But Sanders had needed to be certain – and the only human volunteer, the *only* 'guinea pig' he could offer, conscience-free, was himself.

* * *

For the guinea pigs in the Mukden camp, the prisoners, the end of their incarceration was quite matter-of-fact. After days of rumour, Major Peaty's diary records for August 16th 1945: 'Six men were brought into camp this evening, and from the fact that they were smoking more than the regulation distance from an ashtray, we knew they were not prisoners of war. After an unusually good supper, all prisoners were released from the guardhouse. Red Cross food supplies are to be 'inspected' tomorrow.'

The six men were an American mission sent primarily, of course, to rescue the American prisoners.

The diary continues for August 20th. Peaty noted: "At about 7 pm a small party of Russian officers arrived and announced that we are now 'svobodo' (free), and that they would enter into conference with our senior officers at once to discuss details regarding our departure. Later in the evening, the Japanese guard were disarmed on the parade ground and, headed by their colonel, they were marched in single file right around, guarded by us now, wearing their equipment and armed with their weapons, and escorted into their own guardhouse in front of every man in the camp. The Russian officer in charge said 'Here they are – do what you like with them, cut their throats or shoot them, it is all the same to me', but this was translated diplomatically as 'he says he hands them over to you...'"

For Major Peaty and the hundreds who had survived the privations of Mukden, the victory was theirs in every sense. They had no need, they decided, to seek reprisals. "It would have been," said Major Peaty, "beneath our dignity. It would have reduced us to their level.

"After all, they had to live the rest of their lives with what they had done..."

The Hart family, who sailed aboard the Titanic - Mr Benjamin Hart, Mrs Esther Hart and their daughter Eva. Benjamin Hart died in the disaster.

The Titanic prepares to sail - and Mrs Hart had a premonition of the disaster that lay ahead.

The New York Times breaks the news in April 1912 of the full horror of the sinking of the Titanic.

Titanic, surrounded by tugs, during her sea trials off Belfast in March 1912

Eva Hart, then in her seventies, relaxes at home.
AUTHOR'S COLLECTION

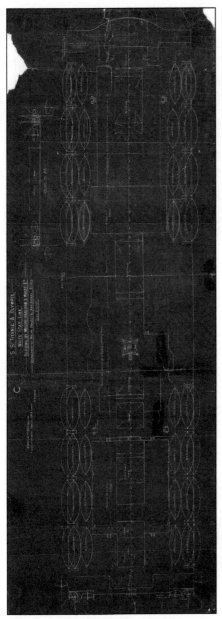

Alexander Carlisle

Axel Welin

TOO FEW LIFEBOATS?
Rival versions at the
British Inquiry into the
Titanic disaster.

Harold Sanderson

THE TELL-TALE BLUEPRINT
that supported Alexander Carlisle's version of events,
now in the Merseyside Maritime Museum, Liverpool. Space
for three lifeboats under each of the davits is clearly shown.
MERSEYSIDE MARITIME MUSEUM, LIVERPOOL

Lord Pirrie

A White Star Line advertisement for the Titanic and her sister ship Olympic, 'the Largest Steamers in the World'.

The Harland and Wolff shipyard in Belfast, with the gantry for the construction of the Titanic in the background.

Figure 1

Figure 5

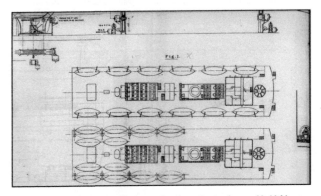

The new Welin davits, Double Acting Quadrant Davits that enabled lifeboats to be double-banked on a liner's deck, and a plan to show how they would be accommodated. This was an important advance in the technology of saving lives at sea, and was offered to the builders and owners as the Titanic was being constructed. After Titanic, the sales of these davits boomed.

The official British Inquiry into the sinking of the Titanic, in session.

A pencil sketch of the Titanic as she slipped beneath the waves, drawn from memory by survivor,
Leo James Hyland, a steward aboard the stricken liner.
PEARSON

The Olympic and the Titanic (right) together off Belfast -
probably the only photograph of the sister ships side by side at sea.
PEARSON

Chapter 2

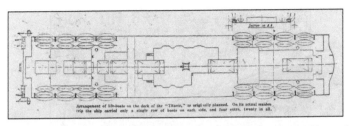

*Another contemporary blueprint found among the Welin papers, showing a suggested lay-out for
32 lifeboats in a double row. When she sailed, Titanic carried only a single row of lifeboats.*

*Robert Ballard, who led the team from the Woods Hole Oceanographic Institution, with our
documentary team on board, that found, photographed and filmed the Titanic wreck site.*
©WOODS HOLE OCEANOGRAPHIC INSTITUTION

*Thousands of feet below the surface of the Atlantic,
a camera peeps through a porthole of the wreck of the Titanic.*
©WOODS HOLE OCEANOGRAPHIC INSTITUTION

The media storm that broke world-wide as a British medical and scientific team announced the birth of the first baby, Louise Brown, born in 1978 through in vitro fertilisation, IVF.

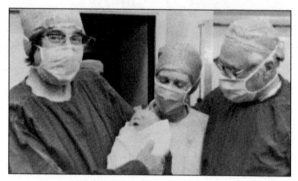

Scientist Robert Edwards, nurse Jean Purdy and surgeon Patrick Steptoe, with baby Louise Joy Brown, moments after Louise had been born in Oldham to her parents John and Lesley.

Elizabeth Jordan Comeau (nee Carr), with her baby Trevor James Comeau, and parents Roger and Judy Carr.
CARR FAMILY COLLECTION

Jean Purdy, nurse extraordinary, and a much-valued member of the British IVF team.

IVF pioneers Robert Edwards (left) and Patrick Steptoe (right), face an often-critical press corps after the successful birth of Louise Brown in Oldham, in 1978

Kershaw's Hospital, in Oldham, scene of the birth of the world's first 'test tube' baby. It is now a hospice.

THE OTHER LOVER
Ruth Ellis photographed with Desmond Cussen on an evening out in London.
ALAMY

STAR-CROSSED LOVERS
David Blakely with Ruth Ellis.
ALAMY

Ruth Ellis - her last resting place, the headstone bearing her maiden name, Ruth Hornby.
ALAMY

John Bickford, Ruth Ellis' solicitor, who knew so much more than the courts were ever told.
AUTHOR'S COLLECTION

Bickford's office at the end of his career, tucked away in a rented room over a High Street shop.
AUTHOR'S COLLECTION

Gladys Yule, who saw Ruth Ellis shoot David Blakeley, and was shot in the hand by a stray bullet.
ALAMY

David Blakeley, playboy at play with his sports car before an event.
ALAMY

Marlon Brando, one of the finest actors of the 20th century, a relationship with the author that began with a phone call at three o'clock in the morning.
ALAMY

Charles Chaplin with Marlon Brando; two of Hollywood's greatest - but they found working together was not easy.
ALAMY

Marlon Brando as Johnny
in The Wild One, *1954*
COLUMBIA PICTURES

Marlon Brando, with friends Belinda Frixou (right) and her sister Andrea, during one of his many
stays in Kent, where he found peace and a degree of anonymity.
BELINDA FRIXOU COLLECTION

Frank Borman, first man to fly around the moon when he captained Apollo 8 in December 1968, and who went on to run Eastern Airlines in the USA.

NASA

The crew of Apollo 1, which burned on the launchpad in 1967 killing the crew "Gus" Grissom, Ed White and Roger B Chaffee. Frank Borman was one of the team who investigated the cause of the fatal flash fire.

NASA

Joan Aldrin stretches to talk to her husband, "Buzz" Aldrin, while he is quarantined after the Apollo 11 space mission in 1969

ALAMY

Walter Marshall, for a decade one of the most powerful voices in Britain's energy industry.

A jubilant Walter Marshall proves that the containers carrying nuclear waste on Britain's rail network are robust enough to do the job safely - by staging a rail crash to test their reliability.
SHUTTERSTOCK

An aerial view of the site of the fast-breeder nuclear reactor, at Dounreay near Wick in Scotland.

*The control room at Chernobyl nuclear power station,
before the disastrous explosion in December 1986.*

An aerial view of the Chernobyl nuclear power station site in 1986, following the explosion.
ALAMY

Thousands of gallons of water are pumped from the sea in an attempt to douse the fire at the Japanese nuclear power station at Fukushima in March 2011.
SUFFOLK UNIVERSITY, BOSTON

Fireball at Fukushima. An aerial view of the disaster that followed the tsunami and explosion.
SUFFOLK UNIVERSITY, BOSTON

The search for the thousands who died in the tsunami and the nuclear disaster at Fukushima.
ALAMY

*Thousands march in Tokyo in protest at the Japanese
nuclear energy policy, following the disaster at Fukushima.*
ALAMY

McIndoe's Guinea Pigs - Sir Archibald McIndoe (far right) with some of his patients, at the Queen Victoria Hospital, East Grinstead.

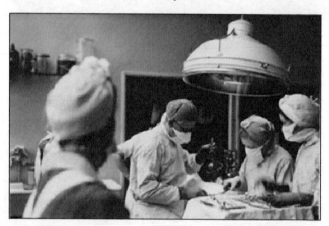

Archibald McIndoe in the operating theatre at the Queen Victoria Hospital.

The Queen Victoria Hospital, East Grinstead, which became a world centre in pioneering plastic surgery.

Sir Archibald McIndoe - "The Boss" to the hundreds of sorely-injured servicemen who received treatment at East Grinstead during World War Two.

"All work and no play..." Relaxation for the Guinea Pigs was part of the reconstruction of their confidence. Archie McIndoe is, of course, at the piano at this early Guinea Pig reunion.

Members of the Japanese Unit 731 at work on a victim during World War Two.

*The Russians brought the Unit 731 scientists they captured to justice,
in a War Crimes trial at Khabarovsk, the Soviet city closest to Japan, in December 1949.
The West took little notice of the findings of the trial, nor of the punishments meted out.*

A rare photograph of some of the members of Unit 731. The photograph, issued through the Japanese broadcaster NHK, confirmed the cover name for the unit guilty of horrific crimes against humanity: The Kwantung Army Epidemic Prevention and Water Supply Department.

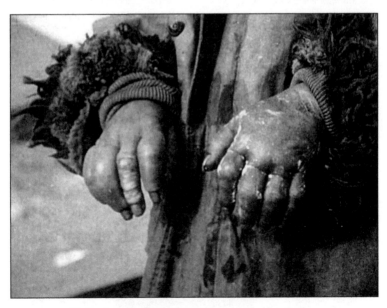

The hands of a victim of a Unit 731 "experiment" on hypothermia.

Murray Sanders, the US colonel who negotiated the deal between General MacArthur and Unit 731.
AUTHOR'S COLLECTION

General Shiro Ishii, commander of Unit 731, taken in 1946 when he and his fellow scientists had escaped justice for their war crimes.

Colonel and Mrs Murray Sanders at their Florida home, visited by the author, his wife Jo and baby Megan in the 1980s. Murray Sanders swore that when he concluded the deal with Unit 731 he had no idea that they had experimented on human beings.
AUTHOR'S COLLECTION

John Aspinall with a special gorilla friend.

John Aspinall
"I think he liked animals more than people."

Aspinall with his first tiger, Tara, in 1960.

Howlett's Mansion in Kent, with John Aspinall's grave in the foreground.
ALAMY

Aspinall, later in life, with his elephant friends.

John Aspinall, his wife Sally and tiger cubs at their home at Howletts.

James Angleton carries the ashes of his old friend and colleague, former CIA chief Allen Dulles, at his funeral in Georgetown, Washington in 1969.

James Angleton, schooled at Malvern College, in England, and at Yale University, lived in Italy as a young man and was multi-lingual.

Lee Harvey Oswald loved guns; a photograph from his family collection.
Angleton knew of Oswald's activities long before the
assassination of the President.
ALAMY

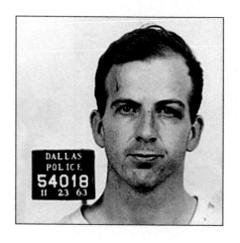

Lee Harvey Oswald, the police
mugshot taken after he had been
arrested for the assassination of
President Kennedy.
ALAMY

Guy Burgess and Donald Maclean (pictured with his family),
British diplomats and Soviet agents, who fled to the Soviet Union in 1951.
ALAMY

Kim Philby, who defected to the Soviet Union in 1963. A close friend of Angleton's
when Philby was in Washington, this "betrayal" hurt Angleton deeply.
ALAMY

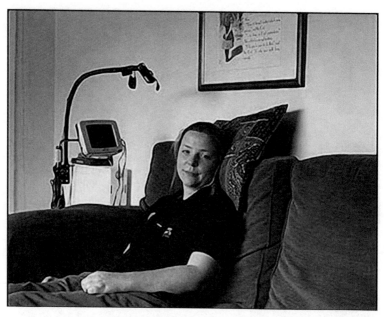

*Hilary Lister's "world" before sailing came along; a sofa in the front room and a
computer she could control with her mouth.*
FAMILY COLLECTION

*TRIUMPH! Hilary Lister celebrates with champagne in August 2009
- with the help of her partner Toby May - after her three-month voyage around Britain,
becoming the first disabled woman to do so.*

Hilary Lister's yacht Artemis was specially equipped with a "sip and puff" system so that she could control sails and steering using only her mouth.

Hilary and her husband Clifford celebrate in 2005 as she becomes the first quadraplegic woman to sail solo across the English Channel.

Hilary's mother, Professor Pauline Rudd, welcomes her back in Dover at the end of her voyage around the coast of Britain.

Hilary at sea - "it's freedom..."
FAMILY COLLECTION

Hilary's long-time friend, labrador Lottie, who went with her support crew around Britain, to greet Hilary at every port at which she stopped.

Alastair Campbell with Tony Blair - Campbell was Blair's spokesman and campaign director from 1994 till 1997.
ALAMY

CLOSE FRIENDS AND COLLEAGUES -
President George W. Bush and Prime Minister Tony Blair.

The ornate staircase behind the polished black front door of No. 10 Downing Street.

Number 10, Downing Street.
ALAMY

Greg Dyke, Director General of the BBC, whose employees took to the streets
to support the BBC's stand against government pressure over the Iraq War.
ALAMY

"Hands off the BBC" hurriedly-made placards deliver the BBC staff's message to the government of
Tony Blair and Alastair Campbell in London and Edinburgh, Cardiff and Belfast.
ALAMY

Donald Campbell's attempt on the world water-speed record in 1966-7 was fraught with financial and mechanical difficulties.
THE RUSKIN MUSEUM, CONISTON

Bluebird K7 at speed on Lake Coniston, the lake on which Donald Campbell died on January 4th l967
THE RUSKIN MUSEUM, CONISTON

CRASH! A sequence of four photographs captured as Bluebird K7 left the surface of Lake Coniston and then sank on January 4th ,1967
ALAMY

BRAVE BUT SUPERSTITIOUS - Campbell's wife Tonia gives him his mascot Mr Whoppit during the land-speed record attempt at Bonneville Flats
TONIA CAMPBELL

*Donald Campbell and
Mr Whoppit - inseperable.*

LIKE FATHER, LIKE SON
Sir Malcolm Campbell and young Donald.

Bluebird K7 on the slipway at the boathouse on the shores of Lake Coniston.

*Bluebird CN7 preparing for the successful attempt on the world
land-speed record in Australia in 1964.*

The Crown Equerry, Sir John Miller, was a skilled and competitive carriage driver.
AUTHOR'S COLLECTION

Confidante of Her Majesty the Queen, Sir John with Prince Charles at an event at Windsor.
ALAMY

Her Majesty the Queen with the author, during the "interview" arranged by Sir John Miller.
AUTHOR'S COLLECTION

Sir John and Her Majesty discuss her Windsor Greys in the Royal Mews at Buckingham Palace.
AUTHOR'S COLLECTION

The author - seconds before he had to chase after Her Majesty to ask her to return to the Royal Mews.
AUTHOR'S COLLECTION

Lt Col Sir John Miller GCVO DSO MC, Crown Equerry to the Queen from 1961 to 1987.
AUTHOR'S COLLECTION

WEAR A MASK - or go to jail... the message during the Spanish flu epidemic of 1918-20.

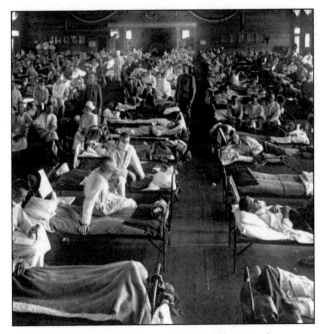

A crowded emergency ward as the 1918 pandemic spread.

The virus spread through personal contact. Public transport carried graphic reminders on how to behave - and did so until the late 1930s.

Unemployment was high, men with no work still gathered wearing makeshift masks.

Masks could become a fashion statement - the more flowing , the more stylish.

Professor John Oxford - "we didn't learn the lessons of 1918".

Chapter 9

JOHN ASPINALL:
A Passion to Protect

John Aspinall led an eventful life. Gambler, impresario, raconteur, eccentric and politician, he changed the gaming laws of Britain. He flirted with the law, both in making his considerable fortunes and in the controversy surrounding the life of his friend, Lord Lucan, and the murder of Lucan's nanny,[204] a subject on which he gave questioners short shrift. He prized as his favourite types of people "gamblers, pirates, writers, soldiers and brigadiers".[205] But it is as a conservationist that he made his most indelible mark, the attribute for which I believe he would most wish to be remembered.

Henry Kissinger[206] once said of him that he "stood for the values and principles precious to our civilisation and relevant to our ability to master our future". I think John Aspinall would have questioned the use of the word 'master' for he was, at heart, both pragmatic about his own achievements and dismissive of the human race's ability to do anything other than seek to dominate and destroy. But he would have appreciated the personal compliment.

---

204. Aspinall said he believed that his friend, Lucan, subsequently committed suicide by tying a heavy stone to his body and jumping overboard from a powerboat near Newhaven
205. Andrew Roberts, The Sunday Telegraph, February 13th 2000
206. Henry Kissinger served both US Presidents, Nixon and Ford, as Secretary of State from 1973–77

Aspinall, who died in June 2000, leaves an extraordinary legacy. He created in a vast corner of Kent, a habitat that encouraged animals to flourish at a time when around the world so many species were struggling to survive against a tide of commercial greed and human irresponsibility. By any yardstick, Aspinall's achievements over 50 years are impressive. Two animal parks at Howletts and Port Lympne transformed 500 acres of East Kent into a nature reserve at a cost to him of £5 million a year, where 72 species, most of them rare breeds, have been cared for and continue to thrive under his son Damian.

It all began at the Newmarket Racecourse at the 1956 Cesarewitch Handicap. John Aspinall was 29 and he had, "even for me", a hefty bet on a horse named Prelone. It won. With the winnings, he bought a neo-Palladian house in 60 acres near Canterbury, called Howletts. The house was built by Sir John Leach in 1787, then bought by Sir Thomas Deering who, like Aspinall, was a famous gambler and who, in a game of faro at White's Club in London, lost the entire estate to a money-lender named Abraham Gipps. The house was renovated by Philip Jebb and John Fowler; the gardens re-designed by Russell Page around the trees which have characterised Howletts for centuries: the Spanish chestnuts, the ilexes and the cedars of Lebanon.

Aspinall had already proclaimed his love for animals in his daily life as a man about town in London. It suited his lifestyle, the image he wished to portray and which he had established at Oxford University as a dandy and an eccentric, a "notorious plunger", as Paul Johnson once said.[207] He was a student who could, and did, feign a fainting fit to walk out of his finals examination in order to attend the Ascot Gold Cup. How better to display his extravagant personality than

---

207. Paul Johnson, New Statesman

to bring up a tigress and two capuchin monkeys at his flat in Eaton Place, London? He then bought two Himalayan bears but "altogether, things became rather crowded and it wasn't popular with the women".[208] In fact, his love for animals can be traced back to a farm near Petworth in Sussex, where young Aspinall had spent his holidays from a private school in Eastbourne and where a farmer, Jack Pring, was to become a "surrogate brother" to him. [209]

All 18 cows on the farm had names and were milked by hand. To farmer Pring, the animals had distinctive characters and personalities. The Jesuits would have you believe that, given control of a child until he is seven, they will give you the man. But the years between seven and the teens are just as formative. These were the years that Aspinall spent at Palfrey Farm.

"The impressions from Palfrey Farm have remained with me always. The saddest day was market day when some animals had to be disposed of for cash, a commodity which seemed always to be in short supply, the shortage of which was the very reason I was staying there in the first place, as Mrs Pring took in children during holidays for a small fee.

"The farmhouse was Elizabethan and almost untouched by the passage of time. There was no electric light or power of any sort. In those days, a farm of this nature was almost self-supporting. The Prings made their own butter and cured their own hams in a chimney vault large enough to hang a horse. Warmth came not only from the huge log fire which was never allowed to die during the winter months, but from the organic affection bestowed upon us by the Pring family – father, mother and daughters. Father Pring was a patriarch and, by his example, encouraged manliness and adventure,

---

208. Conversation with author, 1994
209. The Best of Friends, by John Aspinall, Macmillan, 1976

accompanied as it must be by periods of discomfort."[210]

Farmer Pring gave Aspinall a large, dappled, polecat ferret with which to hunt rabbits and he 'adopted' a jackdaw, which he subsequently took with him to Rugby School. These friendships "stirred something deep within me, some response that was not elicited by my relationship with the numerous dogs that shared my stepfather's home at Framfield in Sussex. I liked dogs and cats but they did not stir my imagination. It is difficult to be uplifted by a Dalmatian or a budgerigar. I needed the tinge of unpredictability, of independence, to invite my full respect. Without wildness, there can be no ingredient of fear; without fear, even fear of a nip from a ferret or a peck from a jackdaw, there must be a lessening of respect. Of course, a dog, cat or horse may bite, scratch or kick, but this is considered an aberration in animals that have suffered thousands of years of guided selective breeding – a process that is intended to reduce them to obedience or, in the case of a cat, compliance".

There was uncertainty in Aspinall's early life. He was not close to his father, Colonel Robert Aspinall, a British Army surgeon. Later, he discovered – and met – his real father, George McIllree Stanton Bruce, a retired major-general. "I was apparently conceived under a tamarisk tree beside a lake in Uttar Pradesh on the night of the regimental ball." Unknown to Bruce, Aspinall supported his birth father for the rest of his life.

The purchase of Howletts in 1956 made it possible for Aspinall to start forming and encouraging small colonies of wild animals. But by 1970, he realised that the size of Howletts, 60 acres, would restrict his ambitions. He needed to expand. Regrettably, this coincided with a global rise in oil prices and the slide towards the market slump of 1973–74,

---

210. Ibid

when shares tumbled by up to 75%. In his grand mansion at Howletts, John Aspinall found himself penniless. He had sold his interest in the Clermont Club in 1972 for around £500,000. His investments and, therefore, his income had now been swept away.

He was "bust, I had lost everything", to use his own words. The pressure to provide for his family, both human and animal, was enormous. His close family helped to cope with the emergency with the prime aim that the growing colonies of animals were always well fed.

He mortgaged his London house at 1 Lyall Street and other properties for a substantial sum. He returned to gambling at other clubs, winning more than £160,000 at blackjack over a period of one month, which was enough to feed the animals and pay the staff for some time. When the revenue from these initiatives dried up, he sold all his wine, then his books and his pictures. His wife, Sarah, sold her jewellery.

A routine was established whereby his half-brother, James Osborne, drove from Kent to London every week with a car-load of *objets*, ornaments or prints, to be delivered to the bank of his friend, James Goldsmith, in return for £3,000, which paid the weekly bill for grain, fruit and wages. On his return, Osborne divided the £3,000 into brown envelopes. Sometimes, Aspinall would gamble the £3,000 in an attempt to increase it before the division was made. Before long, money was owed to fruit and grain dealers and other suppliers all over Kent, but Aspinall generally managed to pay up just before any threatening letters arrived. Every week was a miracle.[211]

From this financial nightmare emerged the opportunity Aspinall had been eager to find. Alan Clark, an MP and friend from his days at Oxford, telephoned him from his

211. The Passion of John Aspinall, Brian Masters, p203

home in nearby Saltwood Castle. A derelict estate of close to 300 acres near Folkestone, was for sale. It was called Port Lympne, formerly owned by Philip Sassoon, politician, art collector and socialite who, in the 1930s had illuminated the mansion every summer with lavish parties for his upper crust friends, who included the Prince of Wales and Mrs Simpson, Winston Churchill, Lloyd George, Stanley Baldwin, Lord Beaverbrook, film stars Douglas Fairbanks, Mary Pickford and Charlie Chaplin. For the rest of the year, Port Lympne had been eerily empty, maintained by a skeleton staff, its fields and woodlands silent. John Aspinall, on his uppers financially, took his friend's advice and went to see the estate, which had been divided at auction into 27 lots.

"I entered the main drive and the moment I saw that amphitheatre of land, shaped down to the sea, with the escarpment all facing south, I began thinking of rhinos over the whole area. Then I saw the house and I thought 'This has got to be it' and I made a bid that afternoon for it. I knew I couldn't afford it – I had the deposit, that's all, and I then had to borrow the rest of the money.

"It was a mad thing to do. Lord White, a great friend of mine, said to me, 'Aspers, it's just a mad ego trip!' I said, 'Of course it's an ego trip.' Fortunately, my ego and my vanity are entirely twisted with my work. It *was* an ego trip, but it was an ego trip I had to take – a gamble – because the animals needed more space."[212]

The grounds at Port Lympne covered a vast acreage, poorly suited to agriculture but an ideal home for animals. It faced south across the English Channel. It cost Aspinall £360,000 as he bought all but two of the 27 lots at auction.[213] Port Lympne itself reflected Sassoon's luxurious tastes – designed by Sir

---

212. Conversation with author, 1999
213. The other two lots were bought by Alan Clark, MP and diarist, who had introduced Aspinall to the possibilities of Port Lympne

Herbert Baker, built of 2½ inch French bricks, roofed with Kent peg tiles, bronzes by Bainbridge Reynolds, interiors by Rex Whistler, a Moorish courtyard with 52 marble columns, an extravagant marble floor with five fountains and, from its escarpment, one of the most striking panoramic views of the corner of England closest to Europe. All this ... but, above all, in that view lay a vision of Aspinall's most earnest wish: to create a haven where his animals could live undisturbed and in safety. The financial challenge was now greater than ever. Aspinall needed a rich partner. In 1974, at the prompting of his wife Sarah's brother-in-law, Geoffrey Keating, he began to negotiate with an oil-rich Middle Eastern sheik who was interested in preserving the larger mammals and, it was rumoured, wished to open a zoo of his own. Aspinall "didn't do zoos", but he looked forward to meeting a man with similar interests. In September 1974, the Arab prince, in a six-car cavalcade with a retinue of 18, arrived at Howletts. They were royally entertained and Aspinall showed his affinity with animals by entering enclosures with wolves, tigers and gorillas. They talked figures. Aspinall told him it would cost £400,000 a year to run Howletts and Port Lympne; £800,000 if the public were not to be allowed in, which was the prince's preference. The sheikh did not blink and hands were shaken on a gentleman's agreement. As he left, the sheikh said that Aspinall and the family "must come to visit us in Abu Dhabi" and the visit duly took place just before Christmas.

John and Sarah Aspinall set off to meet the prince bearing gifts that included a film of Howletts and the animals, an exquisite ruby brooch and two live tigers. They waited five days in a hotel room. They were eventually summoned and, again, negotiations went well, so well that Aspinall was told he would shortly hear from the sheik's lawyers in London with a draft agreement. Back in London, no such agreement appeared. Ten days passed during which Aspinall tried to reach the prince or his people to enquire after progress to the agreement. The response from the prince's representative in London, as Aspinall later described it to his friend Lord (Harold) Lever, was negative and discouraging. Aspinall remembers: "I can't get past the Prince's representative … who refuses to relay the instructions for want of a colossal bribe which unfortunately I cannot pay him." The flirtation with the Middle East was over – and the financial problem was even more pressing. He turned to his old friend, James Goldsmith. Goldsmith moved decisively to raise the money for the outright purchase of Port Lympne, with a further sum for the restoration work through the banking subsidiary of his company, Anglo-Continental.[214] A company known as Howletts and Port Lympne Estates was set up with a limited liability of £220,000, which owned all Aspinall's properties, except the London house at Lyall Street on which a mortgage was raised.

John Aspinall had invested everything he owned into pursuing his vision of conservation. He now had to service the loan raised from and through Goldsmith to buy Port Lympne and to meet the running costs of the parks. He sold shares in the company. He wrote to all his friends around the world. They chose to invest in him as much as in his dream. Aspinall describes those tense weeks thus: "Help arrived in the confidence and understanding of old friends who knew what I was trying to do and enough money was raised to float (and rescue) the project."[215]

Since 1984, both animal parks have been owned by the charity, The Aspinall Foundation. Aside from its success in conservation, it is now big business. At its height in the 1990s, more than 130 people were working at either Howletts or Port

---

214. The Passion of John Aspinall, Brian Masters, pp209–217
215. The Best of Friends, John Aspinall, p16

Lympne and this number was augmented during the summer season. As well as 30 keepers directly concerned with the animals, there were 20 gardeners, four carpenters and three bricklayers, woodcutters and 16 maintenance men. Fourteen people worked in administration. There was no week in the year that building of some sort was not in progress.

In a normal year, Howletts welcomes about 165,000 visitors and Port Lympne, 136,000. Between them they raise nearly £800,000 in gate money (in 1984–85 £450,252 at Howletts, £333,823 at Port Lympne), representing about a third of the running cost of the zoos. The remainder of the parks' income has to be raised from capital – from profits on the sale of Aspinall Holdings and ultimately from gamblers who use the casinos and gaming tables. Most of the money goes on wages and salaries, some on food, but the parks have their own farms in order to minimise expense.

Aspinall bought 138 acres at Coombe Farm close to Port Lympne at the end of 1984 for £265,000, together with more than 210 acres at Chilham and nearly nine acres at Walmestone Nursery, owned jointly by himself and Lady Sarah. This enables the zoo to be self-sufficient, up to a point. The annual crop is extraordinarily varied. At Chilham, for example, 30 acres are set aside to grow nothing but herbal hay for the elephants; mangold, lucerne, maize and kale are grown at Port Lympne for rhinos, elephants and hoof-stock; 150 tons of mangold is needed from January to May. At Coombe Farm, 30 acres provide a red clover mix for water buffalo and American bison.

Thousands of bales of haylage are gathered every year at Port Lympne, yet it is still necessary to buy 12,000 bales or more of lucerne and haylage each year. The parks also buy 30 bales a week of woodshavings to provide bedding for the elephants. Three thousand bales of wheat straw are used for bedding every year and 6,000 bales of oatstraw for the gorillas. Fruit and vegetables, which have to be bought from outside the parks cost upwards of £450,000 for both parks. These include yams, leeks, kiwi fruit, figs and much else to make a gorilla's life pleasant. Good quality produce is provided because, to quote Aspinall, "they don't eat inferior seconds in the jungle".

Eighty-nine different species of animal thrive at Howletts and Port Lympne, comprising nearly 1,200 creatures. For a man born to the wife of a middle-class doctor in India, brought up on a Sussex farm, more or less thrown out of Rugby, receiving an allowance of £1 a week at Oxford, degree-less, career-less and prospect-less when he came down, it is a remarkable achievement.[216]

The objective of the Aspinall Foundation is to contribute to the conservation of global species. Its flagship project is known as 'the western lowland gorilla rescue and re-introduction programme', initiated in 1987 in the Congo and expanded to neighbouring Gabon in 1988.

John Aspinall loved gorillas as brothers. To lose gorillas as a species would have been, to him, a personal tragedy. He believed that "those who know the gorilla well, and they are but few, cannot bear the thought of his passing. Heroic in his pride and strength, magnificent in his self-possession, he is the father of the anthropoids. It seems incredible that nature can combine in his person such gentleness and such power". He quoted George Schaller, from his book *The Mountain Gorilla – Ecology and Behavior*: 'Probably no animal has fired the imagination of man to the same extent, as has the gorilla. Its manlike appearance and tremendous strength, its remote habitat and reputed belligerence, have endowed the beast with a peculiar fascination and stirred popular and scientific interest. It appears to possess some transcendent quality...'

---

216. Ibid, Masters, p346

It is interesting to note that Schaller, the great student of gorilla behaviour, refers to the gorilla as 'it'. To Aspinall, the gorilla is personalised, always 'he' or 'she'.

One of the secrets of the gorilla's appeal to Aspinall was his aloofness.[217] Unlike a chimpanzee, he said, who seemed willing to concede man's superiority at least to the extent of imitating him in his presence, the larger ape retained his reserve. Aspinall endorsed Sir Julian Huxley's dictum that 'no man can feel anything but humble in the presence of an adult male gorilla'. This conscious feeling of distance was characteristic of gorilla posture and expression. They did not invite familiarity and resented, as often as not, any 'unseemly show of affection' on the part of a human. The emotional tempo of gorillas was subdued. More than any other ape, including man, they appeared to Aspinall to live in an inner world of self-containment – a carefully guarded personality to which they alone held the key.

Aspinall first 'met' the great ape in RM Ballantyne's 'absurd' book *The Gorilla Hunters* at the age of about 12. Aspinall later saw him on the screen in *King Kong*. "I can remember even then discounting the stories of his innate ferocity and insatiable libido. For years, I collected every available book on gorillas, but they were a disappointing miscellany: mainly the narratives of trophy- or specimen-hunters and interspersed, for the most part, with photographs of the cadavers of huge sag-jawed males, hand-hoisted to give them the grisly appearance of life. Even in these dim works, the mystic allure of the gorilla came through for me in unmistakable terms – it became my ambition to have gorillas as my friend, to win their confidence and trust.

"To me, the gorilla is the closest thing to an embodiment of Rousseau's dream of the Noble Savage. Power buys respect,

---

but restraint of power buys admiration. In the years that the gorillas of Howletts have lived together, no ape has seriously injured another. Seemingly terrible quarrels take place from time to time and probably serve to act as a tension-release sequence, but the fact remains, that in spite of the noise and the screaming, no permanent damage has ever been recorded. I, myself, after all this time have never been badly hurt in spite of the fact that few weekends pass without my entering their enclosure and spending an hour or two in their company."[218]

Aspinall befriended a 570 lb adult gorilla called Djoum in the 1950s. It was probably the world's first example of a one-to-one human-gorilla bond. No-one had ever before entered a cage and spent hours every week communing with a full grown gorilla.

"I rate Djoum as a friend, just like Jimmy (Goldsmith) was a friend. Over the past 50 years, I was also close to six or perhaps seven tigers. Zemor slept in my bedroom at Howletts and would wait until I woke up and then say 'good morning' in tiger language by licking my neck."

Male gorillas seek and prize dominance, said Aspinall. Females, on the other hand, do not "aspire to leadership and never challenge for primacy". Aspinall noted that for man to seek dominance in his relationship with a male gorilla invites disaster. He gave, as an instance, the story of three gorillas trained from childhood to perform in a variety act in Japan. For years, they complied to a strict regime. The act ended abruptly when they suddenly turned on their trainer and nearly killed him. Powerful animals will not be cowed, he said. Castration had been used in circuses to make primates more biddable, but Aspinall believed this invasion of the

---

218. Ibid

animals' rights "should be outlawed forthwith".[219]

In the wild, gorillas live in bands or extended families numbering from 10 to 30. Aspinall felt at Howletts that it was imperative to create conditions where a large group could run together. All the original apes were obtained as infants and each new arrival had to be carefully assimilated into the group structure. To see them *en famille* and to watch their interaction was "a joy which never palls ... so many gorillas of different ages and sex mixing freely together".[220]

The eternal challenge for Aspinall was to dispel boredom for the animals and to encourage play. Each enclosure at Howletts is equipped with ropes, bars, hand-walks, chutes, a heated swimming pool and artificial trees in which the gorillas can make a nest or take shelter from rain or sun; there are drums to play with and beat, tubular steel spheres, cable reels and tyres.

Hundreds of bales of straw are spread in the enclosures to provide a comfortable surface for wrestling and climbing, leaping and rolling. Each morning, whatever the weather, nuts or raisins are scattered in this deep litter, which require the apes to forage for an hour or two, as they would in the wild. At sundown, fresh bales of clean straw enable them to make their night nests. Only rarely in an average year in England will the apes refuse to go out into the weather. They don't like cold, driving rain and high winds and are most active in still, humid weather. In the height of the summer they may sleep out at night.

It became important to Aspinall that the subtleties of hierarchical structures should be maintained in captivity, just as in the wild.

"The dominant role of the male is indicated at a very early

---

219. Ibid
220. Ibid

age by his overt concern for the safety of his companions. The adult gorilla male who leads a band is usually stable and benevolent, but not necessarily the largest or most powerful. He is the one who carries the confidence of the females and young black-backs. He must be a skilled botanist and topographer and the whole group will draw from him its tone and personality.

"Gorillas have developed an extraordinary capacity to neutralise any over-weening, intra-familial exercise of power. A juvenile, if attacked by a large male or female, is immediately helped by other gorillas in the clan – whatever the cause of the assault. The patriarch can usually stifle a quarrel by a series of staccato grunts or coughs, provided that he is near enough. This tendency to go to the assistance of the weaker or outnumbered, acts as a counterbalance and enables the extended family to survive without injury.

"Fights to the death are almost unknown and often two groups will meet and intermingle without incident."[221]

Over the year, Aspinall's apes are supplied with more than 90 types of food. They include bananas, fruit tea, celery, oranges, nuts, mango, radishes, peaches and a huge selection of herbs.

This detailed description of how the gorillas live in captivity is important for two reasons; one, to indicate through the provision of a varied and top-quality diet how much these animals meant to Aspinall and two, because the animals are much more likely to breed if they are settled and contented. That was the Aspinall priority – to concentrate on rare breeds, breeds under threat and, through increasing their numbers in captivity, to conjure the possibility of returning them to the wild.

The context of this initiative could not be more urgent, for

---

221. Ibid

animals and plants are, in the 2020s, dying out more quickly than at any time since dinosaurs were wiped out 65 million years ago.

Gorillas

The two gorilla populations in the process of being re-established by Aspinall's Foundation in the Congo and Gabon, are both in new protected areas created specifically for the projects. The Aspinall team work with local partners in Africa with the following five areas:

- To reduce trade in orphan apes, through improved law enforcement and through education and raising awareness
- To rehabilitate confiscated apes
- To re-introduce gorillas to protected areas
- To protect area conservation and management and, generally,
- To rouse international awareness of the threat to these primates.

The development of the project has contributed to a major reduction in the trade in gorillas at a national level.[222] The Aspinall Foundation built a sanctuary for orphaned gorillas in Brazzaville in 1987, which received an average of 10 orphan gorillas in each of the early years. The impact of the orphanage project, combined with other conservation activities in the country, reduced the number of orphans, with only 17 gorillas received over the ten-year period from 1998 to 2007. Which delighted Aspinall.

The scourge of the gorilla in Africa is the 'bushmeat

---

222. King et al. 2005, 2009

trade'. On paper, lowland gorillas are a protected species. But on the ground a mass slaughter has been carried out for decades. For the poor African, 'bushmeat' is a fetish with magic powers. For the wealthy, it is the ultimate chic. For years, the centrepiece at the banquets of the elite has been not beef nor chicken, which are 'white man's meat', but gorilla or chimpanzee. Month after month, logging companies are thrusting their roads further into the jungle. In their wake come the hunters with their shotguns and traps. Politicians and lawyers try their best to restrict the trade but, in the Third World, meat and money matter most.

The Aspinall sanctuary is established in the Batéké Plateau region, the first major wilderness area from which the species has been completely wiped out. In addition to rescuing parentless baby gorillas, it is also home to young gorillas born in Kent. Sixty gorillas were released to two protected areas between 1996 and 2013 – 30 in the Lesio-Louna Reserve in Congo and 30 in the Batéké Plateau National Park in Gabon; 50 of the released gorillas are wild-born orphans and 16 are hand-reared captive-borns, most of which originated from the captive-breeding programme at Howletts and Port Lympne; the 16th was born to confiscated orphans in the pre-release phase of the Congo project.[223] The first two captive raised gorillas, Kwa Kwa and Kwam, arrived in Africa from Kent in 2000. John Aspinall said at the time: "This has been the lodestar of my life. Kwa Kwa and Kwam are pioneers for the recovery of their lost lands.

"It's about 40 years since the first gorillas arrived at Howletts. I wanted to form a breeding colony. To do that, I knew I had to get a large number because gorillas live in troops. But hardly a single zoo in the world was doing that at the time. They were just keeping pairs. So, my aim of

---

223. King et al. 2005, 2006, 2012a

forming a breeding group looked very far away. Indeed, it was only in 1956 in Basel Zoo that the first gorilla was born in Europe. And that was only the second born in captivity in the world. So it was a very long shot to think of establishing a breeding colony and then taking them to Africa. But the colony eventually took off and this is a great moment."[224]

That was in the year 2000. Kwa Kwa has since died but the colony now numbers more than 30. Aspinall, reflecting on the success of the African initiative just before he died, said: "Never underestimate the gorilla. If Kwam and Kwa Kwa had been introduced on their own, it might have failed. But they had the others to show them the way. Their instinctive behaviour saw them through. We can always learn from the gorilla; they must never be underestimated..."[225]

The newcomers from Kent have adopted feeding habits similar to the wild gorillas. Indigenous wildlife other than the released gorillas are also flourishing in the security of the protected areas and an added bonus is that a diverse mixture of savannah, flora and fauna is also recovering and spreading.

As for the gorillas themselves, the first births took place in 2004, with several more in 2006 and 2007.[226] Annual birth rates are now similar to what it is in the indigenous population. The numbers both of newcomers and the rescued orphans are on the increase. John Aspinall would have been more than pleased with the judgment of a recent scientific paper.[227] Leaving aside unanticipated catastrophic events, it declared:

'The results of the population viability analysis suggested that the reintroduced gorilla populations have a reasonable

224. Conversation with author, 2000
225. Ibid
226. King et al. 2012
227. The Aspinall Foundation: 30 years of captive breeding, reintroduction and conservation, Tony King 2013

chance of persistence (<90% over 200 years).'

It also illustrated that reinforcement of the population of gorillas could significantly improve the probability of survival of the species and the retention of genetic diversity.

Tigers

John Aspinall had many friends but, of his 12 closest friends, six have been animals.[228] Among those six, at least one was a tiger. The first tiger in his life was Tara, who he found in a pet shop near Regents Park in London. She was nine weeks old and cost him £200. She shared Aspinall's bed for the first 18 months of her life. He bottle-fed her. She lived until she was 13 and gave birth to almost 50 cubs in that time. Aspinall described her as sweet and affectionate and one day he elaborated on the importance of character in the animals he loves.

"Few animals have suffered such a character assassination as the tiger and few animals have warranted it less. The character and disposition of a tiger can vary much like that of a man or a gorilla. Because each animal has a known hunting range which it demarcates and protects for as long as its food supply lasts, its personality becomes known to the other inhabitants of the area, including humans. There are bold tigers and timid ones, honest tigers and treacherous ones, predictable and unpredictable, noisy and silent, hot-tempered and good-natured. From my experience of 70 animals in captivity, about one in 12 is delinquent to varying degrees, though we have not experienced a really psychopathic animal."[229]

One of the problems, he added, was the image that wild

---

228. Conversation with author, 1998
229. Ibid

animals conjure up in the human mind, a feeling of fear that is bred from childhood:

"Fairy tales and legends from deep antiquity tend to ensure that animals retain a primal place in our psyche. 'Little Red Riding Hood', 'Who's Afraid of the Big Bad Wolf?', 'Goldilocks and the Three Bears' and other nursery legends."

I think John Aspinall preferred animals to human beings. Certainly, an argument can be made that he understood them better because, beneath his buccaneering reputation, there lurked in Aspinall a naiveté that was based on trust and that led him to take in the world of commerce, instant and sometimes rash decisions over both relationships and business transactions. He didn't bear grudges. He forgave but he didn't forget. His views on man's attitude to conservation were trenchant and almost wholly critical:

"In Man, of course, tigers have found their nemesis. There is nothing they can do to adapt to him as he sweeps away the environment that – along with prey and water – is a prerequisite of their existence. The cover is never replaced, domestic cattle take over from the wild deer and antelope and the water table falls as the process of deforestation dries up lakes, rivers and streams.

"The tiger has one last card to play before he bows out for ever. He has the capacity to arouse in us admiration and affection. Were his nature and quality known to enough of us, his future would be assured. Is it possible that we will slowly watch the tiger die without stirring from our stupor? If my words help to find for him a dozen friends, they will not have been written in vain – but only a mass reversal of sentiment can hope to save him."[230]

It was a clarion call from the heart. Aspinall's championship of conservation has extended to many endangered species.

---

230. The Best of Friends, John Aspinall, p84

Langurs and Gibbons

The successful initiative with gorillas in the Congo or Gambon has been replicated in Indonesia, with the creation in 2010 of the Javan Primates Conservation Programme, involving the management of two primate rescue and rehabilitation centres in Java and associated langur and gibbon release projects to reinforce and conserve small, isolated and threatened wild populations. Results from the first release of 13 Javan langurs in 2012 were very encouraging with 100% survival during the first six months post-release. The release stock for these projects has consisted primarily of rehabilitated wild-borns, with individual animals provided from the captive-breeding populations at his animal parks in Kent. The Foundation's Indonesia Programme currently manages two primate rescue and rehabilitation centres in Java specifically for the eastern subspecies of the Javan ebony langur. In East Java, an isolated population of vulnerable Javan ebony langurs in Coban Tulun protected forest was reinforced, with the first release of 13 langurs in September 2012. In West Java, reinforcements are planned for the isolated populations of the endangered Javan silvery gibbon and the endangered Javan grizzled langur in the Mount Tilu Nature Reserve. As with the Gabon gorilla re-introduction project, the release stock for these projects will consist primarily of rehabilitated wild-borns, with additional animals from the captive-breeding populations in Kent.

Lemurs

A lemur conservation programme has been established in Madagascar. Often referred to as the world's eighth continent, the island of Madagascar 400 km off the east coast of southern Africa has been isolated from Africa for 160–180 million years and from India for 90 million years and most species occurring there are found nowhere else on earth. A remarkable 105 lemur species are currently recognised, all endemic to Madagascar.

A priority for the Foundation is to save the greater bamboo lemur, one of the world's most endangered species.

Rhinoceros

An agreement in May 1985 between the Foundation and the government of Indonesia led to the creation of the Sumatran rhino conservation project to help save this highly-endangered species. By August 1985, a base camp had been constructed in Sumatra in a forest area where the rhinos were doomed because of the extension of logging activities and on November 25th, the first Sumatran rhino was captured. Named Torgamba, he travelled to Howletts in 1986 and, although he failed to breed during a decade in the UK before returning to the Sumatran Rhino Sanctuary in Way Kambas National Park, this captive-breeding programme initiated by Aspinall, was taken on by several American zoos from 1987. It resulted in a birth in captivity in 2001, in Cincinnati; the only previous captive-birth of the species was recorded in Calcutta in 1889.

Rhinos have been a key focus for the Foundation's conservation efforts. Rhino horn is prized for its alleged aphrodisiac qualities, as well as for medicinal properties and as a symbol of wealth. Realising that poaching was the single biggest threat to the survival of rhino, the Foundation has repeatedly funded efforts to uncover and disrupt international trade in rhino horn. So critical is the situation that there are now only two northern white rhinos in existence.[231] Both females, Kenyan conservationists in 2020 were attempting in-vitro fertilisation with frozen sperm from dead males in order to save the species.

Several eastern black rhinoceros have been taken back to Africa. The first, a male, went to a semi-wild breeding programme at Addo National Park in South Africa in 1995, the first captive-bred rhino ever to be returned to Africa. Having already sired at least two offspring at Addo, he was moved in October 2000 to Thabo Tholo, a private reserve in a northern province of South Africa where he rapidly became the dominant male and continued to sire offspring. Two female rhinos were subsequently also sent to Thabo Tholo in 2004 where both have given birth several times. Another two females went to the 140-hectare Grumeti Park in Tanzania in June 2007 and, in June 2012, one male and two females joined the re-introduction programme in the Mkomazi Rhino Sanctuary, Tanzania.

Other Key Species

Other species sent back from the UK to their indigenous habitat include two ocelots to a conservation-breeding programme in the Chamela-Cuixmala Biosphere Reserve, Mexico, in April 1994; a pair of clouded leopards sent to Phnom Tamao Wildlife Rescue Centre, Cambodia, in August 2006 and another female in January 2011.

In the last 40 years, the Foundation has also embraced the Przewalski's horse, the European bison, the crowned Sifaka and the Scottish wildcat. The Przewalski horse project was negotiated with the Russian authorities in the early

---

231. The i newspaper, UK, May 2020, p14. Three viable embryos have been created and stored

1980s. This species is the holy animal of Mongolia, where Mongolians name it 'takhi', or 'spirit'. Virtually extinct, it is probably the last link with the original wild horse and there are now around 2,000 of them in Russia, China, Kazakhstan and Mongolia.

Aspinall built a herd of this rare breed at Port Lympne and pioneered its return to China. The Foundation sent 10 horses, five stallions and five mares to the Milv Ecological Centre in Beijing in 1992 and they are now in a semi-wild enclosure in Gansu Province.

* * *

Aspinall's success as a conservationist is established. He confirmed with his drive and his money that his commitments to conservation that he expressed so fiercely, were not empty words. He also acknowledged and embraced the danger that inevitably was part of his worldwide initiative. Five keepers, all remarkable men who believed in the Aspinall creed, have died over the years – two killed by the same tiger in 1980, one crushed by an elephant in 1984, one savaged by a tiger in 1994 and one trampled to death by an elephant in 2000.[232]

Aspinall, too, has experienced his narrow escapes. Two bears, Esau and Ayesha, lived in a large enclosure in Howletts and they welcomed Aspinall as a regular visitor with whom they teased and rolled and made merry. In play, he said "they liked to suck my neck". Together, the bears were so powerful they could knock him down, which was not unusual in his play with gorillas and tigers as well. On this particular afternoon, Aspinall had forgotten his keys to the entrance gate, so he dropped down from the high wall into the enclosure itself. Unfortunately, he timed his arrival just as Esau was trying to

---

232. The names of those keepers who died can be found in Appendix 7

mate with Ayesha, who was not in the mood. Esau turned, saw Aspinall and charged at him. Aspinall fled. The bear chased him from tree to tree. Aspinall threw his coat at him. Esau tore it to pieces. "I shouted for help. No-one heard. I had no keys, no way out. I had no doubt that I was the prey. He chased me for what must have been about 10 minutes and I was exhausted. I made a break for it and landed in the ditch near the wall. But I was too tired to try to climb out…"

At that moment, he considered his death.[233] "I felt an almost trance-like numbness steal over me. Looking back, I recall that David Livingstone had recorded a similar experience with a lion – 'the shock produced a stupor similar to that which seems to be felt by a mouse after the first shake by the cat … a sort of dreaminess … no sense of feeling or terror'. I feel, and I also felt this in an encounter with one of my tigers, Jhelum, that prey are to some extent anaesthetised by fear. The fear inspired by the great predators is probably very much like the *ivresse de profondeurs* experienced by deep-sea divers.[234] I was in that ditch, literally defenceless."

Aspinall's reflections were vivid, even 40 years after the event. At the time, he "yelled for help and threw rocks at the bear. But he kept coming. I gave myself a 20-to-1 chance of survival. But I was determined to die fighting, a crude flint in either hand".

In the classic manner of a silent movie, help arrived in the nick of time. Aspinall's mother-in-law, together with a friend, Richard Parkes, happened to be in a cottage 100 metres away. They heard the bear's roars if not Aspinall's cries. They distracted Esau by banging saucepans and dustbin lids and Aspinall was dragged to safety. He clasped the hands of his rescuers, said little – and went off to bed.

---

233. Conversation with author, 1998
234. Literally, an acceptance, a light-headedness felt by divers in ocean depths

John Aspinall died from jaw cancer on June 29th 2000, aged 74. He used to hope for what he described as a "romantic, violent death rather than just fading away with this cancer" and he had thought it quite possible that he might be killed by one of his own animals. Not that he wished to die in this way "because it would have brought the animal into disrespect and people would have clamoured for it to be put down". But he hankered after a brave, extravagant, noble death, the death of a warrior.

Those who gathered for his funeral and his burial at Howletts did their best to reflect those wishes. Zulu tribesmen – Aspinall was an honorary Zulu – danced as his coffin was laid to rest amid the avenue of trees leading to the mansion that had been his home for 50 years. Zulu Chief Buthelezi, described him as "a true romantic … my best friend".

And at the funeral, politicians and environmentalists, Thatcher and Goldsmith, animal keepers and Sir John Paul Getty, racing drivers and top models, nodded their agreement. It was left to the Greek writer, Taki Theodoracopulos, to pose a question to which no-one that day chose to provide an answer:

"Why was John Aspinall, this great man, never honoured by his country for the unique conservation initiatives he inspired? He could have been one of the richest men in Britain if he hadn't spent his money on trying to save a world that is disappearing before our very eyes…"

Dame Jane Goodall,[235] who visited Aspinall at Howletts, thought "John's work was ahead of its time. I loved his programme to re-introduce Przewalski horses to China and admired his breeding of endangered species to re-populate the wild creatures. His lasting legacy is that he surely made

---

235. Author's conversation with Dame Jane Goodall, 2020, renowned for her 60-year-long study of the social and family interactions of wild chimpanzees

a difference to many endangered species. He will long be remembered".

As John Aspinall was laid to rest, the wolves nearby in their spacious homes, howled…

Chapter 10

SUPER SPY:
Presidents, Power and Betrayal

In October 1976, *Rolling Stone* magazine ran a gallery of portraits of the most powerful men in the political life of America: Henry Kissinger, George HW Bush, Presidents Ford, Carter and Reagan, the editor of *The New York Times*, AM Rosenthal, and *The Washington Post* publisher, Kenneth Graham, all made the list. And then there was a gaunt, bespectacled image of a man less recognisable to the magazine readership. His name was James Jesus Angleton, spymaster of the CIA[236] for more than two decades of the 20th century and one of the most influential unelected officials in the federal government of the United States.

From World War II through to the Cold War, James Angleton toiled relentlessly and controversially in the mysterious field of counter-espionage, out of sight of the public, members of Congress, the Senate and even the President – often without their knowledge. He either controlled or was involved in many of the most high-profile espionage scandals that followed World War II, from the defection to Moscow of the Cambridge spies – Burgess, Maclean and Philby – to the Bay of Pigs fiasco and the assassination of President Kennedy. He was – according to Richard Helms, the USA's Director of Intelligence, who

---

236. CIA – Central Intelligence Agency

shared space with Angleton in the *Rolling Stones'* 1976 Gallery of Stars – "recognised as the dominant counter-intelligence figure in the non-communist world".

He was also devious, untruthful, paranoid, manipulative and ruthless. But perhaps that's a prerequisite of the job he did and of the influence he wielded. More surprisingly, he could be both loyal and naïve in his loyalty.

Angleton served five Presidents. His opinion of each depended on the degree with which their view of the world corresponded with Angleton's, which was that, although in 1945 the war against Germany and Japan had ended in victory for the Allies, another war had immediately begun.

"In 1945, we began to acquire information which showed that there were two wars going on. The Soviet Union had no desire whatsoever that the world be moulded in a Western fashion: (The Soviets) sought world domination. It was a global war, an ideological war."[237]

Angleton and I were talking in the faux Colonial Georgetown Inn, in Washington in 1976 and I asked if, in the intervening 20 years since the end of World War II, he had seen anything to make him change his views.

"There has been nothing."

Angleton's convictions were seminal, part of his DNA. With an almost religious fervour he quoted Lenin to support them: "Lenin was the forefather of practically all the principles of subversion, the deliberate undermining of any opponent. He believed that, in order to reveal the source of opposition (to your objectives), you must create *false* opposition to unmask the real enemy and his methods.

"Lenin was one of the most ruthless murderers in history, as was Stalin. They saw no value in human life. One of Lenin's principal instruments was institutionalised assassination,

---

237. Conversation with author, 1976

murder, maiming – the eradication of individuals. The same goes for his successors. Human life is not important in this ideological war."[238]

For more than 20 years, Angleton contributed these bedrock views with confidence and authority to the foreign and domestic policy of the most rich and powerful nation in the world. His influence was immense. It is instructive to examine his contribution to the West's attitudes and behaviour during those dangerous decades, when the world teetered on the edge of nuclear war.

The location of my last long conversation with James Angleton is significant. It was in that most European area of Washington DC, Georgetown. Only a few years before, Angleton, as ever an enigmatic figure, had carried the ashes of his good friend, Allen Dulles, at his funeral in the Georgetown Presbyterian Church, close to where we were now sitting. Dulles was probably the greatest Director of US Intelligence there's ever been. The congregation who came to mourn him included senior members of the CIA past and present, senators and congressmen, bankers and journalists. CIA Chief, Richard Helms, gave the oration: "For us, as for him," he said of Dulles, "patriotism sets no bounds on the wider pursuit of truth." Angleton set no bounds either in his pursuit of patriotism, nor the dedication to *his* truth. In the death of Dulles, he lost a lifelong friend, a mentor and a father figure,[239] whom he had first met in Italy in October 1945.

Born in Boise, Idaho, in 1917, Angleton was a precocious youngster. He shunned his second Christian name, 'Jesus', which his catholic mother, Carmen Moreno Angleton, had chosen, though there were many in the Georgetown church that day who thought it appropriate. It reflected, they

238. Ibid
239. The Ghost, Jefferson Morley, St Martin's Griffin, New York, 2017, p30

thought, a majesty to which Angleton aspired. In his teens, he had studied at Malvern College in England, and by the time he attended Yale University in 1937, he had lived in three countries, the USA, Britain and Italy, and spoke three languages, English of course, plus Spanish and Italian. He was a brilliant scholar. A friend at Yale described him as "quite British in his ways ... very much at home in Italian literature, especially Dante – as well as the finer points of handicapping horses".[240]

He was also a poet. He had edited the literary magazine *Furioso* at Yale, was friendly with Ezra Pound and had persuaded luminaries such as Pound himself, EE Cummings and Dr Carlos Williams to write for the Yale magazine. On holiday with his family in Italy, he had watched the growth of Mussolini's fascism and in 1939 had seen Britain go to war against Italy and Germany. Angleton then went to law school in Harvard. After Pearl Harbor, which drew America into World War II in 1941, he joined the US Army as an enlisted man and was drafted into the Office of Strategic Services (OSS), which was newly formed as America's foreign intelligence service. The British already had a foreign intelligence agency, the Secret Intelligence Service (SIS), commonly known as MI6 and it was to Britain that Angleton and his fledgling fellow agents went for training at Bletchley Park. He was an enthusiastic pupil. Angleton spent the war identifying and trying to render ineffective, Communist secret agents across Europe. William Donovan, a financial lawyer, in uniform now as General "Wild Bill" Donovan, had persuaded President Roosevelt to set up the OSS. He described Angleton as "the service's most professional counter-intelligence officer".

This, then, was the Angleton who Allen Dulles met

---

240. Ibid

in Rome in October 1945. The war had been won both in Europe and the Far East and the OSS had disbanded. But Dulles was convinced that a post-war intelligence agency would be needed to control and restrict the Soviet Union's political ambitions.

With Donovan's recommendation in mind, Dulles found Angleton "immensely attractive".[241] In 1947, Angleton helped Dulles set up the CIA. Over lunch in Georgetown in 1976, he recalled his motivation which was rooted in his views of the Soviet Union pre-war:

"The prime Soviet objective in setting up the KGB, both for Lenin and under the first great Chief of Soviet Intelligence, Felix Dzerzhinsky,[242] was defensive," he declared. "They adopted clandestine methods in order to deceive the West and to prevent any invasion of Russia as they feared the destruction of the Bolshevik movement. They did it through double agents and deception and the West never understood it nor took any effective action against it. Only later did we discover that defensive measures can easily be transformed into offensive action. Penetration is penetration; once you have the knowledge gained through defensive measures, you can use it equally effectively to attack your enemy.

"Tourism has always been totally controlled in the Soviet Union by the government. This network of knowledge, which they obtained through this control, enabled them to forecast the targets to approach and try to befriend them through their agents and then to strike against the 'targets', particularly if they visited Moscow. Their methods were (pause) and are (longer pause) exhaustive and underhand." He gave an example. "One high-ranking Foreign Minister from the West

---

241. Bill Miller, Oral History, p6–7, Senate Historical Office, 2014
242. Felix Dzerzhinsky created the Soviet's first post-Revolution state security organisations, Cheka and OGPU (1917–26). He was Polish and, ironically, of noble birth

was to attend a conference of great importance in Russia and, when he arrived, he was very security-conscious. They tried to tempt him with women and alcohol. No success. (Another pause). They finally drilled a hole in the wall of his hotel room and introduced a gas which deepened his sleep. They entered his room and found the documents they knew he had. The diplomat woke with a headache in the morning and the secret documents were no longer secret."

A conversation with Angleton is littered with assertions such as this. Would he identify the diplomat? No, he wouldn't. The country, perhaps? No. Every question is considered and chewed over during a pause of varying length. As you wait, the atmosphere hangs heavily with expectation. If cutlery is added to the encounter, say, over a meal, much manoeuvring of knife, fork or spoon may extend the pause. Two forks may be combined, apparently to see if there is any way that they can be locked together.

In passing, one of the least understood tools of an interviewer is the pause. For the interviewee, the pressure builds into an intimidation to break the lengthening silence. It is a challenge both to the veracity of what he or she has just said and to what he or she is going to say. It is an implication that the last answer given has not been understood, is incomplete and/or unsatisfactory and needs elaboration. Invariably, it is the interviewee who breaks the silence. The words then spoken are often among the most revelatory in the entire conversation.

Not so with James Angleton. He was impervious to a pause. He loved pauses. Pauses were his stock in trade. He probably invented the term: the space between words. That is where he lived and had his being. He knew what he was going to say and chose his moment to say it. His hesitance was a façade, a device.

He also loved words. He would roll an 'r' around his

tongue. His eyes would sparkle behind the heavy glasses as he toyed with phrases such as 'diplomatic pouch' or 'hostage situation'. At moments like this it was easy to remember that Angleton loved poetry, especially TS Eliot. *Gerontion* was one of Angleton's favourite poems. The title is Greek for 'little old man'. It discusses themes of religion, sexuality and childhood. It includes the lines:

'After such knowledge, what forgiveness? Think now
History has many cunning passages, contrived corridors
And issues, deceives with whispering ambitions,
Guides us by vanities.'

Angleton was ready to admit that *his* knowledge and *his* actions deceived and destroyed others but he would insist that this was justified by his uncomplicated patriotism. He spoke of his love-hate relationship with Eliot. "Eliot was my favourite … a whole man … and yet he killed poetry by making it so complicated that it became almost incomprehensible."[243]

Like his muse, Angleton transformed spying into "such an involuted, convoluted, labyrinthine maze that the CIA got lost in its own intricacies".[244]

Most interviews are, at least in part, predictable. They have a finite span, usually governed by the willingness and boredom threshold of the interviewee. That was not the case with Angleton on that day in Washington DC. We talked through lunch and into the afternoon; we talked so long that the lunchtime waiters restlessly gave way to a fresh shift who would wait upon those who would come to dine at the Inn in the evening. My agenda, which I had not previously discussed with Angleton, had five headings: the spies Burgess,

---

243. Orchids for Mother, Aaron Latham, Little Brown, 1997
244. Ibid

Maclean and Philby; Watergate; the Senate Inquiry into the CIA, chaired by the Senator Frank Church; the assassination of the Kennedys, John and Robert and Angleton's assessment of the Presidents he had served.

In the event, he seemed eager to embrace them all. He did so as if to get on the record, as he twice put it, "the truth and not the distortions of ill-informed politicians and journalists".

Of all these five subjects, he was most cagey about British spy, Kim Philby. The reason was simple: Angleton was a close friend of Philby's and when Philby defected to Moscow in 1963, it was, I believe, the greatest experience of betrayal in Angleton's life. It hurt him professionally; it also undermined his self-belief that someone so close could fool him so completely. In 1951, Philby spent his last afternoon in Washington taking tea with James Angleton. Had Angleton any intimation that the Englishman was about to defect? "I am not prepared to discuss anything further about Philby." His lips shut like a trap. It was the only time in four hours that he was visibly moved.

Philby and Angleton first met in 1944 in London, at the OSS headquarters in Ryder Street and at Bletchley Park, where Philby taught Angleton the fundamentals of counter-intelligence – how to run double agents, the art of wireless interception, methods of feeding false information to an enemy. Philby was a senior officer in the OSS; he had had field experience in the Spanish Civil War, where he was injured while covering the conflict as an accredited journalist. At the same time, he was feeding information to both the British and Soviet intelligence services.[245]

Since 1941, Philby had been working for Section 5 of

---

245. In Spain, Philby suffered a head injury in 1937 when the car in which he was travelling with three other correspondents was hit by a shell. The three other correspondents were killed. Ironically, Fascist General Franco awarded Marxist Philby the Red Cross Military Merit medal in 1938

MI6 on anti-Fascist propaganda. But in 1944, soon after he met Angleton, it became apparent to the British and the Americans that Russian ambitions for a post-war Europe did not match their own and Philby was promoted to head Section 9 of MI6, the anti-Communist section.[246] The relationship between the two men became personal as well as professional. Angleton later recalled that Philby, twice married, advised him as he went through a difficult period in his own marriage. "He helped me to think it through…"[247] In November 1947, Angleton was recalled to Washington to join the CIA, the formation of which he had discussed with Allen Dulles two years earlier in Rome. Philby soon followed him. He was transferred to Washington to run the UK's SIS station. From December 1949, their friendship developed and they regularly lunched together at Harveys fish restaurant where, as Philby later remembered, Angleton was "one of the thinnest men I have ever met and yet one of the biggest eaters".[248]

No matter how close they were personally, these lunches had their own rules which both recognised. There were always matters that were withheld or only partially revealed. Philby would later outline his tactics:

"The greater the trust between us overtly, the less he [Angleton] would suspect covert action. Who gained the most from this complex game I cannot say. I knew what he was doing for the CIA and he knew what I was doing for SIS. But the real nature of my interest was something he did *not* know."[249]

The Angletons bought a four-bedroomed house on 33rd Road in North Arlington, on the Virginia side of the Potomac.

---

246. The Fourth Man, Andrew Boyle, 1979
247. A Spy Among Friends, Ben Macintyre, 2014
248. My Silent War, Kim Philby, New York Modern Library, p151
249. Ibid, p151

The Philbys settled into a modest home on Nebraska Avenue in Northwest Washington. Both wives began entertaining their husband's friends and colleagues.

It was at a party at Philby's house in 1950 that Angleton met Guy Burgess. Burgess who, with Maclean and Philby, would make up the trio of British defectors 11 years later, was a bizarre figure in the intelligence circus in Washington – flamboyant, a heavy drinker and so openly homosexual that he was frequently castigated for using Embassy cars as he cruised to find new partners. Angleton already knew of Donald Maclean, who had worked in the British Embassy in Washington from 1944 to 1948, where he had risen to be First Secretary. Maclean, like Burgess and Philby, was a Cambridge University graduate and a convinced Marxist and, as early as 1934, while editing the Trinity Hall students' magazine, he had written that England was 'in the throes of a capitalist crisis…'[250] While Soviet Russia had fought beside the Allies against Fascist Germany and Italy, these left-wing views had not hindered either his recruitment to the diplomatic service or his advancement within it. But the world had changed by the 1950s and so had the attitudes of the Free World, the democracies of Britain, France and the USA.

US and British officials had had suspicions for some time that Maclean had been spying for Soviet Russia. Angleton and Philby would have been aware of this. Evidence suggests each kept his own counsel in their lunchtime meetings.

In May 1951, Burgess and Maclean disappeared. Burgess picked up Maclean in a rented car and they left England by ferry. There, the trail went cold. For Maclean, already under suspicion, the motivation for his defection was clear. But the flamboyant Burgess was considered too obviously unreliable to be thought of as a double agent and his disappearance was

---

250. Ibid

more of a surprise. Why had the pair suddenly fled? British and American investigators believed that someone had tipped them off and had warned Maclean that he was about to be unmasked. British intelligence considered whether there could be a 'Third Man' under cover in Washington. Philby came under suspicion as a possible informant, a Soviet spy. Opinions in the CIA were therefore canvassed. Angleton argued Philby's innocence and wrote in a memo to his CIA bosses:

'Philby has consistently 'sold' Burgess as a most gifted individual. In this respect, he has served as Burgess' apologist on several occasions when (Burgess') behaviour has been a course of extreme embarrassment in the Philby household. Philby has explained away these idiosyncrasies on grounds that (Burgess) suffered a severe brain concussion in an accident which had continued to affect him periodically.'[251] Philby should not be blamed for Burgess' treachery, Angleton declared.

His superiors did not agree with him. The CIA told the British that they would not work with the SIS unless Philby was removed from Washington. Angleton's loyalty remained naïvely unwavering. When he was told the British would accede to the CIA request and that Philby would be returning to London, he called his British friend to meet for a drink. "I was trying to find him all day long but he didn't answer his phones." They eventually met "for two or three hours".[252] Philby recalls in his memoir that Angleton seemed confused that day and "oddly clueless" about the reality of the situation.[253] As they were leaving at the end of their meeting, Angleton waved and said he expected they would soon meet

251. Wilderness of Mirrors, David S Martin, Harper and Row, 1980, p53
252. The Ghost, Jefferson Morley, St Martin's Griffin, New York, 2017
253. Ibid, p53

again.[254]

Back in London, Philby pursued his career as a journalist and moved to Beirut where he wrote on policies and finance for *The Economist*. The British SIS continued to investigate him. Philby was probably aware of this. On the evening of January 22nd 1963 in Beirut, he made his excuses and left a dinner party early. Four days later, he was in Moscow.

The news that his friend, Philby, had defected hit Angleton like a hammer blow. The man he had befriended and defended had been spying for the Soviet Union for 16 years and had deceived his friend, James Jesus Angleton, for seven years. Angleton's wife, Cicely, described Philby's defection as a "terrible shock", which had affected her husband "deeply. It was a bitter blow he never forgot". Nicholas Elliott, a close friend of Philby's, later told novelist, John Le Carré, of his surprise that Angleton had "made such a fuss of Philby when he was the head of the service's station in Washington. He had trusted him and confided in him far beyond any routine relationship between the colleagues of two friendly countries. The knowledge that he, Jim, the top expert in the world on Soviet espionage had been totally deceived had a cataclysmic effect on his personality. Jim henceforward found it difficult to trust anybody, to make two and two add up to four".[255]

Soon after Philby's defection, Angleton told fellow CIA officer, John Hart, that he had "always thought there was something wrong with Philby". He had suspected as much as far back as 1951.[256] There is no evidence to support that assertion.

* * *

254. Interview with author, 1976
255. The Ghost, Jefferson Morley, St Martin's Griffin, New York, 2017, p125
256. Ibid, p50

In November 1963, Lee Harvey Oswald was arrested for shooting dead President John Fitzgerald Kennedy in Dallas, Texas. The world was shocked. James Jesus Angleton, however, was less surprised than most. Not that the President had been assassinated but that Lee Harvey Oswald was in some way involved. For Angleton had had his eye on Oswald for some years.

Since the early 1950s, the CIA and the Federal Bureau of Investigation (FBI) had been randomly intercepting, opening and photographing other people's private letters. In 1955, Angleton asked to extend this CIA programme to access *all* mail traffic to and from the Soviet Union so that "new information … could be recorded, indexed, analysed" to help CIA activities. He also proposed that letters could be both opened "and copied", which was a fresh request. He received CIA approval in December 1955.

Angleton rented a room at LaGuardia Airport in New York to accommodate this initiative. New staff were recruited to process up to six bags of mail every day. Letters were steamed open. The steam from a kettle softened the glue on the envelopes and the letters were prised open with a stick. The staff were nicknamed 'flaps and seals' for they could open a letter in between five and 15 seconds. The operation was called LINGUAL. In 1956, 832 letters were opened. In 1958, more than 8,000 letters were opened.[257] During the 20 years that the LINGUAL programme ran before being closed down in 1973, 215,000 letters and packages were opened, copied and filed. Angleton will certainly have seen many of them.[258] The US Postal Service (USPS) was kept in ignorance as CIA agents examined personal mail in this private area. The envelopes were often brought in at night after removing

257. Church Committee Report, Book 3, p570
258. The Ghost, Jefferson Morley, St Martin's Griffin, New York, 2017, p83

them from the routine mail system. Angleton, the Cold Warrior, viewed this illegal interference as totally justified. He later produced the CIA's knowledge of the activities of Lee Harvey Oswald as proof, both of the efficiency of the system and the necessity to use this flagrant breach of confidentiality. He said:[259]

"Our mail coverage was very successful. We had information on Oswald, for instance. When he was arrested as the assassin of the President, we went back into the files and there was correspondence from him while he was in Moscow – his personality traits, an insight into his being and his marriage. One could never have obtained it in any other way.

"Oswald had been a US Marine. We knew he had told the Russians that he had information to impart to them.

"We knew from the letters we opened that he certainly had been briefed and debriefed, by the KGB."

What we also know is that Angleton had opened a file on Oswald as long ago as 1959, that his aides had drafted cables about Oswald's visit to the Cuban Embassy in Mexico City in 1963 and that Angleton had been discussing within the CIA the possible assassination of Fidel Castro. To Angleton, Oswald was a legitimate target, an American serviceman who had defected to Soviet Russia, married a Russian wife, returned to the USA and, under surveillance, had been involved in "handing out subversive propaganda" on the streets of the USA. And perhaps Angleton was right. But legitimate target or not, his methods of intelligence-gathering challenged the US Constitution. Angleton didn't see it that way.

"Let's understand this very clearly. We examined 215,000 letters over 20 years until 1973, working with only a small

---

259. Conversation with author, Washington, 1976

group of six people, who had to know many languages. During the 20-year period, we photographed the outside of some 3 million envelopes, which is not illegal. Our choice of 215,000 represents only, I believe, .004% of Americans who were corresponding with the enemy – and this at a time when we had troops in the field fighting the Communists, in Vietnam and Korea."[260]

But the CIA's LINGUAL programme went beyond taking details from the outside of envelopes which, they argued, would have been legal under the 'mail cover' rules that allowed the government to record all information about both sender and recipient on the exterior of a letter or package. The Church Committee, appointed by the US Senate on September 4th 1975 to investigate the activities of the CIA, the FBI, the National Security Branch (NSB) and the Internal Revenue Service (IRS), revealed that the personal details of many respected US citizens were also on the CIA's files – Edward Kennedy, Art Buchwald, Martin Luther King, Gregory Peck, Walter Mondale, Whitney Young, Frank Church himself and Ralph Abernathy, among others.[261] The chairman, Senator Church, summed up the case against Angleton and the CIA; his committee would find out, he said, why "the mail (of these private individuals), including a letter from me to my mother" should have been "opened and scrutinised by the CIA against the laws of the USA". Angleton's response was pragmatic. LINGUAL, he said, was part of a double bluff. It was so unlikely that, in a democratic country such as the USA, the opening of private mail would be countenanced, that even the Russians would not suspect that it was happening! He said:

"We had reason to believe that the Soviets, neither the

---

260. Conversation with author, 1976. I can find no substantiation of Angleton's .004 percentage
261. NSA tracking of US citizens, NSA archive, 2017

Soviet bloc nor the Soviets themselves, would be aware of the fact that we would violate the cachet of the mails. And therefore there would be a tendency, on their part, to make greater use of the mails than they would do normally. I can also tell you without going further that Philby used the mails and I leave the Philby question there."[262]

His use of the world 'violate' is interesting in this context, surely an admission that rules had been broken. Also the word 'successful' in his overall defence of the policy of prising open 215,000 private letters. Successful, perhaps, in being able to declare that Oswald was 'known' to the CIA. Not so successful in preventing the assassination of President Kennedy. At the end of 1983, the Warren Commission investigated the circumstances surrounding the assassination of President Kennedy and found that Oswald had acted alone. So had Jack Ruby when he shot Oswald dead days later while he was in police custody.

Angleton gave evidence to the Warren Commission. He omitted to tell Chief Justice Earl Warren that he had put Oswald's name on the LINGUAL list so that his letters would be routinely opened, or that he had personally controlled, through the Special Investigations Group (SIG), the file on Oswald for four years, from his defection to Russia in 1959 until 1963, when he shot the President. Or that, in his obsession with security, he had created a special file for Oswald in order to delay information about him reaching the prying eyes of members of his own security service, whom he did not trust. Angleton was asked by Warren: why the creation of a CIA file on Oswald had been delayed by at least a year. He said he did not know the circumstances: "I don't know why it would take that long," he replied. It took that long because it suited Angleton for it to take that long. He was hiding the fact that,

---

262. Conversation with author, 1976

three years before President Kennedy was shot, Lee Harvey Oswald had been very much of personal interest to James Jesus Angleton,[263] but he had taken no action.

The assassination of the President represented for the CIA "the worst failure of US Intelligence since December 7th 1941, when the Japanese attacked Pearl Harbor…"[264] It had happened on Angleton's watch. Yet such was his bureaucratic genius that he managed to ensure that he was put in charge of the Agency's investigation of Oswald. During Kennedy's presidency, Angleton's staff had known more about Lee Harvey Oswald than just about anyone in the US government. After the president was dead, Angleton managed to orchestrate a cover-up of what the CIA knew.[265] He avoided blame. It was a brilliant deception.

* * *

Of the five US Presidents Angleton served, Kennedy was probably his least favourite. He knew the Kennedys socially, they had dined together and, like so many in Washington in the 1960s, James and Cicely Angleton were entranced by Jacqueline Kennedy's grace and glamour, less so by her husband's liberal politics. Cicely said, after Kennedy was elected: "Prince Hamlet is now in the White House." Angleton was a hard-line Republican and almost the same age as JFK. He was doubtful about Kennedy from the outset, partly because he felt that the President was "going through a metamorphosis of his own … he began with what I thought were extreme liberal ideas and misconceptions about the motives of the Soviet Union". But experience in the White House changed Kennedy. Angleton said: "Before his death,

263. The Ghost, Ibid, pp87–90
264. Ibid
265. The Ghost, Ibid, p154

Kennedy was ready to remove practically everybody in the Oval Office, apart perhaps from[266] McGeorge Bundy. If he had lived, those with ultra-liberal views would have been long gone."[267]

During Kennedy's term, Angleton saw the botched Bay of Pigs invasion of Cuba in April 1961 as a turning point and the CIA's involvement in it as "a disaster. It was a major failure … the germ seed of the worst the Agency has ever suffered. Our reputation was sadly undermined". He agreed, he said, with his mentor, Allen Dulles, that "the operation should have been in the hands of the military, the Joint Chiefs of Staff. Then, we would have had the military power and supremacy in the air. The operation would not have failed. And Castro would not have survived". As it was, "we (the US) were on the back foot, particularly in the President's subsequent negotiations with the Russians. It was humiliating and so unnecessary".[268]

Angleton's favourite President was undoubtedly Dwight D Eisenhower. A confrontation with the Soviet Union over Cuba became likely in 1960, when Eisenhower approved the CIA arming and training a group of Cubans to invade and overthrow the Castro regime. In what would later become the Bay of Pigs fiasco, Angleton saw in Eisenhower, a Republican like himself, a man who "had achieved victory militarily and knew how to handle the Russians".[269]

Angleton summed up Eisenhower's years in the White House with words of total approval: "In all my years in counter-intelligence, it was the one period in time when every item of information of value which could lead to political action – in other words, where intelligence operations had

---

266. McGeorge Bundy was National Secretary Advisor to Presidents Kennedy and Johnson (1961–66)
267. Conversation with author, 1976
268. Ibid
269. Ibid

political objectives – these items found their way rapidly into the hands of those who could execute action. And they did execute action. Eisenhower's Presidency was excellent. It was the era of containment."[270] Angleton's longtime friend, Allen Dulles, was director of the CIA. Allen Dulles' brother, John Foster Dulles, was now US Secretary of State, a post he held for six years from 1953 to 1959. John Foster Dulles was Eisenhower's most respected advisor. Angleton must have reflected that, like the pop song of the 20s, he had "danced with the man, who danced with the girl, who had danced with the Prince of Wales". He now had a direct line to the President.

Throughout his term in office, Dulles advocated an aggressive stance against communism. It was indeed, a "period of containment" involving diplomatic confrontations over Suez, the Lebanon and 'indo-China'. If he could have done so, Angleton would have rolled this team into his knapsack and carried it with him wherever he went. "We were strong", he said, and "we were also technically at peace throughout President Eisenhower's term in office".[271] Which is 'technically' correct. But during this 'peace', Angleton was urging a tough policy against Cuba, "this communist in our own backyard", and the CIA were training an invasion force of 1,500 men,[272] preparing for armed intervention against Castro. The situation would become an explosive issue for the next President of the United States, John F Kennedy. And it would give rise to the Cuban missile crisis of 1962, which would be described by historian, Arthur Schlesinger, as "the most dangerous moment in the history of the world..."

The death of Kennedy in 1963 brought Lyndon Baynes Johnson into the Oval Office. To Angleton, who knew that

---

270. Conversation with author, 1976
271. Ibid
272. Ibid

Kennedy had threatened to destroy the CIA over the Bay of Pigs affair, President Johnson was a man "with whom we (the CIA) could do business". He admired, in particular, LBJ's attention to detail:

"He was a man who would read into the wee hours of the morning any report that interested him. He was terribly interested in intelligence and the detail of that intelligence. And, once he'd taken a view, he certainly implemented action." At the height of the Vietnam War, Angleton remembered "going into his office and he was watching four television sets at once: there were also two headphones nearby, as he was taking advice on a particular phase of the Vietnam War". Johnson had "contacts and an ability to deliver, unlike his predecessor (Kennedy)". He "talked straight with the Agency. He got on with the Director. If there was a disagreement, he was blunt but he knew how to keep secrets".[273] For Angleton, who traded in secrets all his life, there could be no higher praise.

The presidency of Richard Nixon was again a challenge for Angleton. He knew President Nixon of old. They had first met in Rome, after World War II "when I had taken over OSS[274] in Italy". Angleton recalled that it had been a "difficult first meeting". Nixon had questioned why, in the Greek Civil War,[275] the US was "supporting the monarchist, Fascist army. I had been asked by the High Commission to brief him and other Congressmen and we had a lively discussion as I stressed the power of the Soviet bloc and its ambitions in Europe. There was a lot that Richard Nixon and the others did not understand".[276]

---

273. Conversation with author, 1976
274. OSS – Office of Strategic Services
275. The Greek Government troops fought the Communist troops (KKE) for three years from 1946 until 1949
276. Ibid, 1976

Angleton had begun his career in Italy and, given the choice, had already shown his preference for right wing politicians during disputes between the Allies over the allocation of local power in the post-war shape of Europe. At the end of World War II, Italy had a formidable Communist Party. Opposing them, on the political right, Junio Valerio Borghese was an Italian naval commander, a Fascist and a confidante of Il Duce, Benito Mussolini. Both the British and the Americans wished to interview Borghese about war crimes. The left-wing Italian Partisans, who mobilised on the side of the Allies and were clearing the country of German troops and Italian Fascists, wanted to find and execute Borghese. In May 1945, Angleton smuggled Borghese to a safe house in Rome, hid him there, disguised him as a US serviceman in a US Army uniform and drove south to Caserta. There, Borghese was arrested but he was never accused of war crimes. He served a prison sentence on lesser charges and was released in 1949. He then resumed a career as one of Italy's leading Fascist politicians. Angleton believed that it was in the "long-term interests of the US that he should not be executed and that his services be retained".[277]

Angleton's first judgment of Nixon as President was that he would "lean too far to the left". But Nixon was to confound Angleton. Two years after their first meeting, he led the move to indict US State Department official, Alger Hiss, as a communist and a Soviet spy. Still a Congressman, Nixon pursued Hiss and insisted on giving evidence himself to the Grand Jury of Hiss' treachery. Angleton said: "I thought I knew Richard Nixon's politics. He amazed me." The Hiss case "made Nixon's reputation". Though he always protested his innocence, Hiss went to gaol for five years. Nixon went on to become a Senator, Vice-President and President of the

277. The Ghost, Morley, pp21–7

United States.

As President, Nixon's relationship with the CIA "began very well. We all met him, we shook hands". The major problem was that Henry Kissinger, the Secretary of State, stood firmly between the CIA and the President. That was an intolerable situation. Unlike Angleton, Kissinger believed in détente with the Soviets. Angleton said: "That was never going to work."[278] Nixon's presidency ended in 1974 amid the debacle of the Watergate Scandal, when the headquarters of the Democratic Party National Committee (DNC) were burgled during the Presidential election campaign. Sixty-nine people were involved either in the burglary or in the cover-up that the Nixon administration attempted in order to conceal its involvement in the failed break-in. They were indicted and 48 people were convicted; Nixon resigned on August 9th 1974 after an impeachment process had begun a year earlier. To Angleton, the fact that Nixon had resigned was to his credit. The CIA had been involved in Watergate, Angleton said, only from the sidelines. Director Richard Helms had refused to try to influence the FBI to stop its investigation into the affair. But Angleton had very definite views about the way those involved in Watergate, the 69, had behaved. "No-one ever resigned on principle. They all paraded themselves, were humiliated publicly – Liddy, Dean, Haldeman and the rest of them – and none of them submitted resignations. None of them stood up for principles. I was brought up in England, in some of my formative years and I went to Malvern College and I learned certain features of life and what I regarded as duty. I recall you British had a Chancellor of the Exchequer

---

278. Conversation with author, 1976. Henry Kissinger, US Secretary of State to President Nixon

and there was a leakage on the Budget.[279] Something about a tax increase, a ha'penny on tobacco or pepper and some other commodity...

"And I recall that Dalton stood up in Parliament and, even though he was not tried or under investigation, he voluntarily admitted he'd played golf with the man on Friday, or something like that. He submitted his resignation and he walked out. And that left a very deep impression on me. I saw none of that within Watergate."

James Angleton practised what he preached when, on Christmas Eve 1974, he resigned from his position of Chief of the CIA's Counter-Intelligence. His friend, Dick Helms, had gone and William Colby was appointed eighth Director of the CIA. Angleton and Colby were very different men. Colby declared at the outset that he believed the CIA had to function "within the American Constitutional structure". The implication that the CIA had *not* done so, was very clear. Angleton had no confidence in his new chief. He told the press that, after 31 years, he felt his "usefulness was over".[280]

"I found myself in a situation in which I had a choice.[281] I could go quietly, or I could stay and oppose the decentralisation and destruction of men who'd been with me for 31 years and who were now being taken over by a group of people who had never been in counter-intelligence.

"I went. And three of my men went with me – my Deputy Chief, my Chief of Operations and my Executive Officer.

"It was the right thing to do."

Did you have regrets about leaving in this way?

"Under the circumstances I have no regrets. But I regret

---

279. In 1947, Hugh Dalton, Chancellor of the Exchequer, leaked part of his Budget speech to a journalist. He admitted this to the House of Commons and Prime Minister Clement Attlee accepted his resignation
280. United Press International, 1974
281. Ibid, conversation with author, 1976

not being in the CIA."

You miss it?

"Totally."[282]

Angleton, the Cold Warrior, told a television audience of millions on September 24th 1975: "As a nation, we have to face the facts that certain individual rights have to be sacrificed (in the interests of) national security."[283]

In April of that year at the CIA headquarters at Langley, Virginia, Angleton received one of the Agency's most prestigious awards, the Distinguished Intelligence Medal, for 'the performance of outstanding services ... of a distinctly exceptional nature ... which constitute a major contribution to the mission of the Agency'.

No-one would dispute that James Jesus Angleton's achievements were both major and exceptional. The only question must hang over the Agency's mission during the years he was in charge. The truth is that, in that period, the CIA played fast and loose with the Constitution of a country to which Angleton gave, throughout his life, a passionate and unquestioning allegiance.

---

282. Ibid
283. NBC Nightly News

Chapter 11

THE GIRL IN THE BOAT
or How Hilary Lister Sailed Away...

Hilary Lister, vivacious, talented and determined, was 46 years old when she died in August 2018. For 30 of those years, she was paralysed from the neck down; there was a tiny, precious place on her cheek where she still had feeling, a sensitivity to touch. But her short life and her achievements are a definition of courage in adversity.

Hilary Lister lived not two miles from my home. When she could, she attended the same church. Disabled as she was, she filled her 46 years with bravery, success and ambition, which was as praiseworthy as it was remarkable. She would be the first to say that she had her moments of suicidal despair, but her life is an examination of pragmatism and sheer grit, hope and music and love – and, of course, sailing which, for Hilary, was the reward for all the hours of pain and frustration that she endured. It is instructive to contrast the stifling nature of her daily lifestyle with her ambitions.

"I sit at home on my sofa all day, working on my computer, answering my e-mails and after that – well, it's daytime telly or staring into space.

"Carers visit me three times a day at home – in the morning to get me up, at lunchtime and in the evening to bathe me and put me to bed. They also sort out my drugs every day, the morphine and the other painkillers. One of the most draining things about my disease is that it leaves me in continuous pain. I've had seven operations to insert implants into my spine to try to override the pain but, at its worst, it's like knives being inserted in my joints and turned slowly. It can be rough. The ultimate frustration is that I can't move and sometimes I can't get to the tablets that will relieve that pain."

The pain began when Hilary was 12 years old. At that time, she was at Northbourne Park, a prep school in Kent, where she was in the top teams at most sports and, as an accomplished clarinettist, a music scholar.

The pains were misdiagnosed at first as Osgood–Schlatter disease (OSD), which is sometimes dismissed as 'growing pains'.

By the age of 13 she was in pain every day. By 15, she could barely put one foot in front of the other.

She had been seeing the doctor at school, but "I hadn't even told my parents about it because I just thought it would go away".

Eventually, she went home to her family in Oxford and sought a specialist opinion. "I remember getting off the train, where my mother was waiting and seeing all the colour drain from her face. I looked like a little old woman, bent over and incapacitated. I couldn't even hold my own bag."

At 17, consultants correctly diagnosed reflex sympathetic dystrophy (RSD), a degenerative disease of the nervous system, but two psychiatrists disagreed and declared that her problems were psychological.

"They called me a hysterical teenager. They said it was all in my mind."

For eight months, the whole family had counselling sessions. "They pulled us apart. They tried to make me say I was unloved as a child, that my father had abused me. None of it was true and it was horrific."

Hilary was the daughter of a vicar, the Rev Colin Rudd, and Pauline Rudd, a professor of glycobiology at Dublin University. Hilary Claire Rudd had three brothers – Martin Nicholas, Simon Christopher and Jonathan Richard. Hers was a testing childhood, as we have already seen, which involved the entire family. Her father says: "It has been heartbreaking watching this illness take hold of her – but she never gave up." Her mother says: "She took every setback as something to be coped with and accommodated." Her godmother, Anne Brown, has a daughter, Allison, who in her teens had ambitions to be a dancer:

"In my memories of Hilary, she was always smiling. Happy girl. I can remember saying to her how sorry I was that this illness, this disease had hit her. She looked at me straight in the eyes and said, 'But, Auntie, it's better it happened to me than to Allison,' and then, 'Allison would never be able to dance again,' and I thought, for a teenager, that was just extraordinary. She was always determined to achieve something for herself but, beyond that, she wanted to do something to help others in a similar plight."

By the age of 17, she was at the King's School, Canterbury. She was now on crutches. She moved on to Radley, in the sixth form, an all-boys school and there she sat her A-Levels. Despite the incessant pain and having completely lost the use of her legs, Hilary won a place at Jesus College, Oxford to read biochemistry. The pattern of Hilary's life was set. Problems that were also opportunities; the impossible would simply be a greater challenge. Her final year at Oxford was "difficult". That adjective conceals the fact that she dictated her finals from a sickbed and took the examination while on pain-killing drugs. She got a good 2:1. She was now a qualified biochemist. But she knew she was not well enough to pursue a full-time career.

While at the King's School, she had met the man who

would become her husband, Clifford Lister. Lister taught music at King's and sang as a lay clerk in the cathedral choir. He was a recently separated 31-year-old with two children. She was 17 and a gifted clarinettist. He taught her singing. They kept in touch when she went up to Oxford and, in 1999, they got married at the tiny Betteshanger Church, close to the Northbourne Park School where Hilary was once a pupil. By her wedding day, Hilary had lost the use of her arms. Her bridesmaids helped to feed her. Pragmatically, Hilary insisted on one change in the wedding vows that she took that day. There was no reference to blessing the union with children. "I didn't want a child if there was any chance of their inheriting the disease from me. If it *was* genetic, I couldn't take the risk." Hilary and Clifford set up home in Faversham, near the town's recreation ground where she could hear the sounds of the sport in which she could no longer take part. Two years later, they moved to a bungalow in the nearby village of Dunkirk. They adapted it to Hilary's needs and this was Hilary's home for the last 20 years of her life. They settled into a routine that was as enervating as it was secure.

"It's truly a delightful house, with fields and woodlands all around. As I sit on my sofa, I can see through the window a willow tree and sometimes a woodpecker hammering away. But, for all that, it's still like a prison, because I can't leave without someone helping me by opening the door. I am trapped in a cage."

Clifford went about his business as a music teacher. However caring he was, Hilary frequently sat alone hour after hour, her only companion the complaint that was gradually killing her. "It's a genetic blip that's just turned into a bit of a monster. I don't fear it. But I personalise it. Like a spider, I try to ignore its presence. I don't want to face up to it, to be honest, but I *do* face up to it every day and I say 'You're not going to beat me today.'"

The effort required to remain positive in the circumstances is difficult to imagine. Hilary Lister had more than her share of God-given talents. She had trained as a clarinet teacher but she couldn't teach music because she could no longer hold a clarinet. She had qualified as a biochemist emulating the achievements of her mother but, physically, she could no longer work as a biochemist. And she was in constant pain. On some days, she was in despair.

"I felt worthless. There seemed no reason to exist. When Clifford went to work, my carers would come to get me out of bed. They would wash me, brush my teeth, take me to the toilet, then put me in front of my computer. I had a headset and I could explore the Internet. That was the morning routine. In the afternoons, they moved me to the sofa where I could watch daytime telly. What was the point of it all?"

She and Clifford discussed the possibility of suicide. He tried to dissuade her but Hilary was, as always, logical in argument and focused in determination. She had assembled a supply of tablets which she judged would end her life. She called them her Get Out of Jail Free card. She recorded her will on the computer. She wrote her goodbye letters. Two things stopped her. Firstly, her love for Clifford. "I didn't want to leave him, nor did I want him to feel that in some way he had failed." And secondly, sailing entered her life.

Around the corner from Hilary's home in Dunkirk lived Sue and Julian Owen. They were members of the same church as Hilary and they took her not only to services but to the occasional hospital and medical appointment. Julian knew of a sailing club for the disabled at Westbere Lake in Canterbury. In 2003, they took Hilary there and for the first time, she took to the water, strapped to a chair that was firmly attached to the yacht. It was the first of many visits. All the 350 or so disabled folk, regularly helped by Richard Gaskell and his fellow volunteers at Westbere,[284] enjoy the experience offered by their time on the water. For Hilary, it was all that and much more. "From that first moment, I saw in sailing the chance of freedom."

In 2005, she steered her 26 ft yacht through the busiest stretch of water in the world, the English Channel, from England to France. She was the first quadriplegic to cross the Channel solo. She used a technology that was complex and innovative, a 'sip and puff' method that allowed her to control the craft by blowing through straws that altered the steering and trimmed the sails. 'Control' is the operative word. She said, as family, friends and supporters celebrated at their Dunkirk home: "I was in control of my own life. I'd forgotten what that was like." That same day, a reporter asked her in the moment of triumph what was coming next. She replied immediately: "Oh! I don't know. Maybe sailing around Britain."

And that was how Hilary's great adventure began, an adventure that became a race against time. As a practice run in 2007, she sailed solo around the Isle of Wight. Both then and when she had crossed the English Channel solo from Dover to Calais, Clifford had been in the backup boat, which would have tried to rescue Hilary if there had been an emergency. Sailing solo around the coast of the United Kingdom was a different kettle of fish altogether. The areas of risk were two-fold: she would need a 24-hour, highly experienced team to guide her at sea and a medical staff to care for her both on the boat and when she came ashore. The risks she would take medically were such that no insurance company would provide her with any cover. The boat would be insured as would her carer, Jo Meakins, her organiser, Paul

---

284. Westbere Sailing Opportunities offer sailing twice a week to the disabled. Of Hilary, Richard Gaskell, the club chair, says: "She lit up life. She was dealt a poor hand of cards but she made the most of it"

Taroni, and her 'rescue' crew of Toby May, Simon Robinson and Huw Fernie, who would travel in a motorised 'RIB'[285] near Hilary's craft as she sailed. But the odds against Hilary completing the journey and surviving the experience were too high for the insurance assessors to accept.

Hilary found a leader for her backup rescue crew at the 2007 Boat Show at Earl's Court. Her major sponsor, Pindar, had dropped out. Hilary was working with another of her supporters, Vizmarine, on their Boat Show stand. Toby May was visiting the show on a day off from his ocean yachtsman course at the UK Sailing Academy in Cowes. They met and talked. Later, Hilary mentioned that there was a vacancy to be filled by someone who was prepared to devote the next year of his life to a project. She spelled out the details. Toby May remembers: "It sounded risky then. Looking back, it was, to use one of Hilary's expressions, a madcap[286] idea."

The logistics of a unique project usually grow from a combination of experience and guesswork. In 2008, Hilary went about assembling her team in an all-embracing way. She placed an article in the local newspaper declaring her plans to sail around Britain and inviting anyone interested to contact her, e-mail address attached. Paul Taroni who was living in Deal at the time, read the article and, with his experience as an HGV driver and in management, he applied to join the team. "Very little was in place in March that year and we were due to leave Dover in June. My first impression of Hilary was her determination, no matter what. The next two years only confirmed that impression. My job was to be the organiser, a co-ordinator – and to drive the truck that towed the yacht."

In the next two months, the strategy was laid down. They

---

285. RIB – Rigid Inflatable Boat
286. 'Madcap' was one of Hilary's favourite words to describe anything between 'disastrous' and 'lunacy'

would start from Dover, sail along the south coast round Land's End, push north to Wales, cross the Irish Sea, come back to Scotland, pass through the Crinan and Caledonian Canals and then sail south to the finish line in Dover. The details were then addressed – stop-overs en route, not least to accommodate Hilary's disability, berthing for her yacht Artemis ("Arty"), parking for the vehicles, food and drink, spare parts for the convoy and the yacht, fuelling points, "and 101 other tiny matters which could assume giant proportions if we don't get them right", as Hilary put it.

They set out from Dover on June 16th 2008. Four weeks later they were back again in Kent. They had travelled as far as Falmouth in Cornwall and had given up. Bad weather and technical problems with the boat had beaten them. It was not the most auspicious of starts.

Almost a year later, in the early morning of May 15th 2009 and with an air of *déjà vu*, the Hilary convoy of five vehicles assembled at Dover and headed for Devon, this time by road. In the intervening nine months, Hilary had decided to resume the attempt to navigate around the British Isles from the point at which they had stopped the previous August. The plans for the 3,000-mile journey were altered, arrangements were reviewed and confirmed. Hilary's surgeon, Christopher Chandler, was among the scores of well-wishers who sent her a message of good luck. Of the challenge, he said: "Just imagine being wrapped up like a mummy so that you can't use your arms and legs and all that is free is your head. And then you set out to sail a boat through some of the roughest and unpredictable seas in the world, unable to move. How remarkable is that?"

On May 21st at 4.30 am, Hilary was lifted into her yacht at Plymouth heading for Mylor.[287] Winds were light but what

---

287. See map, Appendix 5

had been calculated to be an eight- or nine-hour journey took 13 hours. Hilary's breathing gave cause for concern and, on arrival, she apologised to the hundreds waiting to welcome her and was taken straight for a hot shower, a meal and an early bed. She was well enough the next day to sail to Newlyn, where there was a campsite "with fantastic disabled facilities and grass in abundance, which Lottie (Hilary's brown Labrador dog) loves. We are about to discuss the weather for the long sail around Land's End...",[288] she reported.

Hilary kept a detailed blog of the 36 days' sailing on this unique voyage – detailed, that is, except for a single omission. There is no mention of the six times she collapsed during the three-month journey or of her visits to hospital for treatment and resuscitation. None of this surprised Christopher Chandler. He knew the syndrome from which Hilary was suffering was destroying her body and that, combined with the drugs she had to take because of her intense, intractable pain, she might suddenly stop breathing. This twice led to her being rushed to hospital in Ireland, the ambulance once arriving during the dockside ceremony to welcome her on her arrival.

But, for Hilary, there was joy amid the pain. "Sailing is freedom. It's me alive. Just one wave at a time. Where am I going? Are my sails set right? Where are the winds coming from? Where is the next wave? I'm talking about being independent in my life and that's something that is new, completely new."

On the way to Ardglass, Hilary found herself in the middle of a family of whales. Playfully, they acknowledged her presence and swam beneath Artemis. This could have been awkward. Hilary said: "It was just a great sound. Suddenly, I saw a blowhole and a spray of water and then

---

288. Hilary's blog of the journey

there was this animal out of the water – the whole, complete whale. We counted maybe up to five individuals. Obviously a family pod. We think they were fin whales, but we're not sure. They're not often in the Irish Sea – we were so lucky. It was fantastic."

But bad weather again and Hilary's illnesses were pushing the project behind schedule. The equipment, too, was feeling the strain under the weight of expectation. Her vessel, Artemis was, after all, designed more for sprints than marathons and, after crossing the Irish Sea, the engine of the RIB, the rescue dinghy and Hilary's lifeline, developed a fault during the Portpatrick to Troon leg. The engine would cost £8,000 to replace. It would be difficult for the charity, the Hilary Lister Dream Trust, to find £8,000. There were important decisions to be made: to try to repair the engine and delay further, or to replace it? The mechanics and the crew – all male – discussed the options and Hilary was not part of the discussions. She was less than pleased and Toby and Paul were made aware of this. Hilary said:

"This is *my* RIB, *my* project, *my* money. *My* work over two years. At least involve me."

Toby: "But we're trying to get it sorted out…"

Hilary: "You cannot take the engine out and ship it off before you know what's wrong with it. If it's just bearings, you can fix it on site, perhaps."

Toby: "I'm sorry. I'm trying to do my job. I'm trying to get this sorted."

Hilary: "But you can't actually make a decision about anything without *me*."

Toby: "I haven't made a decision about anything. I'm trying to find out what we can do."

Paul slipped into the role of referee. He told Hilary:

"Honestly, everyone is pulling out so many stops to try and get this... this done. You're being really negative. The guys here are brilliant. They are absolutely fantastic. They will do the job without any–"

Hilary: "Okay, I'll go back to my box!" Later, she explains: "Because it's been my baby for such a long time, it's very hard to let go and let other people make decisions. And the hardest part really was that, because I wasn't part of the conversations, I was getting fragments of information rather than the whole picture. The frustration is off the scale. Yeah, it's off the scale. It's one of the penalties of disability that you can't move yourself to the place where you actually need to be. That's why sailing is such a freedom because in a boat I can move myself to wherever I want to be."

The engine was replaced.

At Stonehaven in Scotland, on July 28th and well into the journey, she had what she described as one of her 'bad days'. She is caught in a storm. The voyage is hard work. Hilary is in her tiny boat for 9 hours. She has to be towed into harbour.

"We sailed through some really wet weather and some of the towing is quite bumpy. By the time I got here, I was pretty uncomfortable. I had to take an extra 100 mgs of morphine. My body started to have muscle spasms where things had got cramped or bashed and eventually my body started to go into shock."

Hilary is cold, wet and tired. They have to haul her bodily up the steep, slippery quayside steps. As in all the 46 ports at which she calls, there is a crowd of hundreds, waiting to greet her. She grumbles to her carer, Jo: "Whose stupid bloody idea was it to try and get me up steps? Just listen... don't let's *ever* do that again! Right, sit me up, because I've got to be nice to people now."

She is exhausted. The next day, she is still recovering:

"So, it was a pretty horrible evening and the worry was that all the morphine would stop me breathing and you can't just roll up to an A&E and say, 'I'd like some morphine, please'. They tend to think you're an addict, especially if you're white and shivering. Today, I'm still in quite a lot of pain but I'm just maintaining it. Self-medicating, as usual. Just taking a bit more. If I'm a bit spaced out, that's why." Her speech is slow and slightly slurred. For 20 years her life has been a constant battle against pain. Christopher Chandler remembers the moment when, before the last operation to insert a pain-controlling stimulator in her spine, she requested a 'Do not resuscitate' sign on her bed. "If I stop breathing for any reason, it's just my body saying, 'OK, I've had enough, mate.'"

She still feels that way. Each time Hilary collapses, she has made Toby promise he will tell the ambulance men and the doctors that she does *not* wish to be resuscitated.

They rest and recover for four days at Stonehaven and then make for Arbroath. Hilary is still very tired. She and Toby take a one-night break so that she can sleep in a proper bed with an *en suite* bathroom. At two o'clock in the morning, there's a fire in the hotel kitchens and severe damage to the flat above. The smoke and fire alarms had awakened Toby. He said:

"I got dressed, I got Hilary dressed quickly and into the chair and pushed her down the corridor."

Hilary: "The kitchen vent was just absolutely pouring smoke."

Toby: "There was a lift and I did actually open the door of the lift."

Hilary: "And I was saying, 'We can't use the lift, we can't use it!' Anyway, we opened the lift doors, smoke was pouring out."

Toby: "Luckily, the lift is right by the stairs."

Hilary: "I said, 'Leave me here. You've got to leave me. You've got to.' The protocol is you leave someone in a wheelchair at the top of the stairs in a fire because carrying them down causes danger for too many other people. But Toby wasn't going to leave me."

Toby: "Someone else had come out of their room and they kindly carried Hilary's chair down."

Hilary: "So, that'll teach me for trying to take a day off."

There is one other aspect not recorded in Hilary Lister's log of this journey. She is in love with Toby May.

* * *

Coincidentally, the subject of love had characterised a conversation I had with Hilary's husband, Clifford, in the week before the expedition began. In the previous six years, sailing had become increasingly important to Hilary until, now, it dominated her entire thinking. Husband Clifford reflected on the change in their lives. "There's 'before sailing' and 'after sailing' in our relationship. In the early years of our marriage, we shared a love of music and she was full of zest and life and ambition. I didn't know her when she could walk unaided, remember, and the wheelchair seemed to have very little significance."

But the deterioration in Hilary's health was rapid. "As she lost the use of her arms she couldn't any longer play the clarinet. That was devastating for her.[289] Hard as she tried, she became increasingly frustrated and depressed. We discussed it but Hilary is Hilary and her ability to bounce back is phenomenal. You have to realise that she takes an enormous quantity of morphine and all these other drugs every day and sometimes she must have felt depressed. But I didn't actually know that until I read it on a doctor's report because she doesn't want me always to know how low she's feeling. There have been times when she would gladly have taken too many tablets and not woken up. People come in and say, 'Oh, isn't it lovely, you're so lucky to live in such a nice place', but actually, when you're stuck in that place and you can't move until the next carer comes, you are in prison, however beautiful a place it is. I know she has felt that because, if she is unable to reach her tablets and therefore commit suicide, she's a real prisoner.

"Because I love her, I began to feel helpless. There was nothing I could do."

Over the years, Clifford has come to admire her ability as an organiser. "If she'd been on *The Apprentice*[290] nowadays she would have been a brilliant team leader because she just sees what everybody's strengths are and she plays to those strengths."

And he must admire her bravery.

"Brave..? Did you say, foolhardy? I thought you did. [He laughs]. Yes, I mean in the terms of what she's doing now, I mean completely mad. But yes, 'Isn't she brave, your wife?' No, she's foolish but it's what she loves doing."

The irony of the situation is not lost on Clifford Lister. Sailing has lifted Hilary from the couch in her bungalow

---

289. Hilary confirmed that her clarinet was "a sort of freedom. When I got mad, that is where I went. When I was happy, that's where I went. I miss it terribly. I can't listen to clarinet music now", conversation with author
290. A BBC television programme seeking natural leaders

in Dunkirk and given her a new and special freedom. At the same time, sailing is taking her away from him. He considered: "But Hilary deserves the chance. I'm no good at sailing but she has her friends who are. She would be so unhappy if she couldn't sail and, goodness knows, she's had enough pain and misery in her life. If it's anything to do with sailing, I say, 'Go and do it – you *must* do it.'"

I remember pointing out that he could lose her in the process: "If that's the price, I would be happy to be a loser. Why should I clip her wings? I can't do that."

There are many definitions of love but surely this must be one of them.

Two months later, in Arbroath, Hilary is as ill as at any time in the voyage. She has just survived the fire in the hotel in which they are staying and she will rest for four days before going back to the sea. The voyage is more than a week behind schedule. She is on the homeward leg of her journey. She says: "Part of me never wants the voyage to finish because this is living. I don't even want to consider going home at the moment. I don't see it. Don't look at it, don't think about it. I don't want to be trapped again." I remind her that her husband, Clifford, had described it as a prison for her. "It is. Yeah. He knows that. (Pause). You know, that's an incredible thing for him to have said…"

On the quayside at Arbroath, Toby May is taking a break. I say that Hilary is not really thinking about going home again. He says: "I can understand that. If there is another, different project, she'll be sailing away from her life in Dunkirk, as you say." I ask if he will remain part of that project. "That's up to Hilary. That's her choice."

Toby May sees his job as a jigsaw with two pieces; one, to keep the project moving by judging wind and weather and two, deciding every morning whether Hilary is fit enough to survive the day's demands. The second requirement is the most difficult. I told him I noticed that he looked 'deep into her eyes'.

"It's the only way that I've worked out to tell how she's really feeling. Hilary is petite, blonde and vulnerable. You kind of get dragged into that world and I am very keen for Hilary to do what she wants to do because I think it is a worthwhile thing to do."

What do you feel for her?

"I can't answer that question."

Too deep?

"Yup, too deep."

I ask Hilary later whether she and Toby ever had doubts, ever considered whether it was still possible for them to complete this voyage. She said: "Yes. We did last night. And the answer is yes because we have to. This is why we're doing it. You know, this is as much about the battle against my disease as anything else."

But Toby obviously loves you and you can understand his concerns.

"Yes, and I love him very much as well and I fear for him because actually waking up with someone who's died in the night or, worse, died on the water, is horrific. But the alternative is to let me rot for the rest of my life."

* * *

It takes another three weeks to sail down the east coast of England. Amble to Scarborough, Bridlington to Grimsby, Wells to Lowestoft and on to Harwich where she is greeted by the skirl of bagpipes and a full military band. Then back to Kent where, at Ramsgate, she rests for two days after a long sail in high winds. On August 31st, she is hoisted into Arty for the last time for the final leg to Dover. She says: "It's just another sail." But it isn't. Later: "It's hard, this last one. I don't really want to get out of Arty. Ever."

She sails past the pier at Deal; the pubs on the shoreline are packed and the customers wave as the music from the jazz band floats across the water. Hilary dips her yacht towards the welcome. She is in control.

A flotilla of small vessels emerge to embrace her as she sails into the port of Dover. It is a triumphant return. Her mother says to me, over the din: "There's a glory here. There's a magnificence that supersedes all the pain and the grief. The disease will take its inevitable course but the glory ... that's the human spirit, isn't it? The hope, the knowledge that you are able to overcome the things you can't control." She is in tears. Hilary has travelled 3,000 miles in three months – solo. Once ashore she is wheeled through the welcoming crowd and suddenly there is Clifford. She stops. Amid the din, she mouths a single word to him:

'Thankyou'.

* * *

Hilary Lister was one of the most remarkable of human beings. From a professional point of view, making this film was, also for me, a significant experience. The facts speak for themselves. We started researching this film in 2008. In 2009, we took the idea of filming Hilary's epic journey to the BBC. The BBC liked the idea and gave us £5,000 development money. Hilary sailed around Britain between June and September in that year. Yet, the film was not transmitted on BBC until 2013. Question: So, why did it take four years to get her story on the air? Answer: Because that's how long the negotiations with the BBC lasted.[291]

---

291. This was noted by the television magazine Broadcast; my article which appeared in the July 2013 edition is reproduced with their permission in Appendix 6

First, just as Hilary was about to set sail, the BBC decided they no longer wanted the programme. Among the reasons: Hilary wasn't a big enough character for BBC1. And she might die during the voyage.

I remember pointing out that neither was a good reason for *not* making the film.

Now a situation such as this leaves the independent producer with a profound dilemma: to go, or not to go. How much confidence do you have in your idea – and, in this case, how damaging to the project and to the people involved in the project would it be to withdraw at one minute to midnight?

We decided to fund the filming ourselves and bought a campervan. We embedded into Hilary's team. Hilary's journey took three months and three cameramen – George Pellett, Malcolm Berry and Justin Ingham – each filmed for a month.

As a company, we funded the film ourselves (around £60,000) because we believed in the example Hilary was setting: work hard and you'll win through.

We kept the BBC aware of Hilary's (and our) progress but, despite months of negotiation, there was still no commission. So, we edited her story into a feature-length film that was previewed at the Marlowe Theatre in Canterbury and was then released in other cinemas. I sent a DVD to Charlotte Moore, then BBC commissioning editor for documentaries, who was kind enough to describe it as "a remarkable and beautifully made film" and BBC2 controller, Janice Hadlow, couldn't have been more supportive.[292] The BBC decided it would now take it as an acquisition at nowhere near its true cost. More than that, our 75-minute film would be edited down to just 59 minutes with the aid of an edit-producer.

Over some months we had negotiated with composer

---

292. The original film, A Race Against Time, is available from Peter Williams Television (peter@pwtv.co.uk). It contains the Karl Jenkins score

Karl Jenkins, to use his magnificent and inspirational piece, *The Armed Man*, as our soundtrack. This was removed from the film as being "too sentimental". Within two months of transmission, *The Armed Man* was top of the pops on Classic FM.[293]

The role of an 'edit-producer' was one that was new to me. The edit-producer is not involved in any way in the original production of the film. His job is simply to cut and mould the completed film into what his immediate bosses want. When creating a film, the relationship between film-maker and subject is crucial, particularly when a vulnerable and courageous woman is putting her life on the line. Understandably, the edit-producer cannot be part of that, nor can he or she give the appropriate weight to the views and reasons for decisions made far from his kingdom in the cutting room. I would not wish to be an edit-producer.

The shortened programme was well reviewed but it was not the film we made. The experience persuaded me that, at this stage of a 50-year career, I preferred to make films for cinema release rather than primarily for television. I was secure enough financially to make that choice. The past 10 years have done nothing to alter that view as, too frequently, I see those controlling our viewing, reaching for the lowest common denominator, where the sensational or salacious is justified as being in the public interest.

Like many others, I have lived to tell stories, to make films which we hope add to the sum of human knowledge and experience. It's never been about the accumulation of money. The financial risk involved in the decision to go ahead when the BBC decided *not* to support the film telling Hilary's story was difficult, but not novel. As an independent producer, I

---

293. Hilary watched the shortened film and, as a musician, hated the removal of Karl Jenkins' music The Armed Man

recall that it was necessary to fund our first production by offering our house as a guarantee in order to get a bank loan. Over the years I often wondered how many of those in authority, sitting behind desks in comfortable offices, had shared this entrepreneurial, personal, risk-taking experience. And, if they had, how many had forgotten it.

Decisions taken in BBC White City or Horseferry Road[294] often have profound effects on the people who are the subjects of our stories. The contract with them and, therefore, the allied responsibility, always lies with the independent producer. Yet, too often, the power to carry through that responsibility is not in their hands.

We called the film on Hilary, *A Race Against Time*.[295] Looking back, that title chimes with my own experience and that of many other film-makers. Unlike time, ideas are not predictable. They tumble out; there is an optimum moment when action is needed from a broadcaster. Failure to do so can be damaging and cavalier. I was never happier professionally than when making 14 documentaries in a single year for ITV's *This Week* on subjects which, in the team's judgment, really mattered. There is so much to say and *This Week* had a weekly canvas on which to say it. Being given the privileged access to tell stories to millions, is what makes journalism a vocation rather than a career. It is about vision and determination to remain focused on the original objective, even when circumstances change.

Looking back at this experience, the BBC and I at least agree on the most important aspect of this four-year exercise in negotiation: the film got made and Hilary's remarkable achievement is now on the record.

It would have been a travesty had it been otherwise.

---

294. London headquarters of Channel 4
295. A DVD of the original 75-minute film with Karl Jenkins' music, is available. (Contact: peter@pwtv.co.uk)

Chapter 12

POWER – and PRIME MINISTERS

Locating a seat of power can be a struggle. Forecasting with whom the power actually lies can be even more difficult. Take Number 10 Downing Street, for instance.

Behind the shiny black door, the Prime Minister's home is considerably smaller and more compact than you would imagine. A curving, richly-carpeted staircase rises from the entrance hall to the upper rooms and the golden walls bear the portraits of every British Prime Minister, from the Whig Sir Robert Walpole, who led the nation from 1730 until 1742, to David Cameron, Theresa May and Boris Johnson. It is a historic record of continuity and power for every visitor to No 10 to see and to note:

There is no acknowledgement of those close to the Prime Ministers, those who over the years have profoundly influenced their decisions, the Svengalis to their Trilbys.

In Canterbury Cathedral, the portrait of every Dean adorns the rooms and corridors of the Deanery. Every *Dean*, let it be noted, not every Archbishop, because Canterbury Cathedral is the Dean's domain and every portrait is a reminder of who, in the daily life of the mother church of the worldwide Anglican Communion, actually takes the decisions. Relationships in the corridors of power are important. The current Dean, Robert Willis, sees his job in the disturbed politics of the Anglican Church as supporting his primate, the Archbishop, and making his term in office as easy as possible. In centuries past, however, the relationship hasn't always been this amicable. Dean Hewlett-Johnson (1931–63), nicknamed The Red Dean, became a Communist and entertained a number of Soviet leaders in the Precincts. He served three Archbishops, Cosmo Lang, William Temple and Geoffrey Fisher, and Fisher described him as "blind, unreasonable and stupid".

In the beginning, the Dean of Canterbury was a politician first and a cleric second.[296] Nicholas Wotton (1541–67) was simultaneously Dean and the nation's Home Secretary. King Henry VIII admired and trusted him sufficiently to ask him to negotiate his marriage to Anne of Cleves. Later, Wotton also had the task of informing Queen Anne that Henry had tired of her company. The nation's leading clerics no longer have the status nor the influence they wielded centuries ago. We remember the bloody martyrdom of Archbishop Thomas Becket, by King Henry II's barons in Canterbury Cathedral, following a deep political disagreement with the King over the relationship between church and state. We can reflect that an archbishop's view today will still be carefully considered both by the monarch and by the occupant of No 10 – but, though important, because the church's influence has waned, his view will be just that: another opinion to be considered.

If history teaches us anything, it is that centres of power change. Cromwell prised power from the monarchy and in championing Parliament, tried to give it to the people. It was described as "democracy". The British model of democracy in which the clergy, the nobility and the commoners shared power, travelled around the world and crossed the Atlantic, where the Americans created a Presidential version under which a single man was both political leader and commander in chief of the nation and its armed forces.

---

296. Dean Nicholas Wotton was also the only Dean of Canterbury to be the Dean of York at the same time

A 'fourth estate' was added to the model of democracy, embracing the press who, with varying degrees of independence, stood outside the political process of decision-making and judged, encouraged or discouraged the work and methods of elected politicians. This is a delicate relationship[297] even in nations where democracy is a seminal part of their traditional beliefs. Only by retaining a basic independence from each other can press and politician contribute fully to a healthy democracy. When flawed US President Trump was portrayed as Captain America by Fox News, democracy is threatened. When totalitarian regimes, China, Myanmar, persecute their minority populations under a blanket of media denial, democracy dies. When press barons become too powerful, the intimacy between press and politician may also threaten the balance of democracy. Rupert Murdoch assembled a collection of newspaper titles worldwide and flaunted the power of his Sky Television, making his support plainly attractive to any politician. In the run-up to the British General Election in 1997, Murdoch owned *The Sun*, the *News of the World*, *The Times* and the *Sunday Times*, in addition to Sky Television. His was a powerful voice – more powerful even than Beaverbrook's *Daily Express* and Rothermere's *Daily Mail* had been in the salad days of Fleet Street in the 1930s and 40s. Any political party who had the ear and support of Rupert Murdoch would have a clear advantage in any General Election...

* * *

It is in wartime or during a threat of conflict that the relationship between government and media is at its most strained. So it proved in the summer of 2003 when, at seven

---

297. See also Chapter 6

minutes past six on May 29ᵗʰ on the *Today* programme on BBC Radio 4, Andrew Gilligan filed a report that examined the evidence that was driving Britain into a war with Iraq. It was broadcast at a particularly sensitive time in the relationship between the BBC and the New Labour Government of Tony Blair, because the country was almost evenly split between those who opposed the war as an example of post-colonial interference in the affairs of another country and those who believed that British troops and citizens were threatened by assertions that Iraq had weapons of mass destruction (WMD). The facts, even the different versions of the facts, are well-known. They bear re-examination because they illustrate a trend in the way Britain is governed and power is brokered and there are historic lessons, reaching as far back as Becket's martyrdom that are relevant to the situation we face as a nation today. These facts, then, are beyond dispute.

On January 29ᵗʰ 2002, US President George W Bush in his State of the Union address, identified Iraq, with Iran and North Korea, as part of an 'axis of evil'.

On September 12ᵗʰ 2002, President Bush warned Iraq at the UN that military action would be unavoidable if Iraq did not comply with UN resolutions on disarmament.

On September 24ᵗʰ 2002, the UK Government published a dossier warning that Iraq's Saddam Hussein had weapons of mass destruction, both nuclear and biological, capable of being deployed within 45 minutes.

On November 8ᵗʰ 2002, the UN unanimously passed the Security Council Resolution 1441, giving Iraq a 'final opportunity' to disarm and warning of 'serious consequences' if it did not.

In the next four months, UN inspectors on the ground in Iraq, failed to find weapons of mass destruction.

In February 2003, the UK Government published a second dossier setting out the arguments for going to war with Iraq. This was the so-called "dodgy" dossier, which was subsequently revealed to have been based on a student thesis on Iraq that had then been embellished by Downing Street.

On February 15th 2003, hundreds of thousands of people marched through London opposing military action in Iraq.

On March 10th 2003, Russia and France declared they would veto a UN Security Council resolution which would have given Iraq seven days to disarm.

On March 17th 2003, the UK, the US and Spain abandoned an attempt to gain a UN resolution to validate the use of force against Iraq. President Bush gave Saddam Hussein and his sons 48 hours to leave Iraq or face war.

Throughout the months leading up to the war, Rupert Murdoch's limousine was often seen parked outside No 10 Downing Street. All the Murdoch newspapers headlined Prime Minister Tony Blair's argument for going to war and his claim that British citizens were at risk from Saddam Hussein's WMD. *The Sun* and *The Times* repeatedly made the case for military action. *The Sun* was the most outspoken, leaving no doubt in its readers' minds that WMD existed and giving no space to anyone who held a contrary view.

In March 2003, *The Sun* baldly stated: 'Saddam has stockpiled weapons of mass destruction, and he's not going to give them up'. Columnist Richard Littlejohn wrote: 'Don't kid yourself. There's going to be war in Iraq unless Saddam Hussein hands over his weapons of mass destruction. He's got them. We know he's got them. He knows we know he's got them.' As we now know, he had none.

So, where did the seat of power lie during those perilous weeks? Finally, of course, with the Prime Minister. But how effective would that power have been without the baying of the Murdoch papers in Blair's support? The fact is that Blair's cosy relationship with the Murdochs, both personal and political, openly undermined the traditional separation between Fleet Street and Downing Street and made it easier for the British Government to pursue the policies and the intended course of action that Blair had long planned and discussed with US President Bush.

On March 18th, despite the rebellion of 139 of his own Labour MPs, Prime Minister Blair won a majority in the House of Commons to send UK forces into Iraq, beside the US forces.

On March 20th 2003, the war began, with a bombing raid described as a campaign of 'shock and awe'.

By April 9th 2003, US forces had captured Iraq's capital, Baghdad.

On May 1st 2003, President Bush appeared on an aircraft carrier off the coast of California to declare victory in the Iraq War. The battle with the BBC intensified.

* * *

The trigger which brought the media and, in particular, the BBC into a head-on dispute with Tony Blair's Government, was the broadcast by Gilligan on May 29th that cast doubt on the veracity of the Government's dossiers and, therefore, its justification for going to war. Just as disturbing, it set in train a series of events that challenged Britain's claim to champion freedom of speech and it emphasised a trend towards a more presidential approach that had begun under Blair's predecessor, Margaret Thatcher. Thatcher patronised her colleagues as well as her opponents in her decision-making on the way to her declared objectives. Blair, however, with his chief advisor, Alastair Campbell, misread or distorted the intelligence picture he was being given and went to war, fulfilling the promise he had made in 2002 to his US ally, George W Bush. Blair and Campbell had complained to the BBC throughout the weeks leading up to the Iraq War and during the war itself, that its coverage had been biased against the UK Government and, on March 19th 2003, the Prime Minister had written to Greg Dyke, who had been the BBC's Director General since 2000, saying:

'I believe, and I am not alone in believing, that you have not got the balance right between support and dissent; between news and comment; between the voices of the Iraqi regime and the voices of Iraqi dissidents; or between the diplomatic support we have, and diplomatic opposition.'

Blair went on to say that he had never before written to a Director General in this manner.

On March 21st, Dyke replied that for the Prime Minister to question the whole of the BBC's output because he disagreed with some stories that did not favour his views, was unfair. He went on:

'Firstly, and I do not mean to be rude, but having faced the biggest ever public demonstration in this country and the biggest ever backbench rebellion against a sitting government by its own supporters, would you not agree that your communications advisors are not best placed to advise whether or not the BBC has got the balance right between support and dissent? Given these circumstances, they are hardly in a position to make a reasoned judgment about the BBC's impartiality.

'You have been engaged in a difficult battle fighting for your particular view of the world to be accepted and, quite understandably, you want that to be reported. We, however, have a different role in society. Our role in these circumstances is to try to give a balanced picture.'

Some weeks earlier, before the Iraq War broke out, John Simpson, the BBC's respected World Affairs Editor, had written:

'At the times of Suez, Biafra, Vietnam, the Falklands, the American bombing of Libya and the NATO attacks on

Kosovo and Serbia, the BBC reported the opposition to these wars fully. On every occasion the government – Labour or Conservative – tried to bully the BBC into supporting the official line. On every occasion the BBC resisted; sometimes not as energetically as it ought to have done...

'Governments have as much right as anyone to put pressure on the BBC; it is only a problem if the BBC caves in.'

It rapidly became apparent that this Director General was not going to cave in. After the war, Dyke reflected that "Britain's Iraq policy was disastrous for Blair, for the Labour Party and for Britain's reputation in the entire world, other than in the United States".[298]

Gilligan's broadcast, which became the flashpoint of the dispute, was based on a meeting he had had in May 2003 with Dr David Kelly, a 59-year-old former senior UN weapons inspector, an international expert on chemical and biological warfare and a government advisor. Kelly had confirmed to Gilligan that the intelligence community was perturbed that the 'dodgy' dossier had been made more dramatic by Downing Street. Gilligan's notes on his meeting record that Kelly had said that the dossier "was transformed in the week before it was published, to make it sexier". The intelligence community, said Kelly, had challenged Alastair Campbell on its contents. Gilligan also knew that Labour Minister Robin Cook, in his resignation speech to the House of Commons in March 2003, had told Blair that they did not believe that Iraq had WMD. Given Kelly's status, plus the fact that he had worked with him and had known him as a reliable source in the past, Gilligan accepted that the intelligence had been tampered with and he presented his report to the BBC. It went through a lengthy process of questioning and verification

298. Inside Story, Greg Dyke, Harper Collins, 2004, p254

within the BBC. It was then broadcast – but only as a second item on the *Today* coverage of Iraq. It gave precedence to a report about cluster bombs.

Two days after the broadcast, a four-page letter of complaint arrived from Alastair Campbell. It challenged the truth of Gilligan's broadcast and accused the BBC of 'breaking the BBC's own guidelines',[299] in using a single (and then still anonymous) source for the allegations. On June 9th, Clare Short, who would later resign from the Blair Government, wrote in the *New Statesman*: 'My conclusion is that our Prime Minister deceived us … He exaggerated the imminent threat from WMDs.'[300] The leader of the Conservative Party, Ian Duncan Smith, weighed in with: "My concern is the way this (dossier) was twisted and fiddled and spun by people like Alastair Campbell." Campbell was due to give evidence to the Commons' Foreign Affairs Select Committee on June 25th. Two days before that, Labour's Foreign Secretary, Jack Straw, in evidence, described the February dossier as "a complete Horlicks". The media forecast that Campbell was in for a roasting; *The Mail on Sunday* said that he was 'on the brink of resignation'.

On June 25th, Campbell made his appearance before the Commons' Select Committee and gave an extraordinary performance. He launched an all-out attack on the BBC. It was, he said, broadcasting lies. It was running an anti-war agenda. He admitted his involvement with the dossier and avoided further questions that were critical of his behaviour. An article in *The Scotsman* best summed up his evidence:

'Mr Campbell did exactly what he wanted to do. He blunted the attack immediately by putting his hands up for the dodgy dossier and then used the remaining three hours to perform

299. The BBC refuted this allegation
300. WMD – Weapons of mass destruction

the oldest trick in the spin doctor's manual: distract attention from the government's shortcomings by feeding the media with an alternative story.'

Forcefully, Campbell personalised his criticism of the BBC; it had accused the Prime Minister of lying, he said.[301] He claimed that criticising No 10 *or* the Government was a personal and direct attack on Prime Minister Blair's veracity. Tabloid headlines the next day asserted 'Campbell: the BBC are Liars'. By this time, Campbell's behaviour, by his own admission, was loud and very personal. He went on to berate the BBC in a live interview on *Channel 4 News*. He did so with the knowledge of Tony Blair. Gavyn Davies, the BBC's chairman, told the Prime Minister that he thought Campbell's behaviour in his pursuit of the BBC and Andrew Gilligan[302] was "over the top". Blair allegedly replied, "Don't we all?"

The BBC were to discover a corroborative source for Gilligan's broadcast on their own staff. Susan Watts, it would emerge, had been briefed by Dr Kelly before he had spoken to Gilligan. Watts had not filed the story for *Newsnight* – but as the dispute escalated she supported the substance of the information as Gilligan had reported it, although initially she refused to reveal Kelly as her informant.

Early in July, despite public attempts both by the Prime Minister and by Lord (Peter) Mandelson to calm the whole toxic affair, Alastair Campbell's diary indicates[303] that at the same time he was having conversations with Defence Secretary Geoff Hoon in which he (they) had agreed that the name of Dr David Kelly – who was, up to this moment, still

---

301. The BBC refuted this allegation: "The Board wishes to place on record that the BBC has never accused the Prime Minister of lying ... The BBC did not have an agenda in its war coverage"
302. "I want to wreak vengeance on that little shit, Gilligan," Alastair Campbell, quoted by Peter Oborne and Simon Walters
303. Ibid, Inside Story, p279

an anonymous source of the BBC's broadcast – should be leaked both to the press and to the public and that this would "fuck Gilligan". The naming of Dr Kelly was approved at a meeting at No 10, allegedly chaired by the Prime Minister. The BBC still refused to name Kelly. Campbell's reaction was famously colourful. He had a long vendetta against "gullible Gilligan"[304] dating from a disagreement over Europe in 2000 and exacerbated by the tone of Gilligan's reports from Baghdad.

Tony Blair saw Campbell as "a genius".[305] He had coined the phrase 'New Labour' and, as Blair's press officer and, later, Head of Communications, he had masterminded Blair's election victory in 1997. He was nicknamed 'the deputy Prime Minister' and occupied a major strategic role in the Blair Government's decisions. Now that the row over the Iraq War had become as personal as it was political, Campbell pursued his objective to "fuck Gilligan" and oversaw an original method of ensuring that the national press would be aware that Dr David Kelly was indeed the BBC's anonymous source. Over the next few days the Ministry of Defence and the Downing Street press office "jumped through all sorts of hoops"[306] to make sure Kelly's name became known, including the "farcical stunt" of allowing journalists to suggest name after name until finally they hit on the right one, which the Ministry of Defence then confirmed.

Once Kelly had been named, the Commons' Foreign Affairs Select Committee wished to interview him. Kelly insisted he was not Gilligan's source, which was untrue. Kelly enjoyed neither the experience nor the limelight now concentrated on him. As the BBC and the Government did battle, the pressure on the individuals involved grew.

---

304. Inside Story, p270
305. Tony Blair, A Journey, Random House, 2010
306. Inside Story, Ibid, p279

On July 18th 2003, two days after giving his testimony, Dr David Kelly was found dead in a field in Oxfordshire. The BBC's Susan Watts was shocked and she now confirmed to Dyke and the BBC that Kelly had indeed been her source; she had interviewed him on May 7th. In the week after Dr Kelly died, the tape recording of her interview with Kelly was played for the first time to a small BBC group of executives. Dyke recalls, after hearing Kelly's recorded interview:[307]

"Here was Dr Kelly naming Alastair Campbell, talking about Number Ten being 'desperate for information' to put into the dossier and about the 45-minute claim being a statement 'that just got out of all proportion' and about which he was 'uneasy'; he also said that it was difficult to get certain views into the dossier 'because people at the top of the ladder didn't want to hear some of the things'. Talking of Iraq, Kelly said that his concern wasn't the weapons that Saddam had (at the moment) but what he might have in the future. He complained 'that wasn't expressed strongly enough in the dossier because that takes away the case for war to a certain extent'.

"It was remarkable stuff and showed very clearly that Dr Kelly hadn't told the truth either to the Ministry of Defence or to the Select Committee. Everyone in the room that day thought it massively strengthened the BBC's position and Gilligan's. It showed that Gilligan's story had been overwhelmingly true."

In January 2014, the Hutton Report into David Kelly's death cleared ministers of any wrongdoing and declared that Kelly had taken his own life. It heavily criticised the BBC. There were those who immediately disagreed, among them Norman Baker, MP for Lewes, who later declared he was "convinced beyond reasonable doubt that this (Kelly's

---

307. Inside Story, Ibid, p283

death) could not be suicide. The medical evidence does not support it". Kelly had swallowed painkillers and had several cuts to the ulnar artery in his left wrist. This is a relatively small and inaccessible artery. Retired surgeon, David Halpin, and a group of doctors publicly doubted if it was possible to bleed to death by cutting this small artery. If it were true, Dr Kelly was the only person in the UK to die in this way in the whole of 2003. Unusually, there was no inquest. The only certainty, then, was that a 59-year-old, much respected scientist who had spent half his life serving his country and who was preparing to return to Iraq, had blinked under the unforgiving spotlight of publicity and was now dead.

Six months later, the Butler Review was set up to inquire into the validity of the intelligence regarding Iraq's WMD, which played a key part in the Blair Government's decision to invade Iraq. It produced its findings on July 14th. It seriously undermined the Hutton Inquiry. Butler judged that the key intelligence used to justify the war was "unreliable". Information on Iraq's production of chemical and biological weapons was "seriously flawed". "More weight", said Butler, "was placed on the intelligence than it could bear".

It was a judgment that found favour with the bereaved family of Dr David Kelly. They issued a statement saying that too much emphasis and importance had been given to the 45-minute WMD threat posed by Saddam Hussein's forces, which echoed exactly what Kelly had himself said to the BBC.

But this vindication of the BBC's actions came six months too late to affect what had happened at Broadcasting House as a result of this struggle between government and media. In January 2004, the public reaction to the critical Hutton Inquiry had provoked a crisis in the BBC's top management. Within 36 hours of its appearance, the BBC Chairman Gavyn Davies, and its Director General Greg Dyke, had resigned. If at any time the BBC behaved like a chicken during this episode, it also chose to become headless. The irony is that, as the BBC collapsed before the Government's onslaught and Hutton's judgment, there are good reasons to believe that, if the resignations had been delayed, the outcome might have been different. For the public reaction to Hutton was generally supportive of the BBC. When Hutton published his report, Britain's newspapers and other television channels quickly described it as 'a whitewash' and a barely credible interpretation of the facts – a judgment that, as we now know, would be borne out by the Butler Review a few months later.

The major players in the three-day crisis at the BBC that followed the publication of the Hutton Inquiry were the Chairman Davies, the Director General Dyke and the Board of Governors. Davies believed that Hutton's verdict on the issue was so negative that, in the best interests of the BBC, at least one resignation was necessary. As he subsequently said of that first tense and distressing day:

"I was willing to resign in preference to apologising for doing nothing wrong, indeed, for telling the British people the truth about the dossier. I was never going to grovel but I am not sure that a strategy of 'no apology and no resignation' was ever viable after Hutton. Somebody had to go."

Dyke did not agree with that reading of the situation; better, he thought, to wait. If there were to be resignations, the Chairman, the Director General, the Governors and some senior news executives should all go together, as one, to indicate solidarity.[308] If Davies were to resign, Dyke declared that he would remain as Director General only if the Governors supported him.[309] By chance, there was a meeting of the BBC Board of Governors scheduled for the next day. Dyke urged a postponement to take the momentum out of

308. Ibid, Inside Story, p7
309. Ibid, p8

the dispute,[310] to avoid "rash decisions". But the meeting went ahead, starting at 5 pm. It finished in the early hours of the next morning. In that time:

- In the first 40 minutes, some of the Governors had felt that if Chairman Gavyn Davies were to resign, some of them should also resign with him
- Dyke had argued against this, because the BBC would have been left without an effective constitution
- Dyke had left the meeting when a discussion began on what measures might be taken involving his management team.
- Dyke had told the Secretary to the BBC Governors, Simon Milner, before he left that he would remain as Director General only if he had the support of the Governors, and
- Stephen Dando, the BBC's Director of Human Resources, had told the Board that getting rid of Dyke would be a "terrible blow to the staff and morale in the BBC".[311]

Once he had left the Governors' meeting, Greg Dyke went to his office. He sat there for about an hour and a half. Then, Simon Milner came in and told him that two Governors wished to see him, deputy chairman Richard Ryder and Pauline Neville Jones. Greg Dyke remembers: "Ryder was pretty blunt. He said the Governors had discussed the matter and that they had decided that I should go. Typically, Richard told me that he hadn't expressed a view but was reporting the views of the rest. Pauline said nothing.

"I was completely shocked. I had absolutely no idea what to say ... but I made it clear that if they didn't want me, I wouldn't stay. The whole thing took about five minutes."[312]

---

310. Ibid, p12
311. Ibid, p13
312. Ibid, pp14–5

Overnight, Dyke decided he would resign "but make it very clear that I had been given little option by a bunch of intransigent Governors".[313]

Why did he choose to resign?

"Looking back now, I am not sure I know. With the benefit of hindsight I think I should have stayed and dared them to fire me. But at the time I felt isolated. I also felt hurt and had a deep sense of injustice. I didn't believe that I had done anything to justify resignation, nor did I believe the BBC had done anything seriously wrong. What I *do* remember thinking was that if I *was* to go, I wanted to do so with some dignity."

One subject raised at the Governors' meeting rapidly came to pass. The BBC's head of Human Resources had forecast that getting rid of Dyke would be 'a terrible blow' to the staff. At the Television Centre in White City, hundreds of staff left their desks and took to the streets. Hurriedly crafted 'Bring back Greg' posters appeared and the demonstration stopped the traffic. In Cardiff, Glasgow, Belfast, Newcastle and Birmingham, BBC employees swept out of their buildings to protest the Governors' actions. That same night, the staff of the News and Current Affairs Departments clubbed together and collected money to pay for a full-page article in the *Daily Telegraph*. Under the heading 'The Independence of the BBC', it read:

'Greg Dyke stood for brave, independent and rigorous BBC journalism that was fearless in its search for the truth. We are resolute that the BBC should not step back from its determination to investigate the facts in pursuit of the truth.

'Through his passion and integrity, Greg inspired us to make programmes of the highest quality and creativity.

'We are dismayed by Greg's departure, but we are

---

313. Ibid, p19

determined to maintain his achievements and his vision for an independent organisation that serves the public above all else.'

The page included just some of the thousands of names of BBC staff who had paid for the advertisement – so much so, that they couldn't fit all the names on the page.

Greg Dyke said: "When I read it, it was the only time during the whole saga that I broke down and cried."

One of the supporters of that advertisement was my daughter, Claire Williams,[314] who had just started work as a producer at the BBC in Oxford Road, Manchester. On that Thursday afternoon she was preparing a Sunday show for Roger Bolton. She remembers it as "a profound shock. It was very emotional. We felt we *knew* Greg. Huge numbers of us took to the streets, carrying placards: 'Bring Back Greg'. Greg then spoke to the newsroom in Manchester. His words have always stuck with me: 'Don't let anyone pressure you into putting out stories, which aren't fair and true. You are the bedrock of the BBC'".

* * *

So ended one of the most shaming moments in the distinguished history of the BBC. They had bowed the knee to political pressure, to a government that had bullied them into submission. The comparison between the actions of No 10 and the dishonest way the Nixon White House behaved during Watergate is well drawn. Number 10, under Blair and with Campbell as its political genius, had enormous, almost presidential, power. The unwritten rule in Downing Street was: 'Either you're with us, or you're against us'. There was no middle way. It is a method recognised by dictators

---

314. Claire Williams is currently a programme Editor and Executive Producer at the BBC

and feared by democrats. It diminishes the value of debate and, in reaching for the twin tools of untruth and bullying, it encourages overreaching ambition and weak governance. As it was in 2003–4, so too, in 1170, when King Henry II in anger and frustration cried, "Will no-one rid me of this turbulent priest?" Four of his barons took him at his word and Archbishop Thomas Becket, his former friend, was beheaded. The King never overcame his anguish following the assassination. In 1174, he walked barefoot from London to Canterbury, holding his Bible[315] and near the spot where Becket had died, he asked the monks to whip him. It was the pressure of a four-year-long dispute with his old friend over the power wielded by the Church that led Henry to this uncharacteristic and disastrous outburst. Henry regretted his angry words – but his words had killed.

We live in a society where the extremes of language are freely used to wound. Social media is unaccountable, anger is commonplace and tolerance is conspicuous only by its absence. But after the anger is spent, how are the wounds to be healed? In dispute, there are always winners and losers. In a working democracy, how are the losers to be embraced, accommodated? Can a society properly function without empathy and mutual respect? There is a crying need for an increase in self-control and emotional intelligence[316] at every level of society. Greg Dyke's opinion of Alastair Campbell and his leading role in the BBC row is worth recording: "All governments, of whatever political colour, get upset with the media. They all claim that what they are doing is what they promised when elected and that their policy is the right one. If the public disagree, governments always blame the media, saying that the public doesn't understand this or that because

---

315. The King's Bible instructed him to 'bridle his tongue' which, in James 5, verse 6, is described as 'a fire … a restless evil full of deadly poison'
316. The Way of Benedict, Archbishop Rowan Williams, 2020

the media isn't reporting it properly. As a result, they all try to manipulate the media.

"It was just that Campbell took this to new extremes. Quite how such an obsessive man had become so powerful, is interesting. This was a man whom a judge had described in a court action in May 1996 as 'less than completely open and frank'. The judge further said (that) 'I did not find Mr Campbell by any means a wholly satisfactory or convincing witness'. And yet, until he resigned (in August 2003), he was in charge of all the government's information services, … one of the most important men in the Government."[317] The Prime Minister, added Dyke, was now "all-powerful".[318]

Today, we find in Britain an increasing number of major decisions being made with a decreasing contribution from the elected representatives in the House of Commons. Anxiety is heightened by the growth in the staff of the Cabinet Office, whose first loyalty is to No 10 Downing Street rather than to individual ministers. The importance of Britain's Civil Service, traditionally the scaffolding on which governance has assembled, is diminished. Prime Ministers instead surround themselves with appointed 'special advisers', SPADs for short, "political mayflies, who last on average less than two years in government".[319] In 2021, there were no fewer than 40 SPADs on Boris Johnson's staff in Downing Street.

Soon after Greg Dyke left the BBC, Prime Minister Tony Blair invited him for tea. The invitation was refused. Gavyn Davies and Greg Dyke left the BBC because they were criticised in the flawed Hutton Inquiry for allegedly failing to ensure that the BBC's editorial controls were sufficiently sound on a broadcast on the *Today* programme at 6.07 am on a May morning.

---

317. Ibid, p314
318. Ibid, p326
319. The Secret Lives of Special Advisers, Peter Cardwell, Biteback, 2020

It is now recognised that the broadcast by Andrew Gilligan was substantially correct.

As far as I know, neither Tony Blair nor Alastair Campbell has apologised to Greg Dyke nor to Gavyn Davies. Nor to the BBC which, despite arguments about the licence fee and political bias, remains a valued and unique piece in the jigsaw that is Britain's democratic society.

Chapter 13

IN HIS FATHER'S WAKE:
Donald Campbell: The Last 48 Hours

Heritage has a lot to answer for. The Romans put it this way: *Qualis pater, talis filius*, which literally means 'As the father, so the son'. Nowhere is the English proverb 'Like father, like son' more appropriate than in the Campbell family, Malcolm and son Donald who, in the 20th century, dominated British attempts to drive faster on land and water than anyone else in the world.

Malcolm Campbell set the family tradition. On land, he broke the speed record for the first time in 1924 at 146.16 mph (232.22 km/h) at Pendine Sands near Carmarthen Bay in Wales in a 350HP V12 Sunbeam. He broke nine land speed records between 1924 and 1935, three at Pendine Sands and five at Daytona Beach, Florida in the USA.

He named his car Blue Bird after spending an afternoon in the theatre watching a children's fantasy by the Belgian Nobel Prizewinner, Maurice Maeterlinck, which was called The Blue Bird. Prophetically, it was about the pursuit of happiness.[320]

On the water, Malcolm Campbell developed and tested his Blue Bird speedboat on Tilgate Lake in Crawley, West Sussex. He set the world water speed record four times; his highest speed being 141.740 mph (228.108 km/h) on August 19th

---

320. Malcolm Campbell's boats and cars carried the name Blue Bird, separate words that echoed the play's title. His son Donald combined the words into a single 'Bluebird'

1939, in the Blue Bird K4 on Coniston Water, in England's Lake District.

Twenty-eight years later, it was also on Coniston Water that his son, Donald, would make a fateful attempt to regain the world water speed record for Britain. Between 1955 and 1964, Donald Campbell had picked up the baton left by his father and had broken eight world speed records, seven of them on water. He had travelled ever faster, 202.32 mph (352.60 kph) in July 1955 and 276.33 mph (444.71 kph) on the last day of December 1964.

He thus became the first man to hold, in the same year, the world speed record on both land and water as, on July 17th that year, he had driven Bluebird CN7 at 403.10 mph (648.73 kph) on the salt flats at Lake Eyre in Australia. But even this moment of triumph was tinged with dissatisfaction and it seemed written in the stars that the son's pursuit of his father's meteoric career would end in tragedy.

It was on January 4th 1967 on Coniston Water, that Donald Campbell would die.[321] To spend the last week of his life with a man hellbent on achieving his ambition, while knowing that both mechanical and financial odds were stacked against him, is a profound experience. The facts of Donald Campbell's final record attempt are on the record.[322] Campbell had developed his own all-metal jet-powered hydroplane Bluebird K7 in 1953/4; it was powered by a Metropolitan-Vickers Beryl turbo-jet engine and it scudded across the water balanced on three planing points. It was revolutionary in design and was the world's only successful jet-boat for more than a decade. To attempt the record in 1966, Bluebird K7 was fitted with new propulsion, a lighter and more powerful Bristol Orpheus

---

321. Donald Campbell: The Last 48 Hours was transmitted as a This Week special on ITV on January 4th 1967
322. A number of well-written books document Campbell's life and difficulties in that year (see Bibliography)

jet engine, which was taken from a Folland Gnat aircraft. But, 13 years after she had been designed, Bluebird K7 was never going to be anything but a compromise.

The truth was that, in 1967, the ambitious Campbell needed a new boat to attack the water-speed record once more. But he couldn't afford it. The magic of Donald Campbell's name, which had dominated the 1950s during which he had six times held the world water-speed record, had faded. Wealthy sponsors were no longer queuing to partner and pay for another expensive record-breaking attempt. Yet Campbell felt that "the old warhorse had one more great run in it".[323] All the support team did not share his optimism, however. Leo Villa, who served both father and son so faithfully, commented: "You can't put new wine in old bottles." But Campbell and designer, Ken Norris, disagreed. By being prudent, they felt they could modify the ageing K7 into a realistic record-breaker. Privately, they smiled at newspaper reports that they had spent £10,000 on the new engine. In fact, they had bought the entire Gnat aircraft for £200. They then dismantled its engine and manoeuvred it into the waiting Bluebird K7.[324] Money was short; long-time friend, Bill Coley, picked up many of the bills. In the trial runs on Coniston, there were problems with trim. "We needed more weight in the tail. I think we've solved that by strapping down a piece of paving stone in the stern," said Campbell.[325] It was not a high-tech solution. It was not a confident team. Nor was the weather ideal.

Coniston that autumn was grim and unwelcoming. Poet John Ruskin who lived there in the 19th century got it about right:

---

323. Donald Campbell, The Man Behind the Mask, David Tremayne, Bantam Press, 2004, p26
324. Ibid
325. Conversation with author, 1967

Black water, as still as death,
leafless woods or worse than leafless,
the brown oak foliage hanging dead upon them.
Grey skies and far off wild dark moorlands.
The lake is wonderfully sad and quiet.
No sound except the rustling of the boat among the reeds…

The village of Coniston, a name derived from the Norse word for 'king', sits at the mouth of Coppermines Valley and Yewdale Beck, at the northern end of Coniston Water. By January 4th 1967, Campbell and his team had been there 62 days. Long, often grey days, when winds ruffled the surface of Coniston confining Bluebird K7 to its boathouse on the edge of the lake. The crew waited patiently for the flat calm that would be needed before Campbell could even begin his assault on the world record. It was a daily tension, beginning before dawn when the new day pauses to consider the weather it will deliver during the next 24 hours. During those 62 days, plans had been finalised and the boat and the course had been thoroughly explored. Speed trials had been encouraging. For two weeks, Bluebird K7 had been ready to go. But conditions were never quite good enough. Every morning, Campbell and the team gathered on the slipway as the surface of the lake was monitored and forecasts made for the day ahead. Then, heads were shaken, words of sympathy and frustration exchanged. The routine ended as they all trooped back to their hotels for breakfast.

Waiting can be difficult. In these circumstances, when a life is on the line, it can also be draining. Leo Villa said: "By 10 in the morning, I'm exhausted."[326] Everyone sought distractions to relieve the boredom and the tension. On Tuesday January 3rd 1967, Donald Campbell took me out

---

326. Conversation with author, 1967

on to Lake Coniston in a speedboat. He cut the engine and
the boat gave itself to the gentle movement on the surface of
the lake. The breeze across the water was chill and Campbell
was wearing gloves and a high-collared, weatherproof jacket,
which looked enviably warm. His hair was tousled. He
spoke with the familiar mountains of the Lake District as his
backdrop. It would be the last interview he gave.

How does all this waiting affect you?

Campbell: "Oh, it gets on everybody's nerves inevitably
because you do a run, you make a particular speed, you learn
something. You have to wait another fortnight before you get
another quarter of an hour's calm water."

But how does it affect you personally? Do you get edgy?

Campbell: "Well, I can't say I enjoy it, frankly. For this
game, you want calm, calm, calm, so that you can work,
work and work yourself up with the machine. So that you
become one. It isn't a question of, you know, an enormous
engine in an enormous boat just going fast. It doesn't work
that way. Like test flying, you want to work up to it gently.
Methodically. The one thing that this confounded weather
destroys is method. For the rest, we have to wait. It's hard on
everybody."

Ironically, as we looked back at the shore, the hearth
smoke lay flat over the slate grey cottages of the village. Back
on our boat a breeze stirred the lakeland air and rippled the
surface of Coniston. Breaking records is like a marriage. It
takes patience, a lot of hard work and its only justification is
success. Campbell had succeeded eight times before, on land
and water:

Do you prefer boats to cars?

Campbell: "Oh yes, definitely."

Why?

Campbell: "Why do you like blondes and somebody else likes brunettes?"

Is it something about the way they handle? Maybe we're back to blondes and brunettes again...

Campbell (laughing): "Oh dear, oh dear. No, I ... you know, some people like taking still pictures and others like taking moving pictures. Some people like going in the mountains and others like flat country. It's probably the way you were born."

Is there a magic in the boat for you that there isn't in the car?

Campbell: "Oh yes, a boat without any question of doubt is an individual. You refer to a boat as 'she' and probably not without reason. If they're not happy, they let you know and let you know quickly. This goes for any kind of boat, whether sail or power. And when you get into this class of animal like Bluebird – well, it's light, sensitive, very delicate and a very exciting thing to handle."

Do you think you can read her now?

Campbell: "The male animal will never understand a woman and there are always some tricks that she's got that you don't fully understand ... but as far as one can, yes. She is light and very, very exciting and very rapid, of course. You know you can wind up to 200 miles an hour in this one in five seconds, I'd say."

Are you confident in her?

Campbell: "It rather depends what you mean by 'confident'. You treat her with very great respect – you've got a thrust-to-weight ratio here of one-to-one, which means that if I sat in her – just now – and you wanted a static full power run, if we had been upended and pointing at the sky, she'd go straight up."

Bluebird K7 is a boat with a jet engine that, given the choice and without control, would like to fly. The relationship between man and machine is never dull. Donald Campbell looked back a couple of days:

"The other day we were going very fast indeed, decelerating just out towards the end of the lake here and suddenly a flock of birds got off the water. They were going thick and fast and furiously in every direction under, over, sideways. I think they were ducks. I'm not sure. I was personally too busy ducking. I was lucky. Just another foot and it would have been certain 'curtains'. As it was, birds hit the front spire and did some damage but nothing serious. And I regret it because I don't like killing and I was sorry for the ducks."

How did you feel after a narrow escape like that?

Campbell: "Well, it's just one of those things. So, we slowed down and we came back even faster…"

His lips tighten and his eyes narrow defiantly. He is willing me to say something critical.

Didn't you feel that perhaps this was a good time to stop it altogether?

Campbell: "No, on the contrary; you've got to keep going in life. You've got a target and you've got to struggle on until you reach it. You know, life is a succession of meeting mountains and you struggle up and the summit seems so far away and unattainable and you keep on struggling and if you're lucky you reach the summit. Then, time puts it into perspective and you look back and you suddenly, to your horror, realise that the mountain wasn't a mountain after all. It was only a molehill.

"And this is life."

Donald Campbell spent his 45 years trying to emulate the achievements of his father. His wife, his third wife, Tonia, summed up the father-son relationship with a story that Donald had told her in a quiet moment together. His father had said to Donald one day, 'You're a bloody fool, boy. You'll never amount to anything'. Tonia Campbell said: "Children remember those moments. I don't think Donald had ambitions to beat his father; I do think he wanted to win his respect." The Campbells, said Tonia, were not good at giving praise.

Donald spoke about his father: "He was a tremendously courageous, colourful, a bold character and I think I was very close to him. I also admired him greatly as a man. Oddly enough, from a small boy, I was always much more excited by the water than by the land. Father broke the land speed record, I think it was nine times and the water speed record, three times. I've broken the water speed record seven times now."

Which, as an answer, is as interesting in what it omits as in what it contains – a great deal about achievement and rivalry; no mention of childhood or emotion. He was repeating the public perception of his father while concealing the details of a relationship that was core to his being. Malcolm Campbell was short-tempered and self-centred. He was a strict disciplinarian with both Donald and his sister, Jean. He was seldom at home, as busy as any other record-breaker, journalist, yachtsman, businessman or politician – and Malcolm Campbell was all five.[327] He was knighted in 1932. David Tremayne in his excellent book, *The Man Behind the Mask*, tells of a revelatory moment that is recorded on film:

"On one newsreel, a young Donald Campbell rushes up the gangplank to greet his father at Southampton after his successful 1933 campaign. In a poignant little vignette, the boy moves to shake the man's hand but the gesture goes unnoticed. He stands there, hand outstretched. Ignored. If every picture

327. Donald Campbell, The Man Behind the Mask, David Tremayne, Bantam Books, 2004, p57

tells a story, that film clip raises volumes of questions about the relationship between a father and son who, between them, pushed Britain to the very forefront of speed with 11 records on water and 10 on land to their joint record.

"I once happened to mention this film to Donald Campbell's widow, Tonia, who clapped her hands in recollection and shrieked, 'I know! I know the film you mean! You know, it was watching that film when Donald showed it to me, that made me fall in love with him. There was this little boy, so proud of his father and his father didn't even notice…'"

Donald and Jean were both sent to boarding schools at seven and Donald went on to St Peter's Prep School in Seaford, Sussex and then to Uppingham School in Rutland, just as his father had done. Autocratic though their father might have been, the Campbell children have happy childhood memories, particularly at Christmas when Malcolm always assumed the role of Santa Claus. Donald Campbell loved and needed his father. At the end of his life, at Christmas 1948, Malcolm Campbell suffered a number of severe strokes. He was dying. Donald was abroad at the time and he raced to the family home in Kent. He was shocked at the deterioration in his father's health; it was only a matter of months since he had made his last attempt at the world water-speed record on Coniston Water. At his father's bedside, Donald wept. Frail though he then was, Malcolm Campbell reached out, pulled a handkerchief from his son's top pocket and dried Donald's eyes. "It's all right, old chap," he said. "I'm finished."[328] He died soon after Christmas and is buried in Chislehurst, in the same grave as his parents.

Sir Malcolm's will is a guide to, and a confirmation of, his relationship with his son. He left bequests to friends and family and to Leo Villa and some members of his Blue

---

328. Ibid, p83

Bird team. To his two children, Donald and Jean, his legacy was that all his properties and possessions should be sold at auction and the proceeds divided equally between them. That included the Blue Bird car and the two hydroplane boats. If Donald wanted them, he would have to buy them. Which he did. It was as if his father was asking him a familiar question from beyond the grave: 'How important is it to you, Donald, to try to emulate me? Have you weighed up the cost, in money, in dedication and in emotion? Why not give it all up and live a quieter life as a businessman?'

I do not believe Sir Malcolm would have been too upset if his son had chosen the option of the quiet life. But Donald Campbell, despite his lack of experience, was never going to sidestep the challenge. "Speed is my life," he said, once he had made his choice. "Life is to be lived – and lived to the full." As we sat together in that gently-stirring boat on Coniston Water in 1967, he spoke of his father only once more:

"I won't lightly forget that in 1939 I came adrift off a motorcycle. I got two fractures of the skull and I woke up 44 hours later in hospital. The old man [father] said two things after that: 'You'll never ride a motorcycle again, boy, unless you, (a) wear a crash helmet and (b) you will wear this.' And he gave me a St Christopher medallion.

"Well, of course, I felt an absolute fool riding around in those days with a crash helmet on, which he had especially made for me. But of course, again father, typically, father was 30 years ahead of his time. Now you're regarded as a fool if you *don't* wear one. And rightly so.

"As far as the St Christopher was concerned, all was well. I went into the Royal Air Force and everything went much according to plan until I got another dose of rheumatic fever and was invalided out. After I'd been out of hospital for about a week, I went to run an errand for father on my motorcycle: I collected a Canadian army lorry on the way and got struck on the shoulder, hurled into the air and run over by a car coming in the other direction. I ended up in a slightly messy heap.

"And the odd thing about it was that I'd been to a party with some of my air force chums the night before and I had lost my St Christopher. After that, the old man gave me another one and I've been very careful of it."

Is this the one you wear when you make your attempts?

Campbell: "Yes, I wear it all the time. I'm wearing it now."

His friends have described Donald Campbell as 'one of the most superstitious men' they know. Throughout his record-breaking life, he has jousted with rich Americans, such as Craig Breedlove, star speedster among a younger generation of competitors who were generally backed by generous sponsors and who believed Campbell to be the last echo of a tradition that should be laid to rest. Campbell, with his public school accent and his pin-striped suits, did not fit easily into the new, cool company of record-breakers. They viewed him as the last of the gentleman drivers and, privately and sometimes publicly, they mocked his mascots and his superstitions. He didn't like the colour green. The number 13 was unlucky. He would never race on a Friday. Campbell's answer was to keep breaking records. We examined the St Christopher Campbell wore that day and every day.

You're a brave man but you're also superstitious.

Campbell: "I don't know about brave. I think possibly block-headed. But superstitious, yes. Not perhaps in the way you mean it. I think superstition is a luxury which is rather fun but the reality is that, when the chips are down, you trust your training and your judgment and nothing else. Never mind what presentiment you may have had about the job in hand. Eastern people say anyway that, 'no man can escape his destiny.'"

You mention destiny...

Campbell: "And I believe that too. It's a paradox, I know. But you're dealing with a cold, hard, calculating game. And you must play it that way."

Yet, you still have mascots and–

Campbell: "Oh, rather. Yes, rather. Well, most of us sort of have a tie which is a lucky tie or a suit. Wear one suit one day and everything goes wrong, another suit for some unknown reason seems to be worn on the days when things go right. I expect you know this feeling; I think most people do. I've got all sorts of funny charms and what have you..."

Conspicuous among his 'what have you' is Mr Whoppit, a teddy bear mascot. 'The Story of Woppit' was a 1950s cartoon strip about a bear, popular in the children's magazine, *Robin*. In 1956, a nine-inch tall toy 'Woppit' teddy bear was manufactured and marketed. Soon re-named by Campbell and with an 'h' added, it became Mr Whoppit, who proudly wore the Bluebird logo hand-embroidered on its red felt jacket.

Mr Whoppit went with Donald Campbell on all his record attempts, on water and land.[329] When did these superstitions become important to Campbell?

Campbell: "Well, it begins in childhood, doesn't it? My 'ridiculous teddy bear', as the Americans once described Mr Whoppit, has travelled with me now for a long time. I've

---

329. In the 1990s, long after Donald Campbell's death, a second edition of 5,000 teddy bears was produced, this time re-branded 'Mr Whoppit' after Campbell's famous mascot, and now sporting the Campbell spelling and the Bluebird badge

got a great friend, Commander Greville Herd, who drove destroyers with the Murmansk convoys to Russia in the Arctic winter in World War II and that was pretty hairy. Even in the summer months they went through hell, shot at 23 hours a day – torpedoes, bombs and everything. Well, he's got a pair of little penguins. A bit moth-eaten now, but he won't travel anywhere without penguins. You know, chaps I flew with (in the RAF) all had lucky scarfs and rabbit's feet and goodness knows what. This is perfectly normal, good, human stuff. I'm very fond of my teddy bear – whether the Americans like to describe him as ridiculous or not."

Would you attempt the record if Mr Whoppit, for some reason or other, were not with you?

Campbell: "Well, of course. Mr Whoppit sometimes does get forgotten. In fact, he wasn't out with me last Tuesday when I made that very fast run here. (Pause). He'd been given a wife over the weekend, so I think he thought he had better things to do than go boating."

Campbell will joke about his relationship with his mascots. It is the outward sign of his much deeper need to explore and trust in, the supernatural. He wrote frequently on the subject in national newspapers and carried out psychic investigations for the *Sunday Pictorial*.[330] He said: 'If you are born with a curiosity to probe the unknown, then you must do it.' The articles reveal his belief that his dead father was watching over him. He regularly visited mediums and took part in séances, sometimes accompanied by his mother, Lady Dorothy. One of the mediums, Marjorie Staves, became an important figure in his life. Staves was a "careful but sincere woman", a clairvoyant who, through quiet understanding,

---

330. Later, the Sunday Mirror

became Donald Campbell's Mother Confessor, someone with whom he could feel relaxed[331] and to whom he would reveal his innermost needs and thoughts. David Tremayne interviewed the late Ms Staves comprehensively for his book *The Man Behind the Mask*. They met in the front room of her home in London and Tremayne found that, with her staccato speech and nervous movements, she reminded him of "a little sparrow". He wrote:

'Staves had a quirky manner of speaking that sometimes made her conversation tricky to follow, and she cheerfully admitted that she knew nothing of technology. But Campbell certainly drew something from his visits. 'It was with me that he was able to let his hair down', she said. 'He came so often, to tell me matters that he couldn't talk about to anybody else. He wanted to outdo his father, and he wanted to prove his worth. But at the same time he was very nervous and very shy. Really, I think, he felt he didn't have that support that he wanted. Some people put him in Promise Street, but never came over'.

'Staves detected unhappiness behind the superficial glamour of Campbell's image as a world-famous record breaker. She said: 'Let me say this. Besides all the aggro with the boat, he was not very happy in his personal life.[332] I think he liked to come and talk to me as a form of escape. Perhaps nobody else would listen to him. The whole emphasis was a genuine need to be successful, and he allowed his father's image to be the image he wanted to be.'[333]

Campbell truly believed that the spirit of his dead father had intervened on several occasions to save his life. That day

---

331. The Man Behind the Mask, p259, interview with author, David Tremayne
332. Campbell married three times and, at the time of his death, there were rumours that his relationship with Tonia Bern, his third wife, was strained. She opposed this final attempt with, "Anyway, we were flat broke"
333. The Man Behind the Mask, Tremayne, pp224–5

on Lake Coniston in 1967, he told me of one of them:

"I remember the first time on this very lake, at this very point in my father's old boat in 1949 in my first attempt, rocketing up towards that red kilometre marker at 150 miles an hour and I thought the end of the world had come. It appeared as though we were shooting over the edge of a huge waterfall. The noise was unbelievable as this huge engine was braking rather more than two thousand horsepower. I just thought the world was going to split asunder.

"Then, suddenly, this shower of scalding hot oil hit me straight in the face, all over my goggles and windscreen and everything else. That was when Dad took charge and we went off like a well-trained stallion back to where it had all started. We were OK because he had taken over. But that was a narrow one.

"Yet 150 miles an hour, today? If we want to go from A to B, we go trotting down the lake at 200 mph and the water doesn't come up that fast at all at that speed. But at 300, it comes up like the proverbial rocket. Time will pass, somebody else will take over and they will be going down the lake at 500 – and 300 will seem almost slow, very slow. But this is progress, isn't it?"

To the speedster, progress is the magic ingredient, seductive and dangerous. Campbell's declared ambition had been to hold the world water and land speed record simultaneously in the same year. With his reputation at its height in the 1950s, he and his friends had mobilised the British motor industry to build a car to break John Cobb's record of 394 mph (634 kph) set in 1947. The sponsors included BP, Dunlop, Smith's Industries, Rubery Owen and Lucas and forming this consortium was an achievement in itself. Bluebird-Proteus CN7 would be designed by his tried and tested friends and team mates the Norris brothers, Ken and Lewis, who had a speed of 500 mph (800 kph) in mind.

The car (and it *was* a 'car', because the power from the Proteus 700 gas turbine engine drove directly through all four of Bluebird CN7's road wheels) was completed in the spring of 1960. Campbell chose to make his attempt on the land speed record at the Bonneville Salt Flats in Utah, USA, where his father had broken the record 25 years earlier. The trial runs went well. On September 16th 1960, Donald Campbell remembered that he was "slightly impatient ... This was the sixth run we had had and I wanted to accelerate to get some real speed".

It was a Friday. An unforeseen glitch in the system would almost kill him.

"We started to accelerate. Our brief was to do 300 miles an hour by the time we passed the second mile marker. As it happened, we went by the first mile marker at about 327 and, instead of taking the power off and being well content with having reached our target on that particular run, I didn't. I put it on. And when the tail started to go, I felt it. I knew it and I didn't care. Instead of taking power off at that point, I put more power on. The car went again and I still took no notice of it and then, finally, I saw it coming. I thought, 'Oh well, no worries, it's a nice morning...'

"I must have been very close to unconsciousness at that point. And then there was a complete darkness. The curtains came down. And out of the darkness there came a tremendous blow across the right side of my head and then the sensation of pain. And this brought back a sensation of existence. I didn't know where I was – why I was existing or where I was and then it dawned gradually that I was in this car.

"At this point, it was sliding and slithering its way across the salt having been airborne for more than a thousand feet. Then the pain became intense and I was praying it would stop.

"Then it was dark again and I remember thinking the

car was upside down because of this lack of vision. I was frantically groping around, trying to find something to hold on to for fear of my hands being torn off going out through the broken canopy.

"At this point, Bluebird was still travelling at more than 200 mph. As it happened, of course, the car wasn't upside down … it was the right way up but all the capillaries in my eyes and head had burst. And then it all stopped and then the curtain came down again and I woke up half an hour later."

Campbell had suffered what he later described as "a severe case of oxygen poisoning" that had caused "a complete failure of the human system. Oxygen poisoning is a very remarkable thing. You lose all sense of fear, all sense of reality, all sense of existence and you haven't a care in the world".

Campbell had a fractured skull, severe concussion, a ruptured eardrum and middle ear and injuries to his face, neck, arms and legs. He was still conscious. The black box on board Bluebird CN7 indicated that he had travelled at 365 mph. Campbell had had a presentiment of disaster. He remembered:

"When I was able to piece together what had happened, I was heart-broken. All we had worked for was a mangled mess of metal."

Did you ask yourself, 'Was it all worth it?'?

Campbell: "Well, life is for living and these knocks you've got to be able to take in life. We all get them."

Did you honestly think that, even when you were lying there in your hospital bed?

Campbell reflects for some seconds before he answers: "Frankly, that night, I had had a feeling that I wasn't going to come out of it. But the funny thing was that, by the morning, there was no negative feeling whatsoever. I was curiously calm from the time I woke up. I thought nobody else knew how I felt about my premonition – I'd told only one person I'd had this feeling, one of my executives. But, apparently, everybody knew. I'd been sleep-talking apart from anything else. My wife certainly knew it."

What form did the warning take?

Campbell: "It was just a sort of feeling of – oh, this is the end of a trail – you know?"

Campbell had nearly lost his life but his determination remained intact. Two years passed; his body mended and Bluebird CN7 was re-built and improved. A large stabilising tail fin was added and, with a reinforced cockpit cover, she was shipped out to Australia where Campbell would compete once more for the land speed record, on the salt flats of Lake Eyre. Before he could do so however, in July 1963, on the other side of the world, at Bonneville where Campbell had nearly died two years earlier, American hot rod, Craig Breedlove, drove his jet car, Spirit of America, at a speed of 407.45 mph (655.73 kph). He beat John Cobb's record speed by 13 mph (20.92 kph), but he was disqualified from holding the land speed record because his 'car', whose power was not connected to its road wheels, was literally blown along the course by its jet engine. Nor did Breedlove's three-wheel vehicle conform to the Fédération Internationale de l'Automobile (FIA) definition of a 'car'.

So, in 1964 Campbell went ahead with his attempt on Cobb's record. It was not a happy time in Australia. It rained. The track never really dried out. He had disputes with his sponsors. There was talk of postponement. But on July 17th 1964, in less than ideal conditions, Campbell drove Bluebird CN7 at 403.10 mph (648.72 kph) and exceeded Cobb's record by nine mph (14.48 kph). Campbell was disappointed because he knew Bluebird was capable of much faster speeds. He felt dogged by bad luck. Publicly, he said: "We've made it. We've got the bastard at last."

But the experience of surviving the crash on the Bonneville Salt Flats in 1960 had left its mark. As the months went by, he had suffered panic attacks and a well-concealed loss of confidence. Ken Norris felt that Campbell was "more cautious and apprehensive because he had had a nasty one (but), if anything, I think he was a wiser driver".[334] None the less, back in England, as he prepared to attack the water speed record at Coniston, he spent more time with medium, Marjorie Staves, in her rooms in New Cavendish Street:

"He came to see me because I'd got to know him so well. He really confessed to me that the fault (the crash) was partly due to himself – a lack of control … I didn't say I felt sorry for him. I felt it was worth him trying to fulfil his cause. His purpose was to prove his worth; that's what he was after.

"He was always like a little boy at school, you know. Try and help me, please. That's the guy I had. He wasn't the big guy coming in and showing off or throwing his weight about. I remember he phoned me once and he was delighted that a trial had gone well. He was so excited to pick up a phone and tell me. I was pleased that he'd got something at last. But, by the same token, there was always something in the way of him getting off to a good start. Psychologically, that must have affected him."[335]

On the lake that day just after Christmas 1967, Campbell talked about death. He knew that four men had died in pursuit of the water speed record. He knew this – and in assessing his chances of success, he said:

---

334. The Man Behind the Mask, Tremayne, p277
335. Staves' interview with David Tremayne, The Man Behind the Mask, pp257–8

"The whole thing is absurd, really. But life *is* absurd, isn't it? This just happens to be something one loves doing. When you go on to summarise it – why are you doing it? It's a question, quite logically, often asked and the real short answer is: because I want to.

"It will be a sorry day when we no longer do something for the hell of it. Nobody can do anything really if they are motivated simply by considerations of money. Money is important – it's like sugar in tea. But, no amount of money can make a man do a job well; it's got to come from within him. Or beyond ... I don't know. You read the most brilliant books, listen to the most lovely pieces of music. They are not inspired by money. They are inspired by something that comes from within a man. Everything starts in the imagination of mankind. That's where everything comes from."

It is late afternoon and, in silence, he reflected on the truth of that statement. Then:

"Tomorrow, perhaps, any one of us might be dead from any one of innumerable different causes. It's just one of those things. You either take the risk or you don't."

Yet you are voluntarily putting yourself in a position of much greater risk than the average person.

Campbell: "Yes, but to a great extent, you know; it's a calculated risk. Many of us in our daily lives take uncalculated risks like dashing across a crowded road."

Have you come to terms with it?

Campbell: "I think you've got to. That doesn't mean to say you don't have all the normal human reactions of apprehension, fear, excitement and everything else that goes into the human make-up."

What would you say your attitude, then, is to dying?

Campbell: "I have no desire whatever to do that. I enjoy this life far too much. As you say, there's a number of gallant men have lost their lives trying to push forward men's knowledge in this sphere. It's one of those things, you take the risk or you don't. You know, I'm a profound believer in Almighty God and I think Almighty God gave us a brain and a fund of courage and he meant us to use it. You've got to work out your own philosophy in this life…"

As we drifted back towards the boathouse, he looked ahead to the next day. The weather forecast was good. He said, as if re-focusing his mind: "We're trying to beat the existing record and possibly pass this magic mark of 300. It's just another mountain; everything in life's a mountain whether you're building a business, producing a television programme or whatever … we've just got this on our mind at the moment. Just now, it's a very high summit which seems a long way off. But if we're lucky enough to get there, in due time we'll see that, really, it was a molehill all the time…"

At 7.20 am the next morning, there is a chill in the air. Out on the lake at each end of the measured kilometre of grey water, which Campbell hopes to cover in about seven seconds, the stake boats are in position. Campbell is ready. We wait and watch. Campbell is in a hurry. As he passes me, I reflect on the last words we exchanged the evening before:

"At moments like this, you feel the same way as you do when you climb into the boxing ring before the bell goes – or, on to the stage before the curtain goes up.

"There isn't a person alive that wouldn't say that if you're involved in this kind of game, racing or competition ski-ing, that just before the bell goes or the flag drops, they wish to goodness they weren't doing it and thinking, 'What a fool I am. Why aren't I sitting down comfortably somewhere, in front of the fire or in the sun?'"

I don't know if Donald Campbell knew he was going to die. Some said he had a death wish, knowing that he was in debt, in an old boat and at the end of his career as a record-breaker. What I do know is that he felt that the world was losing interest in his attempt to break the record. So was my editor. I was lakeside with a film crew, despite express orders from London that I was to pack up and come home. For three days, my editor had emphatically shared with me his view that "it would all fizzle out. Nothing will happen. It's a non-story and we've spent enough money already". I disagreed and had somehow missed his calls for the next 72 hours. We would follow this man's story through to the end, to success or failure.[336] Donald Campbell's state of mind was disturbing, particularly to those who cared about him. Bluebird historian, Neil Sheppard, said that Campbell, despite the odds against him, was still, as always, desperate to emulate his father. But how desperate? His wife, Tonia, said that, as the financial backing disappeared, he had become increasingly depressed. The previous evening, he had telephoned her where she was in cabaret in Bristol, to tell her that he would be going for the record. She had said: "Listen, I want to be with you. I'm coming up there" and he had said: "Don't worry, Mr Whoppit will look after me. He's always there."

Marie Staves said of her last meeting with Campbell: "He was trying to emulate the glamour of his father ... it was devastating for him because he felt he had never made it. But he deserves every credit for the urge ... and impetus that he put into his quest."[337] Author, David Tremayne, wrote of the "train of cruel circumstances (that) ultimately pushed (this) lovely, beleaguered, frightened and determined man to take

---

336. Donald Campbell – The Last 48 Hours was transmitted by Thames on ITV on January 4th 1967
337. The Man Behind the Mask, Tremayne, p433

the final chance".[338] To those four adjectives, I would add a fifth. Trapped. Donald Campbell was trapped by his own expectations and by the expectations of others.

At 8.45 am, Campbell started his last record attempt. His first run was the fastest he had recorded in all the 62 days at Coniston. The airspeed indicator had touched 300 mph and his average speed was 297.6 mph. Things looked good – but Neil Sheppard noted that during the run, briefly, for 0.7 secs, Bluebird left the water and flew. Campbell now had to make a return run over the course. Uncharacteristically, instead of waiting for the wake from his first run to disappear, Campbell decided to take his second run almost immediately. He would avoid the ripples before they disturbed the course. Four minutes after the first run, Bluebird was on its way again. Campbell gave his usual commentary as he drove ... he continued to do so even when Bluebird, now at 328 mph (528 kph) bounced three times and became airborne...

"Full nose up ... Pitching a bit down here ... coming through our own wash ... er, getting straightened up now on track ... rather closer to Peel Island ... and we're tramping like mad ... bad indeed ... I'm galloping over the top ... and she's giving a hell of a bloody row in her ... I can't see anything ... I've got the bows out ... I'm going ... U-hh..."[339]

Campbell had cheated death before and anxious friends searched the water, waiting for him to bob up. They found the mascot, Mr Whoppit, but of Donald Campbell, there was no trace.

* * *

His daughter, Gina Campbell, said: "Like Princess Diana or

---

338. Ibid, Donald Campbell, David Tremayne
339. The precise words are sometimes unclear on the transcript of the RT. The meaning of what is happening is crystal clear

Ayrton Senna, he died in a way that immortalised him …
Dad's finest hour was his demise."

Craig Breedlove said of Campbell: "I loved Donald. He
was cool … he was almost like a child who had been held
down all his childhood and then, when the Old Man died …
boy!!"

Lawyer Victor Mishcon,[340] who gave the oration at
Campbell's funeral, said that when he had last spoken to
Campbell, he had told him that he was "dead scared" about
the attempt. Mishcon added: "I wonder whether Donald
really knew what Donald Campbell really was … sometimes
I think he thought he was a bit worthless. Other times, he
felt he was his father all over again and therefore worthy
of esteem. But … he could command complete loyalty …
Donald could make people, almost literally, lie down and die
for him."

David Tremayne said: "Brave men often do things without
considering the consequences. The abnormally brave man
has peered over the edge of the pit … and still carries on.
Courage and patriotism were (Donald's) driving forces."[341]

* * *

The wreckage of Bluebird K7 was eventually raised from
the depths of Lake Coniston on March 8th 2001. Donald
Campbell's headless body was recovered 10 weeks later on
May 28th, just east of the spot where the wreckage had lain
undisturbed since 1967.

Around Donald Campbell's neck was the St Christopher
his father had given him 20 years before, to keep him safe…

---

340. Mishcon, later Baron Mishcon (see Ruth Ellis, Chapter 4) was a friend and
confidante of Campbell's
341. Quotes from Tremayne's The Man Behind the Mask, Bantam Press, 2004

Chapter 14

THE QUEEN'S HORSES:
When is An Interview not An Interview?

Tucked away behind the Palace that gives its name to Buckingham Palace Road, London, is one of Her Majesty The Queen's favourite buildings, the Royal Mews. This is where the horses that grace royal ceremonial have their homes and where the carriages and cars that carry Britain's royal family at State occasions are kept and cared for. Coachmen, grooms, chauffeurs and their families form a village where there is a place for everyone and everyone knows their place.

Few people are as close to Her Majesty than the Crown Equerry, who is in charge of the Royal Mews, its cars, carriages and horses and between 1961 and 1987, that position was held with style and humour by Sir John Miller, a Welsh Guardsman and a man of habit as precise as any of the ceremonial processions he organised for his Queen. Sir John was a courageous soldier and a formidable commander. Educated at Eton and Sandhurst, he was twice decorated during the months of the Normandy campaign after the D-Day landings in 1944, once for rallying his men under intense shellfire for which he was awarded the Military Cross (MC) and again, a month later when, by re-establishing two companies that had been scattered during a fierce onslaught, he won the Distinguished Service Order (DSO). He commanded the first British troops to enter Brussels and, in the days leading up to that victory he revealed again his attitude to danger, which he believed to be "an inconvenience". Miller was well-travelled as a young man before the war and had spent time in Flanders. In 1944, his unit of the Welsh Guards had just crossed the Belgian border from France. At the briefing that evening, the Commanding Officer had warned that the next objective, a village, would be difficult to take as it was occupied by crack German troops. The knowledge was digested by the officers assembled and most retired for an early night, with the exception of John Miller. He remembered a particularly fine restaurant in the village in question and he made his way there. He had an excellent dinner within yards of the German enemy he would be facing the next morning and returned to his unit just before midnight. The next day, the Welsh Guards overcame the enemy and occupied the village.

After the war, Sir John was, for two years, ADC[342] to Field Marshal Lord Wilson, head of the British Joint Staff Commission in Washington and he commanded the 1st Battalion the Welsh Guards from 1958 to 1961, when he joined the Royal Household. Miller was Crown Equerry for 26 years. He took part in more than 64 birthday parades and rehearsals. Most of these occasions passed off flawlessly, but the Queen's official birthday celebration on June 13th 1981 was an exception. Sir John, not a superstitious man, later remembered he was "nervous about the date, for some reason". He was right to be. That day, the Queen was shot at in The Mall; the Queen Mother slipped on a staircase injuring her leg as she left the Duke of Wellington's office from which she had been watching the ceremony; Prince Philip's horse went lame and the Prince's groom was injured in an accident. Sir John reflected that "it could have been worse…"

As he passed his 25th year as Crown Equerry, we felt it

---

342. Aide-de-camp

would be appropriate to make a film to mark the milestone. Through a mutual friend, John Minoprio, we successfully approached the Palace for access and for the next year we watched Sir John at work – with the State coaches, the barouches, the clarences, the broughams and the landaus; the State cars, the Rolls-Royce Phantoms IV and VI and the two Bentley State limousines and finally, the carriage horses, the Windsor Greys and the Cleveland Bays. We watched Her Majesty exercise her Canadian-bred horse, Burmese, in the magnificent indoor riding school and we visited the other Royal Mews at Windsor Castle and the old stables at St James' Palace. And, as with most long-term filming projects, we made friends with those whose lives we were recording.

Towards the end of the year, Sir John was showing us how the horses were trained to remain calm during the noise and disturbance they would encounter when the world would watch them during a State occasion. We were moving rapidly from one location in the Mews to another. Not quickly enough for Sir John: "Don't hang back!" he advised a cameraman as he struggled under the awkward weight of his equipment. We marched towards the sound of the drums and watched the fire-crackers explode and the kettle drums whirr as the trim young horses circled, barely turning their heads from the job at hand. Afterwards, being British, we had a cup of tea. John Miller broke off and said quietly: "We'll be seeing Her Majesty again at the stables tomorrow. That will be your last chance to have a word with her."

I thought I had misheard him. We had spoken to the Queen, of course, during the course of the year but informally, never recorded, and always at Her Majesty's instigation. I ventured: "What do you mean, John?"

"Well, if Her Majesty is going to be in this film, this will be your last chance to get her."

But Sir John knew as well as I, that the Queen does not

give interviews. Then I realised what was in John Miller's mind. He wanted Her Majesty to be in the film recording the job he had been doing for a quarter of a century; he wanted to reflect this unique relationship that existed between sovereign and equerry and the horses they both loved. John Miller concluded this very short and revelatory conversation with the words: "I'll see you in the morning. And I'll tip you the wink when to go in."

The next morning began at 3 am. We were filming the Mews as it prepared for a State occasion. The still, crisp air was filled with the clack of hooves on cobbles, the jingle of harnesses, the murmur of steel-clad wooden wheels as coaches were manoeuvred into position. By 8 am, the preparations were complete and recorded – and we repaired to our nearby hotel for breakfast. I had reflected on Sir John's words throughout the short night and, if there were a chance that we were going to interview Her Majesty, the entire crew needed to know. Over breakfast, I raised the subject. "If you were going to interview the Queen, what question would you ask her?" There was much laughter.

Three times I asked the question and eventually, Tony Searle, who was directing the crew, said for a third time in capital letters, "The – Queen – does – not – give – interviews, Peter."

I confided that, on that very day, before his very eyes, that rule might be broken. If any job is to be done well, concentration has to be at a high level. For the rest of the morning, knowing that we would be seeing Her Majesty again in the stables on what could be a momentous afternoon, concentration was more difficult than usual.

After lunch, Sir John escorted Her Majesty to see her Windsor Greys. Traditionally, royal State coaches are drawn by teams of greys and Sir John was discussing with Her Majesty how best to maintain this complement. Then, and there is no other way of describing this moment, Sir John Miller winked at me and nodded. I heard my voice ask: "Roughly what proportion of greys is there, your Majesty, compared with the Cleveland Bays?" and the interview had begun. Her Majesty answered my questions for about 15 minutes. She said that she needed fewer greys because they were "more selectively used. We always need enough to do two carriages". A good horse, she told me, was "quite a difficult one to breed, to get the right colour and temperament and size". It was "much more difficult than a bay horse". Moussaka had been "the first home-bred grey on the Mews". We discussed the temperament of the home-bred bay horses that Prince Philip was, at the time, driving in four-in-hand competition and coach driving and the reasons why it was relatively unusual for stallions to be involved in the ceremonial occasions "because they are a bit troublesome". It was all very instructive. As if from a distance, I heard the interviewer ask Her Majesty if "this particular grey is a whole horse". It was not. As I would have seen on closer inspection. Her Majesty was very patient with me.

The 'interview' finished. Her Majesty remained while our specially-arranged photographer took some publicity photographs and then she left with Sir John, who raised a thumb of approval towards me as he turned to go. The crew heaved a collective sigh of relief and satisfaction. Hands were shaken. It was a great moment. I inquired: "Now, has everyone got everything we needed?" The specially-arranged photographer was examining his cameras. He had two; one for colour and one for black and white photographs. He swore forcefully. "I've used the same camera twice. We have no colour shots."

This Royal access, the Queen with her horses, was to be shown on the front cover of the top-selling *TV Times* programme listings magazine. It had to be in colour.

All this had occurred in the two minutes since Her Majesty had left. I ran out of the stables in the direction she had headed. She was just getting into her Rolls-Royce. I arrived just as she was about to pull away. I knocked on the car window and assured Her Majesty that she was not going to believe what I was about to say but "we need a colour photograph, please Ma'am". She paused for a second. Then, she opened the car door and accompanied me back to the stables. The colour photographs were duly taken – and the specially-arranged photographer kept his job.

You know and I know that Her Majesty didn't have to do what she did. But she is that kind of woman.

* * *

Our jubilation was short-lived. When the Buckingham Palace press office learned that Her Majesty had given a lengthy interview, there was consternation. Didn't we realise what we had done? From now on, the Palace press office would no longer be able to reject requests for interviews with The Queen by simply quoting the rule: "The Queen does not give interviews." I don't know what words might have been shared between the press office and the Crown Equerry but, if there were any, Sir John never referred to them and I never asked.

Our professional task was to retain as much of this first interview as we could without being sent to the Tower. The press office were insistent. If we did so, it would be ruinous. As soon as we publicised the fact that the interview had taken place, "the floodgates will be open". My Director of Programmes, Greg Dyke, and I discussed it. I saw the point that the Palace PR team were making. I also knew that the Crown Equerry had deliberately arranged the circumstances for the interview to take place. We told the Palace that we would split the interview into sections so that it didn't appear to be a continuous interview. This was considered. But the problem was the word itself – 'interview'.

We reached a compromise. The word 'interview' would NOT be used in publicity. Instead, 'Peter Williams had, while making the film, fallen into conversation with Her Majesty'. We were happy with the form of words. The Palace press people were happy that their protective wall had not been breached. Sir John Miller[343] was, of course, happy: he had achieved precisely what he had planned.

Just before *The Queen and Her Ceremonial Horses* was shown on the ITV network in 1984, we were invited to Buckingham Palace. There, one afternoon in the Palace's cinema, surrounded by the people of the Royal Mews whose story it was, we watched the film. The audience laughed in the right places and at the end they all clapped. And the Queen turned to me and said ... but I couldn't possibly tell you that, could I?

---

343. Sir John remained Extra Equerry to the Queen on his retirement in 1987

Chapter 15

PANDEMIC:
The Spanish Lady's Warning

I am always amazed at how old other people are. I still recall
the sense of shock when that slim, vital Avenger Diana Rigg
died; not so much that, sadly, she was no longer with us but
that she was 82 years old. The thing about age is that it creeps
up on you. It takes 30 years to reach the age of 30 – and then,
with birthdays arriving every couple of minutes, in no time
at all, you're 65.

I am white, Caucasian and in my eighties. I am not
overweight and I am 5 ft 8 ins in height – perhaps 5 ft 7
ins now as I seem to have shrunk in recent years. I have
never considered myself "old", not even when the stair-lift
was fitted. But COVID-19 has confirmed that I am. I am
now categorised as 'extremely vulnerable', in need of being
'shielded' for months from the rest of society, sharing my
'bubble' with my wife and soulmate Jo, separated from
children and seeing our grandchildren only at a distance,
leaving them hugless and confused.

The last time the world was shaken so profoundly by a
pandemic was in 1918, when 'Spanish flu' killed some 50
million people. This was more casualties than in the entire
World War I, which was itself central to the spread of the
virus. For, unlike the COVID-19 outbreak in 2019 where the
elderly were most likely to die, in 1918 it was the fit and the

young who had been cut down in their thousands.

The COVID-19 virus, as it has enveloped populations around the world, has fundamentally changed our way of life. But why the world should have been surprised by this pandemic is, in itself, a surprise. For the lessons of 1918 have largely been ignored in the intervening years. Whether one defines it as a crusade or an obsession, John Oxford has the 1918 pandemic at the core of his being. In 1999, we made a programme with him[344] for the BBC's scientific strand, *Horizon*, that examined the attempts of groups of scientists to isolate and explore the genome sequence of the virus H1N1 which had caused the 1918 outbreak. They were seeking human tissue to work on. They dug up bodies of victims preserved in Arctic permafrost. They also sought to solve the mystery of why the 1918 virus had, as they put it, 'disappeared underground'. The programme was titled *Pandemic*. The various expeditions were fascinating enough. But the crucial aspect of the programme were the declarations made on screen in its closing minute:

"The odds are 100 per cent that we're going to have a pandemic in the future. We know that because it's happened once. So the race is on: can we learn something from the past pandemic to help us in the future?"[345]

"It is not a question of 'if' but 'when' a pandemic will strike again … If we're hit by another pandemic, you'd better have a plan to deal with it, otherwise you're going to have millions of dead people on your hands."

* * *

---

344. with Garfield Kennedy's company GOSH Films, February 4th 1999
345. Prof JK Taubenberger, Horizon, 1999

The History

Part of the reason that World War I ended so abruptly was that the military units on both sides were decimated by Spanish flu as much as by enemy action. It was nicknamed 'The Spanish Lady', but there is evidence that the first cases were found among soldiers in Étaples in France in 1915 and 1916. Outbreaks of this 'new flu' were also recorded among troops in Massachusetts, USA, in Aldershot, England, Leeuwarden in Holland, Västerås in Sweden and, of course, Spain.[346] Professor Oxford believes that scientists were slow to recognise this new virus, dismissing it as a 'minor infection' during the routine winter increase in cases of influenza. The outbreak in Étaples fascinated him as a "portent of the disaster to come". It was well-documented. The medical group at Étaples were particularly exhaustive in their record-keeping; not only were the usual examinations made of tissue and sputum but post-mortem examinations were undertaken of every single soldier dying of disease rather than wounds, throughout a seven-week period in 1917.[347]

At the time, up to 30,000 soldiers were admitted each year to British army hospitals in France and England, suffering from typical influenza symptoms. The medical group in Étaples treated hundreds of patients infected with what they described as an "unusually fatal disease" presenting "complex" respiratory symptoms. The bare scientific language cloaks the agonising reality of the experience of dying in this way – collapse, haemorrhage, followed by death both horrible and inexplicable, often within three days. "As blue as huckleberries and spitting blood" as one American doctor put it.[348] And as the troops went home at war's end, the epidemic spread

346. Prof Robert Webster, Ibid, 1999
347. Human Vaccines and Immunotherapeutics, John Oxford, Douglas Gill, 2019
348. Dr Albert Lamb, Columbia Presbyterian Hospital, New York

like wildfire. In London's Middlesex Hospital, Dr Robert Parry commented: "We do little more now than direct traffic, guiding people who had collapsed in the street to the emergency ward or to the mortuary. BID (brought in dead) is now a routine entry in the Administration Book."[349]

Photographs of the time bear an eerie resemblance to the current COVID-19 experience, citizens masked and isolated, hospital wards full and medics under pressure.

This was, of course, a plague of the influenza virus, whereas COVID-19 is a virus more like the SARS[350] outbreak in China that, in 2002–03 affected 26 countries and resulted in 8,000 cases occurring in a single year. Yet both outbreaks resulted in worldwide pandemics and both the threat and the remedies have much in common. As John Oxford put it in 2020: "Once the virus is able to spread from human to human, disaster strikes. Within two to three days, from just three infected patients, a million infections can be caused in around 40 days. And this is probably exactly what happened in 1918–1919."

Oxford warned in a scientific paper in 2019: "Something similar to what happened at the beginning of the 20th century could easily be repeated. As a precaution, governments everywhere need to stockpile, to have a plan ready (for a pandemic)."[351] John Oxford and other concerned scientists have, for more than 20 years, consistently delivered this message to any politician who has cared to listen.[352]

In 2011, a UK Influenza Pandemic Preparedness Strategy declared that, when a pandemic occurs, "large swathes of the population may become infected by the new virus over a relatively short period of time. It may be associated with mild to moderate illness in the population ... or significant severe

349. The Spanish Lady, Richard Collier, Alison and Busby, 1996, p39
350. SARS – Severe Acute Respiratory Syndrome
351. Human Vaccines and Immunotherapeutics, Oxford and Gill, 2019
352. Human Virology, Oxford J, Collier L, Kellam P, Oxford University Press

illness and mortality in certain age or patient groups and may significantly disrupt the normal functioning of society. It is necessary to mobilise the collective efforts of society in order to manage the impact of a pandemic (which) continues to be recognised as one of the greatest threats facing the UK". It advised: "Prepare for a ... pandemic that may have a high impact on the health system and wider society. Whilst influenza pandemics have been relatively infrequent over the past century, a new pandemic could emerge at any time. Pandemic preparedness is therefore an integral part of wider emergency response and preparedness."

This Pandemic Preparedness Strategy also pointed out in 2011 that pandemics in the last century had "not infrequently" occurred every 11 to 39 years. It also modelled the economic impact of the next pandemic at £28 billion and assumed the absence from work through illness of 50 per cent of the nation's employees. It warned: "There are no grounds for complacency and any presumption that the relatively mild H1N1 (of the 2009) influenza epidemic is representative of future pandemics, is dangerous." It concluded that the next pandemic would probably be a "new sub-type of the ... virus, that it could emerge at any time of year, that it would not be possible to stop the spread of, or to eradicate, the pandemic influenza virus, either in the country of origin or in the UK as it will spread too rapidly and too widely", and that all the above "could be adapted and deployed ... for another infectious disease". It advised that the UK must "maintain stockpiles and distribution arrangements for anti-viral medicine ... sufficient for a widespread or severe pandemic... Health and social care systems (must be) ready to provide treatment and support for the large numbers likely to suffer" in the next pandemic. There was a critical need for "clear leadership, with pre-established and tested command and control structures ... ensuring co-ordination".

John Oxford observed: "Scientists had all worked very

hard in 2011 to produce this preparedness document. I thought the advice was comprehensive and realistic."

But would the advice be followed?

The Rehearsal

Five years later, Exercise Cygnus was mounted in Britain over three days in October 2016. Its object was to test the preparedness of the Preparedness Strategy. It involved 950 officials from both central and local government, NHS organisations, prisons and local emergency response planners. The 'war game' took the 2011 document as its sounding board. It assumed the nation was experiencing a worst-case scenario affecting up to 50 per cent of the UK population and causing 400,000 "excess deaths".[353] Officials were told to imagine that they were in the seventh week of a pandemic, facing peak demand for hospital and social care. Mock 'COBRA'[354] meetings were held and critical reports by a fictitious media organisation, in print and on television, were produced to heighten stress and the reality of the experience.

The results of this pandemic 'rehearsal' have never been released. But details have leaked out. *The Daily Telegraph* reported one government source as saying that the document was "too terrifying" to be revealed.[355] The UK health system "would collapse from a lack of resources".[356] Sally Davies, Chief Medical Officer at the time, said that the lack of medical ventilators[357] and the logistics of disposing of dead bodies were a serious problem.[358] *The Daily Telegraph* declared in

---

353. Excess deaths – deaths additional to the 'normal' average yearly death rate
354. COBRA – Cabinet Office Briefing Rooms emergency committee
355. The Daily Telegraph, Cygnus buried by Government, March 28th 2020
356. The Daily Telegraph, March 28th 2020; The Guardian, March 29th 2020
357. New Statesman, March 16th 2020
358. The Times, December 27th 2016

April 2016 that the exercise led the Government to decide that 'herd immunity' would be the best response if such a pandemic occurred. Which, in the UK, in the early weeks of the COVID-19 outbreak, was exactly what happened.

It is not the task of this book to chronicle the history of the COVID-19 pandemic. But these facts seem indisputable. Despite the warnings contained in the 'rehearsal' in 2016:

- Britain procrastinated in the early stages of the epidemic delaying a lockdown while the number of COVID-19 infections rocketed from 200,000 to 1.5 million.
- The sudden increase in the flood of patients put intense pressure on the NHS, and the government's failure to provide adequate PPE[359] or testing equipment made the situation critical and because of a lack of preparedness, later cost the nation tens of billions of pounds in panic-buying of PPE.
- Britain experienced more infections than any other European country and had too few intensive care beds – 6.6 per 100,000 people, which was fewer than Cyprus or Latvia. Germany had 29.2 intensive care beds per 100,000 people.
- Britain's death rate reached more than 60,000 during the second national lockdown, before any other European country.
- Professor Chris Whitty, the government's chief medical officer, commissioned an age-based frailty score system for consultation in the NHS as a "triage tool", which included the instruction that, if the NHS were overwhelmed, patients over the age of 80 should be denied access to intensive care.[360]
- By the time the effective vaccines had been created, and a

---

359. PPE – Personal Protective Equipment
360. The Sunday Times, October 25th 2020

national vaccination programme begun, the daily death rate in the UK had topped 1,000 as the total number of COVID-19 deaths in Britain climbed beyond six figures.

Early on, the vast majority of deaths in Britain were among the elderly, in care homes, hospitals or in their own homes, though later waves of the pandemic would embrace younger victims. During the first wave of COVID-19, more than half the patients who died in hospital were over 80 yet only 2.5% of patients in this age group were admitted to intensive care.[361]

John Oxford, relaxing on holiday in Cornwall in the summer of 2020, said: "We scientists fondly imagined that the Government would take notice of what had been written. We thought all the bases had been covered. But we had failed to account for the behaviour of politicians. However good and detailed a survival plan might be, it needs clear leadership to make it work. The document said as much. A crisis is not the time for soundbites and, with COVID-19, that's what we got."

Oxford points out that, although the Preparedness documents were inspired by previous pandemics of the influenza virus, it was intended to assess the nation's readiness to cope with a pandemic *per se*, which could involve a completely new virus. COVID-19 is, of course, just that. Former Health Minister, Jeremy Hunt, subsequently admitted that, in considering a national strategy, too much emphasis had been given to "discussing influenza rather than to the special measures that had been necessary and so effective in the SARS outbreak".[362]

---

361. Ibid
362. Jeremy Hunt, BBC's Today programme, September 1ˢᵗ 2020; SARS emerged in China in 2002, killed more than 800 people worldwide and infected more than 8,000 people from 29 different countries before 2004

The Fall-out

Professor John Oxford believed that when the COVID-19 outbreak began, Britain would be among the best-prepared nations on earth. "All the tools, the actions necessary for us to take, had been discussed and were in the box. But when the box opened, it was half-empty: austerity and cutbacks had undermined our public health resources. They'd been asset-stripped. I realised this only gradually; as a nation, we were incapable of doing what was planned in the Preparedness documents."

Money had been 'saved', he said, by failing to buy fresh supplies of personal protective equipment (PPE) and by simply re-labelling existing equipment with a later date. "It fulfilled our worst fears. I was profoundly depressed. In February, I wrote to the national press, saying that we had to take emergency action immediately – no hugging, social separation, avoid contact. It was not a popular view to express. I had forgotten it was St Valentine's Day.

"I don't indulge in social media but the reaction was appalling – 'Who *is* this total idiot?' It was all very personal. By mid-March, of course, we had total lockdown which embraced everything I had written. But we should have locked down a month earlier."

Throughout the COVID-19 pandemic, Britain's politicians, in their own words, "followed the science". John Oxford observes that not only was Britain ill-prepared for the pandemic with insufficient personal protection stockpiles, but that the relationship between scientists and politicians was uneasy.

"The problem is that I think many of our leading politicians, our decision-makers, did not fully understand the science. Look at the nations who responded well to the emergency when it came. Chancellor Angela Merkel in

Germany was a research scientist and holds a doctorate in quantum chemistry. In Ireland, Leo Varadkar was, and is, a qualified physician. In Britain, despite the repeated warnings, we were not properly prepared for it and our policies were *re*active rather than *pro*active."

In contrast, Chancellor Merkel "told citizens what she, her ministers and scientists knew and what they didn't know. She never boasted. Most of her decisions went against everything modern Germany stood for. Yet because she is a real leader, she led and her nation followed".[363]

John Oxford went on: "In Britain, we scientists should have been more alert to the fact that politicians were not taking the threat seriously enough. I begin to wonder whether the Prime Ministers – Cameron, May and Johnson – had even read the Preparedness documents, which still, as far as I know, haven't been published. As scientists, it's part of our duty, I think, to try to ensure that what we believe to be necessary to meet a 'danger' is being acted upon. So, this mess is partly our fault. But any action has to involve the politicians. The politicians have a duty, too, and that is to do what is best for the country. They don't seem to have done that."

Short-termism

COVID-19 has emphasised a negative malaise in the strategy of Britain's democratic processes. Elsewhere in this book I mention the short-term thinking that disfigures politics in Britain and undermines strategic thinking. The life of an elected government can now last up to five years. But the reality is that there is, for every government, a honeymoon period which

---

363. Why the Germans do it Better, John Kampfner, Atlantic, 2020. He also writes, 'Half of modern Germany's lifespan has been in horror, war and dictatorship. The other half is a remarkable tale of atonement, stability and maturity'

lasts perhaps a year, during which pledges made in the election manifestos are pursued or discarded. There follows, perhaps, two years while those policies are argued about and sometimes implemented. After that, members of the House of Commons have their eye on the next election. What do they need to do to ensure a second term in office? What will be popular with the electorate? The cynic will add: How much money can be given away to influence the electorate? And what difficult decisions can be avoided so that they become the responsibility of the next government?[364]

Confidence in politicians' abilities to make the right, the best, decisions are at a low ebb. The divisions between right and left, rich and poor, black and white, have been thrown into relief in a society where views have become increasingly polarised. People who hold and try to express unfashionable views have been 'cancelled', giving a new and sinister meaning to the word. Debate is more violent, more abrupt, sometimes absent altogether. There is a growing need to engage in tolerant discussion in order fully to understand the issues in this 'new' normal, rapidly changing world. In the last century, George Orwell[365] described England as 'a nation of flower-lovers, stamp collectors, pigeon fanciers, amateur carpenters, coupon-snippers, darts players and crossword-puzzle fans'. To these attributes must now be added 'screen-watchers, litter-droppers, fly-tippers and innovators'. Innovation to reduce the frustrations of a society crippled by COVID-19 where personal communication may take place only at a distance. The space between words is a physical barrier. The Internet and IT are now centre stage. We buy and

---

364. A prime and public example of this was the note left by Labour's Liam Byrne, then Chief Secretary to the Treasury, in May 2010 to his successor in the Conservative/Liberal Democrat coalition Government, which read: 'I'm afraid there's no money ... Good luck!!'
365. The Lion and the Unicorn, George Orwell

sell, form and sustain relationships, work with and through our computers at home and wonder about the future of our towns and cities – the familiar fabric of our way of life. Will the temples of commerce become urban housing? We see the disruption of our schools' timetables and wonder whether the three-year residential degree courses at universities will, in actual fact, become part-time degrees, packages of short-term on-line experiences with less and less student-lecturer face to face contact? And will there be jobs for those students when they graduate?

One clear and unexpected bonus from COVID-19 lockdown was that it gave the world a chance to draw breath and to consider its priorities. People got used to, in the unfamiliar stillness, blue skies without the tracery of aircraft, empty roads and the sound of birdsong. They liked it. Out of adversity came opportunity. Time to decide whether to struggle to restore the old carbon-dominated normal or to strive to achieve the much-heralded 'new' normal, a cleaner and greener normal. As Britain's last coal-fuelled power station closed down and the cost per unit of wind and solar power fell, strategic thinking now indicated that 'green' might also, in the long run, mean 'cheaper'. If international environmental commitments were anything more than simply lip-service, what was the point of rescuing millions of carbon-related jobs when these jobs would be phased out anyway in a carbon-lite world? Why not concentrate instead on alternative energies and embrace the potential of nature, to which millions had been re-introduced during lockdown? Why not, as in World War II, make a realistic effort to encourage Britain's farmers to make the nation as selfsufficient as possible in the production of food, which would dramatically reduce both transport costs and pollution. [366]

366. See also Chapter 6

I write this in 2021, as nations still wrestle with the scourge of the coronavirus, when concern blurs into depression and fear and when politicians struggle to answer criticism of how they coped with the outbreak. Present problems press in on them, not least public scepticism. It is a huge challenge.

But, in my lifetime, the world has faced such challenges before – in 1945, at the end of World War II, when free nations decided it was necessary to seek a new, caring normality. Millions had come through two World Wars in 25 years, an experience more dangerous and destructive even than our present troubles. And they had survived. The servicemen who had fought in World War II came home determined that society would change for the better. Their determination triggered a huge wave of societal experiment based on the thinking of Liberal social reformer and economist, William (later Lord) Beveridge.[367] Many of the politicians at that time, such as Denis Healey, had fought in the war and the 1945 Labour Government led by Clement Attlee and including Ernest Bevin as Home Secretary, Sir Stafford Cripps at the Exchequer and Aneurin Bevan as Minister of both Health and Housing, were of the calibre to deliver that vision. These politicians fashioned a major change in British society, not least with the establishment of the NHS.

Now, in 2021, we are living through a similar moment of challenge. Will we also see this as a unique opportunity? Hope and fear compete in our minds to occupy the same space. It was another giant of the World War II era, US President Franklin D Roosevelt, who reminded the world that "the only thing we have to fear is fear itself".

Society must be optimistic and do its best until it knows better. Once it *knows* better, it must, of course, *do* better.[368]

---

367. The recommendations of the Beveridge Report (1942) formed the basis of Britain's post-World War II welfare state.
368. With acknowledgements to Maya Angelou, poet and philosopher.

APPENDIX 1

Filming the Search for the Titanic

In 1986, a film crew from TVS, the ITV franchise – holder for the South and South East of England – sailed with Robert Ballard's team to find the wreck of the *Titanic*. TVS was one of the newest ITV companies and the negotiations over the access were tortuous, so complex that I kept a diary of events.

They began in September 1985 with an approach through TVS' New York office from a Canadian lawyer, Michael Levine, who was seeking "a return of around a million dollars" for access to Ballard's voyage. We were non-committal. He took away a documentary I had made three years earlier, called *Titanic – A Question of Murder* (see Chapter 2).

We offered Levine no money upfront. Instead, Peter Clark (TVS International) and I tell him that we would put a crew on board the mother ship, shoot the film for him and then make that footage available to the expedition to use at their will. We would simply want British rights plus certain minimal world rights. This offer never changed.

"The BBC," Levine warned, were "very interested. As, of course, are the American networks." Of course.

November 28

We speak to the French in Paris. They have footage of the first voyage "but no-one is interested".

May 2nd 1986

Levine says he can't get any sense out of the French. They don't trust Ballard, he says. They feel he dominated most of the good publicity over the last visit. I listen. Yes, we would like to close a deal – but how exclusive is exclusive if the French go separately and make a film of their own?

May 6th

ITN call. They are talking to the French. They hear we have a deal with the Americans. I deny it. Anyway, says Rosie Hayes of ITN, we should talk. Nigel Hancock and Norman Rees talk. Peter Clark and I talk. No-one can provide an answer to the dilemma – how can any arrangements be made if the French and the Americans are determined to hunt separately?

May 23rd

I am at home in the garden inspecting my roses for greenfly when the telephone rings. It is Rosie Hayes of ITN. The French are in Britain trying to raise money for their expedition. They are looking for £500,000 upfront, for the television rights.

June 4th

I call Rosie Hayes. She has spoken to the French. They will sign a deal later in the week. She does not think it will be with us. The Americans have gone quiet.

June 6th

I call David Weill, the West Coast lawyer now acting for Dr Ballard. He is talking in-depth to CBS, he says. I urge him to look again at the detail of the TVS bid. "I'm sorry, Peter, the CBS offer is very attractive." It looks as if we have fallen between two stools.

June 7th

ITN call. The French are definitely going.

June 9th

Weill calls. Cautiously he asks what rights we would require if it were our crew on board. I spelt it out again. Has the CBS deal gone cool? "They want to transmit their programme a week after the expedition returns. We can't go along with that…"

June 10th

"Ballard is a difficult man." If I've heard this once over the past 24 months, I've been told it a dozen times, in France and America. I travel to the town of Falmouth, Massachusetts. Bob Ballard and I meet in the office at Woods Hole. The meeting continues at a Mexican restaurant.

June 11th

We start thrashing out an agreement at 8 am. David Menair, our North American representative, joins us at the table. It is 4 pm before we finish. The Ballard team *will* go. TVS *will* be the only crew on board. We still don't know what the French plans are.

June 14th

The French are going to pull out.

June 15th

The French have pulled out…

June 16th

We have a deal.

* * *

We produced a one-hour documentary, *The Nightmare and the Dream*. It was executive produced by the author and directed by Graham Hurley. These are his thoughts:

By July 1986, Ballard was very important in the aquanaut world and was very obviously relishing his moment in the spotlight. Finding the *Titanic*, as he'd done the previous summer, was an undisputed triumph but now he wanted to go a whole lot further. The French, with whom he'd worked on the 1985 voyage, were fans of sonar mapping the deep seabed whereas Ballard, acutely media-conscious, was determined to return to Woods Hole with hi-resolution stills and video. Remotely-controlled hi-tech exploration was, in his view, the way to go and the world's favourite wreck would be the perfect showcase. Yes, he was still having to use a manned submersible for the two-hour and forty-minute descent, but in time he was convinced that everything could be launched, directed and recovered from a shipboard control room. Pictures, he kept saying, not sonar read-outs.

En route to the wreck site there was a huge sense of anticipation. Ballard, remember, knew exactly where the wreck lay – he'd discovered it at the very end of the previous season's outing – and therefore there was no moment of discovery in its purest sense. But what lay ahead was the proof – in video and stills – that his core mission was going to succeed. Would *Alvin* and *JJ* (the remote swimming eyes) between them, justify all that faith, all that money? In other words, would we get to see this fabled wreck up close and personal? After the first dive, the answer was yes. And after that, the pictures got better and better.

We took a crew of four: Cameraman Paul Houlston, sound recordist Maurice Hillier, editor Christopher Wentzell and myself. Conditions on board were intimate. The boat wasn't huge under normal conditions but Ballard, understandably, had filled it with brainpower and hands-on expertise in the shape of his Woods Hole team. Ballard's gang of mega-bright young engineers and software wizards were deeply engaging, with that wonderfully beguiling 'Yankee doodle' mix of scruffiness (lumberjack shirts and patched jeans), dry humour and awesome talents. They seemed dauntless in the face of any challenge, any unforeseen disaster – on the one hand, having to work all night on a heaving deck to repair an ailing *Jason Junior*? No problem. Ballard, on the other hand, while omnipresent, remained the man apart. In charge? Emphatically. On a mission? Well, yes. Given to the odd soapy moment of televisual grace under extreme pressure? Again, yes.

He knew exactly where to find the wreck and the dives started as soon as we arrived. Nothing comes easy at those kinds of depths and he was beset by recurring technical glitches, but he weathered the worst of the technical storms and quickly began to deliver truly amazing images. Half five every afternoon was magic time. *Alvin* would surface and Ballard – the Wizard from the Deep – would emerge to hand over yet more astonishing rushes for Chris Wentzell and I to carry off to our portacabin for a preliminary look. The editing set-up comprised three machines with adjustable lighting and a heating system – because it got chilly at night. Ballard would pop by to check on the pictures but, apart from that, he pretty much left us alone.

Working nights suited us very well. We were supernumerary to the central thrust of the voyage, outriders as Ballard urged the wagons on, but Chris Wentzell and I were more than happy to agree the gems and begin to shape the rough cut. In this sense we occupied a bubble, partly of our making, partly of Ballard's, but what was beyond dispute was the feeling that we might just be part of something truly historic. We had a VHS of the feature film *A Night to Remember* on hand, and as *JJ* began to penetrate deeper and deeper into the *Titanic's* hull, it became possible to mix between identifiable locations. The moment when *JJ* spotted a chandelier hanging on a thin twist of flex from the rusting remains of the ceiling over the grand staircase, will remain with me for ever. Kenneth More, in black and white on our VHS of the feature film, had occupied that very spot only moments before.

We'd take a break in the middle of the night, crack a Rolling Rock (beer) or two and hang over the rail.[369] Even in July, it was often cold and still, the boat barely stirring and at times like those it was impossible not to ponder the wider implications of what we were up to. More than 1,500 souls had perished in the blackness of these waters and all credit to Ballard for treating the wreck – the jewel in his crown – with the reverence and respect it deserved. His were truly fabulous pictures, gathered and preserved in the face of constant 'buggeration'. We were truly privileged to be there.

Before every dive, we inscribed polystyrene coffee cups with longitude and latitude details and personal messages to loved ones. Gathered in a special net tied to *Alvin*'s hull, the cups journeyed two-and-a-half miles down to the wreck site. The pressure at those depths crushed them to the size of your thumb and once the sub was back on board *Atlantis*, we retrieved our booty. They'd settled on the *Titanic* and as long as you'd used indelible ink, the messages are still there to be read. *Quel souvenir.*[370]

---

369. The British film crew took a crate of the popular lager beer of the time, Rolling Rock, on board with them. In the wee small hours, Hurley and Wentzell refreshed themselves with a bottle or two and then tossed the bottles overboard. Some days later, intact bottles were identified on the film rushes brought up from the wreck. They caused much excitement in the Ballard team. In some embarrassment, the British team confessed there might be a connection between the bottles on the rushes and the bottles tossed overboard the night before. The practice was discontinued

370. Both Graham and I still have our souvenirs. Mine is inscribed 'Peter Williams, Titanic Dive, July 21, 1986'

APPENDIX 2

What was THIS WEEK?

To mark the 35th anniversary of *This Week* in 1991, the then Director of Programming of Thames Television, David Elstein, wrote the foreword to a book recording the work of this current affairs programme. Associated-Rediffusion produced the first edition on January 6th 1956. The final programmes went out when Thames Television lost the London weekday ITV franchise in 1992. Elstein wrote:

'It is difficult to view *This Week* objectively, for it has been so prominent a part of my life and that of ITV.

'So many outstanding journalists, directors and technicians have brought their talents to the programme, helping build its reputation for intelligence, courage and integrity. The series can count on its credits names such as James Cameron, Robert Kee, John Morgan, Jeremy Isaacs, Jonathan Dimbleby, Desmond Wilcox, Phillip Whitehead, Peter Williams and Peter Taylor.

'Aside from professionalism and dedication, perhaps the greatest contribution they and their colleagues have made to the series has been their passion for the subject in hand. The personal determination to investigate circumstances, expose scandal or illuminate the truth of a situation has earned *This Week* wide respect.

'Teamwork has always been the keynote of *This Week* operations and I am proud to have been part of the team. At a time of stocktaking such as the present, I am inclined to think most of those who are no longer with us – John Morgan, Llew Gardner, who died recently and Alan Stewart, killed on location in the Sudan so tragically young. But I also know that every one of the hundreds of people who have worked on *This Week* will always have for me a special claim of comradeship: even those I have never met!

'Television is ephemeral, current affairs even more so. It is fitting that through the National Film Archive and the Thames Television Programme Library the work produced by *This Week* teams is assured of a permanent place in the television canon. At the same time, *This Week* itself continues to preserve the calibre of current affairs journalism that has earned it a significant place in the public service television system of which Britain is justifiably proud.

David Elstein *Director of Programmes*
Thames Television'

Author's note:

It has been my privilege to work, often for *This Week*, with great producer/directors, such as Jack Gold, Martin Smith, Ken Ashton, Ian McFarlane, David C Rea, Andrew Barr, John Edwards, Phillip Whitehead and many others who will, I hope, forgive me for not mentioning them by name, but from whom I have learned so much.

THIS WEEK Production Team at a Friday meeting in 1969. The author (second right) was seated opposite Phillip Whitehead, the then Editor.

APPENDIX 3

Jean Purdy

Jean Purdy's work was admired throughout the world of reproductive medicine. I quote two tributes to her; firstly, a personal 'letter' written as a blog soon after her death[371] by Professor Roger Gosden, entitled 'Dear Jean':

'I wish I had asked you if you ever wanted to be famous. Had you stayed, you would have been queen of the realm – earning awards, dinners in your honour, and guest lectureships everywhere. I guess you were happy to be spared that kind of attention, preferring the undisturbed backroom where you could counsel patients and care for their embryos. You were content for Bob and Patrick to be the front men. Bob will go down in history as a scientific pioneer ... Did you ever mind standing in Bob Edwards' shadow? He was generous with compliments, saluting you as the third pioneer of IVF beside Patrick Steptoe and himself, but as the assistant to a famous scientist and a gynaecologist *(and being female)* you didn't have much visibility with biographers and the press. The longer you are away the deeper the mystery of your part in the programme, and, now that both men are gone, there is no-one left to tell the full story.'

---

371. Professor Roger Gosden, physiologist, Female Reproductive Medicine, Edinburgh University

Secondly, this and what follows, appeared in The Oldham Notebooks, 1969–78, a paper by Martin H Johnson and Kay Elder on Jean Purdy's role in IVF. Alan Dexter, Bourn Hall's first Business Manager and later its chairman, declared in August 2014:

'In all the time that I was involved with Bob (Edwards), both at my initial meeting with him in his lab in Cambridge, and through the early years of Bourn Hall, Jeannie was an integral part of his work and data-gathering and analysis. Bob never omitted reference to Jeannie's contribution whenever he was questioned about the history of the extent of research undertaken ... Further, when Mary Warnock[372] (as she then was) and her team visited Bourn Hall as part of their work into the ethics of IVF, before the HFEA was formed, I recall all of the papers and excerpts from publications, etc, laid out meticulously in the then Board Room (obviously Jeannie's work), which so impressed the visitors.'

---

372. Philosopher Baroness Mary Warnock, chair of the Human Fertilisation and Embryology Committee, 1982–4

APPENDIX 4

The lyrics

EVERYONE'S GONE TO THE MOON

by Jonathan King

Streets full of people, all alone
Roads full of houses, never home
Church full of singing, out of tune
Everyone's gone to the moon

Eyes full of sorrow, never wet
Hands full of money, all in debt
Sun coming out in the middle of June
Everyone's gone to the moon

Long time ago
Life had begun
Everyone went to the sun

Cars full of motors, painted green
Mouths full of chocolate-covered cream
Arms that can only lift a spoon
Everyone's gone to the moon

Writer: Kenneth King: publisher: Marquis Songs USA

APPENDIX 5

Hilary Lister's Round-Britain Journey

Graphic: Kevin Watts

APPENDIX 6

Getting an epic tale to TV against the odds
(Broadcast magazine article, July 2013)

A Race Against Time is the story of quadriplegic Hilary Lister's successful attempt to sail solo around the UK. But she completed her voyage in 2009 – so why, asked *Broadcast*, is it on air four years after the event? Answer: Because that's how long the negotiations with the BBC lasted.

In 2009, we took the idea of filming Hilary's epic journey to the BBC. They were receptive and gave us £5,000 development money. The relationship between film-maker and subject is crucial, particularly when a vulnerable and courageous woman is putting her life on the line. We bedded into the process of planning the voyage and became part of 'The Team'.

As Hilary was about to set sail, the BBC – as was their right – decided they didn't want the film. Among the reasons: Hilary wasn't a big enough character for BBC1. And she might die during the voyage.

I remember pointing out that neither was a good reason for not making the film.

Now, a situation such as this leaves the independent producer with a profound dilemma: To go, or not to go? How much confidence do you have in your idea – and, in this case, how damaging to the project and to those involved, would it be to withdraw at one minute to midnight?

We decided to fund the filming ourselves and bought a

campervan. Hilary's journey took three months and three cameramen – George Pellett, Malcolm Berry and Justine Ingham – each filmed for a month.

They were part of The Team, their campervan part of the convoy of vehicles carrying the men and women that made Hilary's solo journey possible.

As a company, we funded the film (around £60K) because we believed in the example Hilary was setting – work hard and you'll win through.

The film's post-production was helped by grants from a number of Kent-based trusts – the Crown Community Foundation, the Roger de Haan Charitable Trust, The Rooney Foundation and the Kent Community Foundation.

We kept the BBC aware of Hilary's (and our) progress, but despite months of negotiation, there was still no commission. So we edited her story into a feature-length documentary that's now on limited release.

Charlotte Moore (BBC Commissioning Editor for documentaries) was kind enough to describe it as "a remarkable and beautifully made film" and BBC2 controller, Janice Hadlow, couldn't have been more supportive. The BBC decided they would take it now, as an acquisition.

Our 75-minute film was edited down to 59 minutes with the aid of an edit-producer, our music was also completely changed and that's the film you'll see on Sunday night[373].

The BBC and I agree on the most important aspect of this four-year exercise in negotiation: The film got made and Hilary's remarkable achievement is now out there. To be given access to anyone's life is an enormous responsibility. Hilary Lister is indomitable. This is a film about the triumph of the human spirit. Her spirit.

---

373. A RACE AGAINST TIME was broadcast on BBC2 on Sunday July 14th 2013, at 6.30 pm.

Author's note: The price the BBC paid for this programme, as an acquisition, was roughly one-fifth it would have cost them had they supported the project throughout.

APPENDIX 7

JOHN ASPINALL: In Memoriam...

The names of those keepers who died working for John Aspinall are:

Brian Stocks – killed by female tiger, Zeya, at Howletts on the 21st August 1980. He was 29.

Bob Wilson – killed by female tiger, Zeya, at Howletts on the 22nd September 1980. He was 28.

Mark Aitken – killed by male Indian elephant, Bindu, at Port Lympne on the 24th May 1984. He was 22.

Trevor Smith – killed by male tiger, Balkash, at Howletts on the 13th November 1994. He was 32.

Darren Cockrill – killed by female Indian elephant, La Petite, at Port Lympne on 7th February 2000. He was 27.

APPENDIX 8

LYNMOUTH: *The Warning*

Local records indicate that a major flood had taken place in Lynmouth in 1769, when it was simply a small fishing village. The storm had 'brought down great rocks of several tons each... and lessons do not seem to have been learned'. Damaged buildings were repaired and new buildings erected "on flood detritus on the floor of the valley or on shattered and erodible rocks on the side".[374]

In 1933, when the UK Government assessed nationally a Normal Maximum Flood (NMF) index, the flow in both the East and West Lyn rivers "considerably exceeded" this NMF.

Yet, in 1952, neither the East nor the West Lyn rivers was designated nationally as a 'main river', which would have qualified them for a higher standard of maintenance. This is taken from 'Lynmouth Flood: 40 Years On', a report by William Brown Harris, written in December 1992. In conclusion, Harris considered the 1952 disaster and wrote:

'The devastating forces of nature ... seemed so extraordinary that it was felt that nothing like it would be seen again during a lifetime if ever.' But he warned on page 37 that even in 1992 'the chance of flood disasters (in Lynmouth) are considerably lessened but there is no cause for complacency. Pressure for building or encroachment into flood plains continues...'

---

374. History of the Parishes, JF Chanter, 1907, p89

Bibliography

During the research for *Being There*, I have been helped by reading several outstanding books and magazine articles. I am grateful for the co-operation of their authors and for their diligence from which I have learned so much:

DONALD CAMPBELL: The Man Behind the Mask, by David Tremayne, Bantam Books, 2004. *David, a UK-based motor racing journalist, has himself driven in world speed record attempts.*

INGENIA, Royal Academy of Engineering, Carlton House Terrace, London SW1Y 5DG.

BLUEBIRD AND THE DEAD LAKE, by John Pearson, Collins, 1965.

BLUE BIRD, play for children, by Maurice Maeterlinck, 1908.

THE LIFE OF JOHN RUSKIN, by WG Collingwood, 1906.

A MATTER OF LIFE, by Robert Edwards and Patrick Steptoe, ISBN 978-1-908374-48-6.

LOOK ME IN THE EYE, by Jeremy Isaacs, Little Brown, 2006.

BRANDO: SONGS MY MOTHER TAUGHT ME, by Marlon Brando with Robert Lindsey, Random House, 1994.

McINDOE'S ARMY, by Williams with Ted Harrison, Pelham Books, 1979.

THE GUINEA PIG CLUB, by Edward Bishop, Macmillan, 1963.

INSIDE STORY, by Greg Dyke, HarperCollins, 2004.

RUTH ELLIS, by Laurence Marks and Tony van den Bergh, Macdonald & Jane's, 1977.

MATERIALS ON THE TRIAL, The Khabarovsk Trials, Foreign Languages Publishing House, Moscow, 1950.

UNIT 731, by Williams with David Wallace, Hodder & Stoughton, 1989.

FACTORIES OF DEATH, by SH Harris, Routledge, 2002.

A NIGHT TO REMEMBER, by Walter Lord, Longmans, Green & Co, 1956.

THE NIGHT LIVES ON, by Walter Lord, Viking, 1986.

TITANIC, by Michael Davie, Bodley Head, 1986.

THE BEST OF FRIENDS, by John Aspinall, Macmillan, London, 1976.

THE PASSION OF JOHN ASPINALL, by Brian Masters, Jonathan Cape, 1988.

THE GHOST, THE SECRET LIFE OF A CIA SPYMASTER, by Jefferson Motley, St Martin's Press, New York, 2017.

THE PLAGUE OF THE SPANISH LADY, by Richard Collier, Allison & Busby Ltd, 1996.

REASON FOR HOPE, by Jane Goodall, Thorsons, 1999.

TALES FROM WHITELEAVED OAK, by Brian Haynes, Ragged Stone Publishing, 2013.

My Thanks...

I also wish to convey my thanks to my wife, Jo Taylor, a fellow journalist, with whom, over the years, I have discussed much of the contents of this book and who will have heard many of the stories before!

My thanks, too, to davit makers, Welins, to Fred Walker and Graham Hurley for their advice on *Titanic* and to Lorna Hyland at the Merseyside Maritime Museum; to Andrew Steptoe, Martin H Johnson and Roger Gosden, Judy and Roger Carr and Elizabeth, on the story of IVF; to Laurence Marks on the Ruth Ellis story; to Brian Haynes and Ted Harrison, the North Devon Athenaeum and Naomi Ayre, Dr Bridget Gillard, Registrar, Devonshire Association and the sharp-taloned 'East Devon Owl' on Chapter 6; to the Queen Victoria Hospital, East Grinstead, Sam Gallop, Ted Harrison and the McIndoe Guinea Pigs Memorial Trust on Chapter 7; to James Osborne, Amos Courage and the Aspinall Foundation on Chapter 11; to Clifford Lister, Professor Pauline Rudd, Toby May, The Hilary Lister Dream Trust and composer Sir Karl Jenkins on Hilary Lister's journey around Britain; to Dean Robert Willis and Greg Dyke on Chapter 12; to Gina Campbell, Tonia Campbell, David Tremayne and the Ruskin Museum, Coniston, on Chapter 13; and to Garfield Kennedy and Professor John Oxford on Chapter 15 on the Pandemic.

The photographs in this book have come from many sources, often personal collections, and I am particularly grateful to the Rudd family for permission to use the photographs in the chapter on Hilary Lister; similarly, the Aspinall family for the photographs in Chapter 11; the Steptoe family for the photographs in Chapter 3; Belinda Frixou for the photographs of Marlon Brando in Chapter 5; former colleague Ted Harrison for his permission to reproduce all the caricatures of the Guinea Pigs in Chapter 7 and of the author in the Appendix; to Steve Bergson for his advice on our photographic research, and to Patricia Holland for her help with the history of *This Week*.

My thanks, too, to my colleagues Gabriel Morgan, Stefan Proudfoot and James Willis at Spiffing Covers for the flair and skill they brought to the production of this book, and to my always encouraging editor Caroline Ahern.

I have had seven much-loved children - six from my first marriage, Deborah, Jacqueline, Mark, Gareth, Claire and Rebecca, and Megan from my second marriage. I have had the joy of working professionally at TVS and at PWTVI with Mark, Claire, Megan and my eldest daughter Deborah, who was cruelly taken from us by cancer when her life promised so much. This book is also for them.

Finally, my thanks to Peter Crook, my friend and Business Manager, these many years; to Lynn Marston for her transcripts and to Lizzie Talbot for tirelessly typing the draft of this book and for her skill in deciphering my handwriting.

Index